London: A Short History of the Greatest City in the Western World

Part I

Professor Robert Bucholz

THE TEACHING COMPANY ®

PUBLISHED BY:

THE TEACHING COMPANY
4840 Westfields Boulevard, Suite 500
Chantilly, Virginia 20151-2299
1-800-TEACH-12
Fax—703-378-3819
www.teach12.com

ISBN 1-59803-530-4

Credits begin on page iv and constitute a continuation
of the copyright page.

Robert Bucholz, D.Phil.

Professor of History, Loyola University Chicago

Robert Bucholz received his undergraduate education in history at Cornell University. He graduated magna cum laude and Phi Beta Kappa in 1980, whereupon he received a Keasbey Memorial Scholarship for study at the University of Oxford. At Oxford, Professor Bucholz studied under G. V. Bennett and P. G. M. Dickson. He took his doctorate in Modern History from Oxford in March 1988. He taught at Cornell University; the University of California, Los Angeles Extension; California State University, Long Beach; and Loyola Marymount University before joining the faculty in history at Loyola University Chicago in 1988. He currently holds the rank of professor.

Professor Bucholz's primary research interest is the English court and royal household for the period from 1660 to the 19th century. He is the author of *The Augustan Court: Queen Anne and the Decline of Court Culture* (Stanford, 1993); coauthor, with Sir John Sainty, KCB, of *Officials of the Royal Household, 1660–1837* (Institute of Historical Research, 1997–1998); and coauthor, with Professor Newton Key of Eastern Illinois University, of *Early Modern England, 1485–1714: A Narrative History* (Blackwell, 2003; 2nd edition, 2009). He is the project director of the Database of Court Officers, which contains the career facts of every person who served in the British royal household from the restoration of the monarchy in 1660 to the death of Queen Victoria in 1901. The database was launched online by Loyola University Chicago in 2005 and was archived by the British Library in 2008.

At Loyola, Professor Bucholz teaches both halves of the Western Civilization survey as well as upper-division courses in early modern (Tudor-Stuart) England, English social history, and early modern London. He has received several awards for his teaching, most notably the Sujack Award for Teaching Excellence (the highest such award from Loyola's College of Arts and Sciences), which he received in 1994, the first year of its presentation. He was also Loyola's Honors Program Faculty Member of the Year in 1998 and 1999.

Professor Bucholz was named Prince of Wales Foundation Scholar for Architecture in America, which led to his being invited to speak on the etiquette of the public rooms and the experience of going to court in the 17th and 18th centuries to Royal Collection Studies at Windsor Castle in September 1997. (Professor Bucholz's week-long stay at Windsor coincided with the death and funeral of Diana, Princess of Wales.) This talk was repeated in 2000 and published in 2001 in *The Court Historian*. Professor Bucholz's work has been solicited and commented upon by the Prince of Wales. For his work, Professor Bucholz has been named a Fellow of the Royal Historical Society.

Professor Bucholz is past president of the Midwest Conference on British Studies. He is occasionally asked to comment on British history and the activities of the British royal family to the Chicago media, most notably *Chicago Tonight* with John Calloway and *Extension 720* with Milt Rosenberg.

Table of Contents

London: A Short History of the Greatest City in the Western World
Part I

Credits

S. J. Perelman's letter of 12/13/53 to Laura Perelman: Reprinted by permission of Harold Ober Associates Incorporated. © 1986 by Abby Perelman and Adam Perelman.

Siegfried Sassoon's poem "Blighters": Copyright Siegfried Sassoon by kind permission of the Estate of George Sassoon.

London: A Short History of the Greatest City in the Western World

Scope:

Samuel Johnson famously said that "the man who is tired of London is tired of life, for there is in London all that life can afford." After all, London is the seat of an ancient monarchy, yet a stronghold of modern democracy; home of the language of Shakespeare where you can now hear the music of myriad tongues; a treasure trove of priceless ancient artifacts and a wellspring of art, literature, theater, music, and fashion both past and present. No other city in the world offers such bounty, and no city on earth has had so profound an impact on worldwide culture for so long in so many areas of life.

In fact, this course will argue that London, more than any other city on the planet, catalyzed modernity. It was in London that constitutional monarchy, participatory democracy, a free press, public concerts of music, and viable commercial theater first flourished in modern times. Throughout the early modern period, London was a leader in world trade, the capital of a rich and powerful global empire, and (despite a few notable flare-ups of intolerance) a community that became a home to people of all nations, all faiths, and all political beliefs. On a more sober note, London was arguably the first city to demonstrate that bombs—whether from the Luftwaffe in 1940, the IRA in the late 20th century, or terrorists at the beginning of the 21st—could not break its will.

Over its 24 lectures, this course will ask: Why London? Why did it increase 10-fold in size to become the largest city in Europe by 1750? Why did it come to dominate a world-encircling empire of trade and finance? Why did it come to represent freedom and economic opportunity for persecuted religious groups, immigrant groups, artists, and thinkers, and how successfully does it assimilate all these groups? How did London weather repeated bouts of plague, fire, and warfare? How did it remain a world city even after the loss of empire and manufacturing? How is London facing a new millennium? Equally interesting and important is the question of why and how people become Londoners. In other words, this course is not merely about a place and a structure; it is about people. The course considers not merely the growth of London or its rise to world prominence or its forging of many of the milestones of modernity, but also how London's people coped with each of these things to forge that combination of proud humility, recalcitrant loyalty, and spirited resilience that we know as the Londoner.

We examine this great city in terms of six of its most remarkable characteristics: its growth, wealth, diversity, modernity, resilience, and ambiguity. Chronologically, this course traces how Johnson's hometown rose from a tiny outpost on the fringes of the Roman Empire to dominate the economic, political, and cultural life of first England, then a worldwide Empire, and now an informal but powerful global network of finance, communication, and culture. During the 24 lectures, we will confront the best recent work in urban history, accounts by contemporary Londoners and tourists, and fictional works in which the city is a character.

We will start our examination with London's Roman foundations (Lecture Two), then watch the dramatic changes through the Middle Ages and the Tudor and Stuart periods (Lectures Three, Six, Seven, Ten, Twelve, and Thirteen). In the 19th century, we will meet the Victorians and Edwardians (Lectures Thirteen, Sixteen, and Eighteen) and watch the city's evolution through the two World Wars (Lectures Nineteen and Twenty-One) and postwar bleakness into the swinging '60s, the millennium, and beyond (Lectures Twenty-Two through Twenty-Four).

We will also pause frequently to experience London's life as it was actually lived by some flesh-and-blood Londoners who were also its brightest literary stars—Geoffrey Chaucer (Lectures Four and Five), William Shakespeare (Lectures Eight and Nine), Samuel Pepys (Lectures Eleven and Twelve), Samuel Johnson (Lectures Fourteen and Fifteen), and Charles Dickens (Lecture Seventeen). Then our own eyes and others' will show us the contemporary experience of millennial London (Lecture Twenty-Four).

These sources will expose us to "all that life can afford" in London, ranging from the contemplative splendor of Westminster Abbey, St. Paul's Cathedral, and the parish church; to the opulent galleries of Whitehall and Buckingham Palace; to the damp and sooty alleyways of the East End. Along the way we shall meet Boudicca, Dick Whittington, Will Shakespeare, Sam Pepys, Jack the Ripper, the Bloomsbury set, and of course Dr. Johnson. We shall brave the dangers of plague and fire and Blitz; witness the diverse spectacles of royal coronations, the Lord Mayor's Show, and the hangings at

Tyburn; and take refreshment in the city's pleasure gardens, coffeehouses, music halls, and pubs.

So, to quote another famous phrase, "Let's to London, for there's variety."

Lecture One

There's No Place like London

Scope:

This course is an interdisciplinary introduction to the history of the greatest city in the Western world. Proponents of other cities will disagree, but just to name three, New York never fought the Nazis; Paris wasn't burned to the ground in four days and rebuilt within six years; and Rome had no Samuel Pepys. No city on earth has had so profound an impact on worldwide culture for so long—as a center of political significance, trade, finance, media, etc. This lecture lays out that significance as well as the themes to be addressed in the course: Why London? Why between 1450 and 1750 did it increase 10-fold in size to become the largest city in Europe? How did it come to dominate a world-encircling empire of trade and finance? How did it weather repeated bouts of plague, fire, and war? How is London facing the new millennium?

Outline

I. Samuel Johnson said, "The man who is tired of London is tired of life, for there is in London all that life can afford."

- **A.** Arguably, no city on earth has had so profound an impact on worldwide culture for so long in so many areas of life: politics, trade, finance, media and the arts, etc.
- **B.** This course will argue that London, more than any other city on the planet, catalyzed modernity.
- **C.** This lecture poses several questions to be addressed in the course.
    1. Why between 1450 and 1750 did London increase 10-fold in size to become the largest city in Europe?
    2. How did it come to dominate a world-encircling empire of trade and finance?
    3. Why did it come to represent freedom and economic opportunity for persecuted religious groups, immigrant groups, and artists and thinkers?
    4. How, and how successfully, does it assimilate all of these groups?

5. How did it weather repeated bouts of plague, fire, and war?
6. How did London remain a world city even after the loss of empire and manufacturing?
7. How is London facing a new millennium?

D. Equally interesting and important is the question of why and how people become Londoners.

II. This course traces how Pepys's and Johnson's hometown rose from a tiny outpost on the fringes of the Roman Empire to dominate the economic, political, and cultural life of first England, then a worldwide empire, and now an informal but powerful global network of finance, communication, and culture.

A. It confronts the best recent work in urban history, eyewitness accounts by contemporary Londoners and tourists, and fictional works in which the city is a character.

B. The course will trace London's history in several ways.

1. First, we move chronologically from its Roman foundations through the Middle Ages, Tudor, and Stuart periods; then the 18th century, the Victorians, and the Edwardians; the two world wars; and through postwar bleakness to the swinging '60s, the millennium, and beyond.
2. We will also pause frequently to experience London's life as it was actually lived by flesh-and-blood Londoners, such as Chaucer, Shakespeare, Pepys, Johnson, and Dickens, as well as the contemporary experience of millennial London.

III. For as long as it has existed, London has been important—but not always in the same way.

A. Londinium, founded by the Romans, was the central garrison and chief port of the farthest-flung outpost of the Roman Empire (c. 50–410 C.E.).

1. It was hardly central to the defense of the empire.
2. It was easily abandoned by its founders when the empire started to crumble at the end of the 4th century.

B. During the Middle Ages (c. 410–1485), London took centuries to recover, but once it did, it established itself as the country's chief harbor and financial center, a crucial military chokepoint, and a major religious center.

1. From about 800 on, London was so crucial to the political and economic health of the country that as London went, so went the nation.
2. Still, the country of which London was capital remained itself on the fringes of Europe, hardly the center of world civilization at this time.

C. During the Tudor and Stuart periods (1485–1714), London grew from fewer than 50,000 people to well over half a million.
1. Those people had to be fed and clothed, heated and housed, leading to the diversification and greater efficiency of the national economy.
2. More people patronized entertainment possibilities: the pleasure garden and public theater at the end of the 16th century; the public concert, coffeehouse, and club at the end of the 17th century.
3. During this period London weathered great disasters, including civil wars, revolutions, plots and counterplots, six deadly visitations of plague, innumerable fires culminating in the Great Fire of 1666, and the perception of high taxes and repeated crime waves.

D. During the 18th century, London was still the seat of government and greatest city in England, but England was now the most powerful country in the British Isles, which had, in turn, become a dominant player in Europe and the proprietor of a worldwide empire.
1. London was now the capital of that empire, the greatest port in Europe, and its financial and banking center.
2. The resultant wealth generated immense real estate and entertainment opportunities, but also massive problems and anxieties.
3. By 1750 London was inhabited by nearly 700,000 people, making it the greatest city in Europe.
4. London had become the great entrepôt for Europe's most desirable products from overseas.
5. London was the headquarters of a constitutional monarchy with more elements of democracy and popular participation than any Western country before the United States.

6. It was an artistic center with a vibrant theater and musical life and a thriving and relatively free press.
7. Finally, London was gripped by crime, disease, and poverty.

E. Nineteenth-century London grew to 8 million people, the largest city in the world.
   1. It was the capital of an empire covering one-fifth of the world's land mass and one-quarter of its population.
   2. It was a site of political demonstrations leading to governmental reform and a wider democracy.
   3. It was still an infamous concentration of poverty, disease, and crime.
   4. London and the national government would make some attempt to solve those problems by creating citywide administrative bodies and pouring public money into public works and regulatory agencies.

F. Twentieth-century London would have to adjust to Britain's declining role in the world. London nevertheless recovered and remained a thriving center of culture and finance.

G. Twenty-first-century London has faced the millennium with exuberance and dogged determination in face of terrorism.

H. As London becomes ever more diverse and ever more interconnected globally, it is no longer a purely English or British city but a world city.

IV. This brief chronology raises themes that we will highlight again and again in the course.

A. London's growth: From a sleepy port town on the fringes of Europe to "the Great Wen," a vast megalopolis, London became a world financial and cultural capital.

B. London's wealth: We will look at London in trade and high finance.

C. London's diversity: There will always be two—or more—Londons economically and ethnically.

D. London's modernity: London pioneered or was at the forefront of many developments that produced our modern world.
   1. London pioneered modern democracy, opposing the Stuarts and creating a constitutional monarchy.

2. London was a leader in world trade and experienced a financial revolution in the late 17th century.
3. London was an early printing center, with, from 1695, a relatively free press, including the first real newspapers and essay magazines.

E. London's resilience: London has survived—from the burning and massacre by the Iceni in 60 C.E.; to the Black Death and the Great Fire; to the ravages of war; to the unexpected madness of terrorism, culminating in the bombings of July 7, 2005.

F. London's ambiguity: Commentators either love or hate London.

Suggested Reading:

Inwood, *A History of London*, introduction.

Manley, *London in the Age of Shakespeare*, chap. 1.

Questions to Consider:

1. Why does London remain a world city despite its relative slip in size of population?
2. How have Londoners managed to cope with the many disasters the city has experienced?

Lecture One—Transcript
There's No Place like London

Welcome to a course on the greatest city in the Western world. Now, that statement is bound to raise some eyebrows. What about New York? What about Paris? What about Rome? To which I reply: New York never fought the Nazis, and Paris did not burn to the ground in four days and rebuild itself in a mere six years, and Rome had no Samuel Pepys.

At one point, circa 1900, London was the largest city in the world, with perhaps 8 million people. It has stayed more or less steady at between 7 and 8 million for a century. But that has dropped it down to something like 25th in the world table of big cities, dwarfed, for example, by Greater Tokyo's 28 million and Mexico City's and Mumbai's 18 million.

Still, in this course, I'm going to argue for greatness as a function of far more than size. It was another famous Londoner, Samuel Johnson, who made the case, saying, "The man who is tired of London is tired of life, for there is in London, all that life can afford." Indeed.

Where else in the Western world can you see the Queen of England, Scotland, and Northern Ireland at Buckingham Palace, or at least the changing of her guard. Or see another queen's lyre from ancient Iraq, as well as countless mummies, the Rosetta Stone, and Elgin Marbles, just a mile away at the British Museum?

Where else can you witness the debates of the oldest continuously sitting legislative body in the world—Iceland's was interrupted at the beginning of the 19th century—the very mother of parliaments at the Palace of Westminster, or take part in all manner of uncensored debate yourself at Speaker's Corner in Hyde Park, where freedom of speech is nearly total?

Where else can you watch authentically produced Shakespeare at Sam Wanamaker's brilliant recreation of the Globe Theatre on the South Bank? Or throw money at itinerant street players whose life experience may actually reflect the Bard's a little more closely?

Where else can you hear five major symphony orchestras and two international opera companies for a state-subsidized song? Or take part in the free singing in pubs, or listen to the music of cockney speech in the shadow of Bow Bells, the Church of St. Mary-le-Bow, within whose earshot one must be born to be considered a true cockney?

Where else can you patronize Harrods, the world's most prestigious department store? Or Foyles, the world's largest bookstore, or Dickens's Old Curiosity Shoppe, or Johnson's and Dickens's local pub, Ye Olde Cheshire Cheese on Fleet Street?

More seriously, it's an arguable point, but I believe that no city on earth has had so profound an impact on worldwide culture for so long in so many areas of life—politics, trade, finance, media, and the arts, etc. It was in London that constitutional monarchy, participatory democracy, a free press, the first public concerts of music, the first viable commercial theater since ancient times, first flourished in modern times. Though Amsterdam is a serious competitor in some of these areas. In fact, this course will argue that London, more than any other city on the planet, catalyzed modernity. There is perhaps one more rather sobering first on London's record. It could also be argued that London was the first city to demonstrate that bombs, whether from the Luftwaffe in 1940 or the IRA in the late 20th century, could not break its will.

This lecture asserts that significance and poses several other questions to be addressed in the course. For example, on a very basic level: Why London? Why was London the first place where so many of these features of modern life flourished? Why between 1450 and 1750 did it increase tenfold in size to become the largest city in Europe? How did it come to dominate a world-encircling empire of trade and finance? Why did it come to represent freedom and economic opportunity for persecuted religious groups—Protestant reformers and Huguenots in the 16th and 17th centuries, all sorts of similarly persecuted groups in the 20th century; immigrant groups—the Irish from the 1600s on, more recently Indians and Pakistanis, West Indians, Africans, Cypriots, etc.; as well as artists and thinkers from Anthony Van Dyck to Karl Marx? How, and how successfully, does London assimilate all these groups? How did it weather repeated bouts of plague and fire, and in our own times, the Blitz? How did it remain a world city, even after the loss of empire and manufacturing? How is London facing a new millennium?

Equally interesting and important, why and how did people become Londoners? In other words, this course is not merely about a place and its buildings; it's about people. We'll be interested not merely in the growth of London or its rise to world prominence or its forging of many of the milestones of modernity, but also in how London's people coped with each of these things to forge that proud combination of proud humility, recalcitrant loyalty, and spirited resilience which we know as the Londoner.

Now, like any tourist, we had best be advised to have a plan. Here's ours. A history of London is an interdisciplinary course tracing how Pepys and Johnson's hometown rose from a tiny outpost on the fringes of the Roman Empire to dominate the economic, political, and cultural life of first England, and then a worldwide empire, and now an informal but powerful global network of finance, communication, and culture.

Over the 24 lectures, we will confront the best recent work in urban history, eyewitness accounts by contemporary Londoners and tourists, and fictional works in which the city is a character. These sources will expose us to all that life can afford in London, ranging from the contemplative splendor of Westminster Abbey, St. Paul's Cathedral and the parish church, to the opulent galleries of Whitehall and Buckingham Palace, to the damp and sooty alleyways of the East End. Along the way, we shall meet Boudicca, Dick Whittington, Will Shakespeare, Sam Pepys, Jack the Ripper, the Bloomsbury and Carnaby Street sets, and of course, Dr. Johnson. We shall brave the dangers of plague and fire and the Blitz, we'll witness the diverse spectacles of royal coronations, the Lord Mayor's Show, and the hangings at Tyburn, and we'll take refreshment in the city's pleasure gardens, coffeehouses, music halls, and pubs.

More specifically, this course will trace London's history. First, chronologically, from its Roman foundation in Lecture Two; through the Middle Ages, Tudor and Stuart periods, in Lectures Three, Six, Seven, Ten, Twelve, and Thirteen; through the 18th century, the Victorians and Edwardians, in Lectures Thirteen, Sixteen, and Eighteen; to the two world wars, Lectures Nineteen and Twenty-One; through postwar bleakness to the swinging '60s, the millennium, and beyond, in Lectures Twenty-Two through Twenty-Four.

But the chronology of demographic trends, plagues and wars, kings and municipal ordinances, is only the barebones of London's story, interesting as those bones may sometimes be. In this course, we'll also pause frequently from the examination of those bones and take to the streets to try to experience London's life as it was actually lived by flesh and blood Londoners. Six times we're going to tour London through the eyes, or at least our imagination of what the experiences were, of some of its most famous and observant residents: Geoffrey Chaucer in Lectures Four and Five, William Shakespeare in Lectures Eight to Nine, Samuel Pepys in Lectures Eleven and Twelve, Samuel Johnson in Lectures Fourteen to Fifteen, Charles Dickens in Lecture Seventeen. And if you'll indulge me, the lecture on millennial London is also in some ways the lecture on Bucholz's London, for this is the London that I came to know as a graduate student in the '80s, and then as a returnee in the '90s, and in more recent years. Finally, we'll devote full lectures to two great periods of crisis, from which London's recovery was anything but certain. That of plague and fire in Lecture Twelve, and that of the Blitz in Lecture Twenty-One.

Now, before going further, I need to make a point about London's relationship to English, British, and European history. This course will, of necessity, refer to a lot of those histories, for the history of a capital and its country are necessarily intertwined. When it does so, I'm going to do my best to explain briefly the historical context. I'm going to try to explain to you why the Roman Empire fell, and before it did, pulled back from Roman Britain. Why Princess Elizabeth was put in the Tower. Why 18th-century England was almost constantly at war with France. Why there was a great depression, and why Neville Chamberlain opted for appeasement in the 1930s. One of the major reasons, it turns out, was that he felt that he couldn't protect London from German bombs. But I'm going to be unable to provide lots of depth and background on these topics. If you want to know more, many of them are covered in greater depth in other courses for The Teaching Company, including my own, England from the Tudors to the Stuarts, and also Foundations of Modern Western Civilization II.

Now, to return from our commercial break: For as long as it has existed, London has been important, but not always important in the same way. At its foundation, Roman London was the central garrison and chief port of the farthest flung outpost of the Roman Empire. It was locally crucial, a toehold of Roman culture in a sometimes hostile sea of Celts, but it was hardly central to the defense of the empire. It was easily abandoned by its founders and conquerors when the Roman Empire started to crumble at the end of the 4th century.

During the Middle Ages, London took centuries to recover. But once it did, it established itself as the country's chief harbor and financial center via the river and the bridge; a crucial military chokepoint via the Tower of London, or at least enforced by the Tower of London; a major religious center via St. Paul's Cathedral and Westminster Abbey. From, say, 800 on, London was so central to the political and economic health of the country, that as London went, so went the nation. Any conqueror who took London took England—the Vikings, William the Conqueror, the Yorkists, then the Tudors during the Wars of the Roses. Any who failed—Wat Tyler, Jack Cade, the Lancastrians during the Wars of the Roses—ended up on the ash heap of English history. Quick, how often have you thought about Wat Tyler or Jack Cade lately?

Still, at the same time, the country of which London was capital remained itself on the fringes of Europe, itself hardly the center of world civilization at this time. It could be argued that London's greatest significance at the end of the Middle Ages was as the funnel through which the ideas and products of other more powerful European countries passed into England. In other words, my point is that medieval London was the biggest fish in a really rather small pond.

During the Tudor and Stuart periods, roughly 1500 to 1700, or more accurately 1485 to 1714, both the fish and the pond got bigger. London expanded enormously in size, growing tenfold in population from less than 50,000 people to well over half a million. Those people had to be fed and clothed, heated and housed. This led to the diversification and greater efficiency of a national economy.

London forced farmers to grow more crops and cattle. It forced counties to build better roads and canals. It forced the whole country to establish better communication at the rise of the printing press, and later, a free press. This period saw the rise of new financial institutions, government funds, an informal stock exchange, which enabled London to assist, but also to control, the economic development of the rest of the country.

More people in London patronized entertainment possibilities during this time, in part because of the thriving economy. The rise of the pleasure garden and the public theater at the end of the 16th century, the rise of the public concert, the coffeehouse, and the club at the end of the 17th century, are developments of this period.

During this period, London weathered great disasters. Tudor and Stuart Londoners lived through—when they did not die in—two changes of royal dynasty, two civil wars, two revolutions, frequent constitutional crises, numerous plots and counterplots, repeated wars, some of which—in 1588 and 1642 and 1667 and again in 1745—came very close to being waged on London soil. Six deadly visitations of plague, innumerable fires culminating in a great conflagration in 1666, and the perception, if not necessarily the reality, that Londoners' taxes were too high and that they suffered from repeated crime waves. During this period, individual Londoners died at alarming rates, much faster than they could reproduce themselves, and yet, London itself was replenished and rebuilt and flourished. Finally, by the end of the Stuart period, as Britain began to acquire a world empire and challenge France and the Netherlands for the leadership of Europe, London began to be a world capital.

During the 18th century London was still the seat of government and the greatest city in England, but England was now the most powerful country in the British Isles, which had in turn become a dominant player in Europe and a proprietor of a worldwide empire. In keeping with Britain's imperial pretensions and economic growth, London was now thc capital of that empire, the greatest port of Europe, and its financial and banking center. Now, the wealth generated by empire and trade led to immense real estate and entertainment opportunities, but also massive problems and anxieties. Like Los Angeles or Hong Kong today, London in 1750 was a shock city of new buildings and slums, concert halls and gin joints, churches and brothels, possibility and fear. Anyone familiar with the prints of Hogarth or the writings of Johnson will know exactly what I'm talking about.

By 1750, London was inhabited by nearly 700,000 people, making it the greatest city in Europe, but that population had long ago overflowed London's walls, which were being haphazardly torn down. While many people still lived in the heart of the old city, others had expanded its borders west to include the West End and Westminster, or they'd moved south across the river to Southwark and beyond, or northward to the suburbs of Islington and Highgate.

For contemporaries, the growth of the suburbs and the development of better roads and coaches meant that one could try to actually avoid the worst features of city living by commuting. You could work in London, but you could live in Surrey or Hertfordshire. In fact, one of the many problems for the historian of early modern London is that it's sometimes kind of hard to figure out where it ended. Given its commercial reach across the English Channel to Antwerp, Amsterdam, Hamburg, Lisbon, and the Mediterranean, given the tentacles of trade and government it extended across the Atlantic, Pacific, and Indian Oceans, one could make an argument that London never really did end.

By 1750, London had become the great entrepôt for Europe's most desirable products: sugar and tobacco from the Americas; fabrics, spices, and tea from the Indies; Europe's financial and banking center, in rivalry to Amsterdam—it would surpass Amsterdam by about 1800. London was the capital of an empire which by 1763 stretched from Canada to India, Gibraltar, to, well, just about Tahiti. That would come a little later in the decade. It was the headquarters of a constitutional monarchy with more elements of democracy and popular participation than any Western country before the United States. London was an artistic center, including a vibrant theater and musical life, a thriving and relatively free press, it was home to the British Museum, but also to a cynosure of problems, many of them age old: crime, disease, poverty. Still, this led to innovative modern solutions. For example, the Bow Street Runners were a primitive municipal police force. The London Foundling Hospital was founded to stem the tide of abandoned children. We'll talk about both in later lectures.

Nineteenth-century London would grow even larger, becoming, at 8 million people, the largest city in the world. It was the capital of an empire by this time covering one-fifth of the world's landmass and one-quarter of its population. It was also the site of political demonstrations leading to governmental reform and a wider democracy—demonstrations over the Reform Bill of 1832, over the National Charter in the 1830s and '40s, though these failed, and, by the end of the century, demonstrations over votes for women. But London was also, in the 19th century, an infamous concentration of poverty, disease, and crime. Detailed in fiction by Charles Dickens and many others, detailed by Henry Mayhew at mid-century and Charles Booth at its end, in scathing works of sociological fact.

London and the national government would make some attempt to solve these problems by creating citywide administrative bodies and pouring public money into public works and regulatory agencies.

Twentieth-century London would have to adjust to a new reality, Britain's declining role in the world. But I would argue that, unlike the country itself, the city has done rather well for itself. True, 20th-century London was, after say 1919, no longer the capital of a great worldwide empire, or at least one that was still expanding. It was threatened by German bombs twice, it was subject to strikes, depression, killer fogs, and the Blitz. And nevertheless, London recovered and remained a thriving center of culture and finance, as it remains today.

Twenty-first–century London has faced the millennium with exuberance. The Tate Modern Gallery, which showcases the most avant-garde and participatory art; the Millennium Dome, and the London Eye, and Queen Elizabeth's Golden Jubilee in 2002; the successful Olympics bid in 2005. Millennial London has also faced the future with dogged determination in the face of terrorism throughout the 1970s, '80s, and early '90s, particularly from the Irish Republican Army, and just 24 hours after the Olympics announcement, the coordinated bombings of London Tube trains and buses. As London becomes ever more diverse and ever more interconnected globally, the city's identity has changed yet again. London is no longer a purely English city, or even a British city; it's a world city.

Now, this brief chronology of London's importance raises themes that we're going to highlight again and again in this course. First, London's growth: From a sleepy port town on the fringes of Europe to "the Great Wen," a vast megalopolis that became a world financial and cultural capital.

Second, London's wealth: Wealth from trade, wealth from high finance. London began first by dominating England's economy, to eventually being one of the world's great money markets and financial centers.

Our third great theme in this course will be London's diversity. There will always be two or more Londons. Economically, contrast the great palaces and the aristocratic townhouses of the West End with the cruel slums of the East End and South Bank. Ethnically, because London is a port city, it's always been diverse, welcoming Jewish, Flemish, and Italian merchants in the Middle Ages. It's always been a haven for refugees. We've mentioned Huguenots in the early modern period, refugees from Eastern Europe and the Middle East today. London is now home to large concentrations of Africans, West Indians, Pakistanis, and Indians, who came because of economic or political freedom.

Our fourth great theme will be London's modernity. London pioneered, or was at the forefront, of many developments which produced our modern world. Take democracy: London was active in opposing the Stuarts and in creating a constitutional monarchy. From 1500 to 1800, it boasted the largest electorate for city offices and members of parliament in the Western world. There was in London lots—always, dating back to Roman times—lots of local self-government via parish and ward, as well as mass popular participation in politics from the Middle Ages. In other words, Londoners were never afraid of mounting a demonstration or a riot, or signing a monster petition with thousands of signatures, culminating in the great Chartist movement of the 19th century.

Recalling modernity and economics, London was a leader in world trade, it experienced a financial revolution. Following the example of Amsterdam, but going well beyond it; creating stock companies and an exchange, government lotteries, banks, the Bank of England.

In communication, London was an early printing center. Intermittently in the 17th century and permanently from 1695 on, it had a relatively free press. That free press produced the first real newspapers, the first essay magazines. Today, London is the place from which more international long-distance calls originate than anywhere else in the world. In sociability, London gave us the coffeehouse and gave us the club.

Our fifth theme will be London's resilience. London experienced burning and massacre by the Iceni in 60 of the Common Era; abandonment by the Romans; sacking by the Vikings; burning by William the Conqueror; the Black Death and repeated visitations of plague to 1665; repeated conflagrations culminating in the Great Fire of 1666; spectacular riots culminating in the Gordon riots of 1780; catastrophic health crises—the gin craze of the 1730s and '40s, cholera epidemics in the 19th century, deadly fogs culminating in the Big Smoke of 1952; the ravages of war culminating in the Blitz of

1940–1941; and of course, most recently, the unexpected madness of terrorism, culminating in the bombings of 7/7/05. In every case, London has rebuilt; London has not knuckled under. London carries on.

The final theme about London is London's ambiguity. As we read contemporary accounts from London's past, we'll be struck by the fact that they generally fall into two categories. The first is wildly positive, not unlike my own opening to this very lecture. As if written by a real estate agent. In the 16th century, William Dunbar thought London "the flower of cities all." His contemporary, Andrew Boorde asserted,

> There is not Constantinople, Venice, Rome, Florence, Paris, nor Cologne, cannot be compared to London, the qualities and quantity considered in all things. And as for the order of the city in manners, and good fashions, and courtesy, it excelleth all other cities and towns.

William Wordsworth, standing on Westminster Bridge in 1802 grew positively sentimental: "Earth has not anything to show more fair." Even today's modern guidebooks emphasize London's size and variety. Here's one:

> This British capital is alive and well and culturally … vibrant … a mammoth metropolis. … The core of London is one of the most fascinating places on earth. With every step you'll feel the tremendous influence this city once exerted over global culture when it had an empire on which the sun never set.

But note this part: "London is a mass of contradictions."

As you may recall, the title character in Stephen Sondheim's *Sweeney Todd* has a rather different view of London, calling it "a hole in the world like a great black pit," inhabited by immoral vermin. Sweeney Todd's alternative take on London also dates back as far as the positive ones. In the 18th century, that great London lover himself, Samuel Johnson, warned of its streets, "Prepare for death, if here at night you roam, and sign your will before you sup from home."

The anonymous contemporary author of *A Trip Through the Town* elaborates:

> The Town of London is a kind of large forest of Wild Beasts, where most of us range at a venture, and are equally savage and mutually destructive of one another: … The strange Hurries and Impertinencies; the busy Scramblings and Underminings; and what is worse, the monstrous Villainies, Cheats and Impostures in it, the innumerable Equipages and outward Appearances, that we see in every Corner, are but the dismal prospect of an Universal poverty, and Crowds of Miserable people, either wrack'd with Agonies of their own Guilt, or Folly, or groaning under the terrible Apprehensions of Bankruptcy.

Indeed, it would be a lie to ignore the facts that London grew at the expense of the rest of the country, draining the countryside of people and thus destabilizing hundreds of towns and villages. No wonder that James I complained that, "soon London will be all England." For centuries it killed off most of these immigrants, murdering more people than it birthed, victims of overcrowding, disease, accident, and crime. As late as the 1960s, government planners worried that London's economic vibrancy and tourist attractions were actually siphoning off jobs and pounds from the rest of the country. In the 1930s, the Barlow Commission actually studied how to stifle London's economic growth in order to stimulate the rest of the country.

Nor should it be forgotten that within living memory, London was home to some of the worst slums in the Western world, as well as always gross inequalities of wealth and privilege. So while George Santayana might have thought of London as "the paradise of individuality, eccentricity, heresy, anomalies, hobbies, and humors," Percy Shelley thought "Hell is a city much like London— / A populous and smoky city." While Sir Arthur Conan Doyle, who perhaps inadvertently did so much to romanticize Victorian London, referred to it once as "a great cesspool."

But of course, it is part of the tradition of city dwellers to call their cities of abode the worst, the most dangerous sinkholes of human inequity imaginable. New Yorkers revel in their city's supposed toughness and callousness. But also part of London's myth, one to which Sir Winston Churchill obliquely referred during the city's greatest crisis, when in July 1940 he said, "The vast mass of London itself, fought street by street, could easily devour an entire hostile army."

I don't know that all Londoners agreed, but there was something of their stubbornness and toughness when he said, "We would rather see London laid in ruins and ashes than it should be tamely and abjectly enslaved."

So once again, even in the midst of criticizing London, we fall back to celebrating it. It is time now to confront this vast monster of a city, neither apple nor orange, nor a city of light, but something perhaps tougher and more stubborn, an immovable feast, a festering wound, "the Great Wen," as it came to be called in the 19th century. So, without further ado, to quote a famous phrase, "Let's to London, for there's variety."

Lecture Two

The Rise and Fall of Roman Londinium

Scope:

There was no London before the Romans, who founded the city on a site very much like that of Rome itself: on a river, at a bridgeable point, forming a north-south/east-west crossroads. Despite a terrible massacre led by local tribes in 60 C.E., Londinium grew quickly to become the political, military, and economic heart of Roman Britain. The Romans established many of the principal features of London: a harbor, a bridge, a wall, a fortress, and what was at the time a more-or-less regular street plan. But as their empire crumbled, London was left defenseless and, eventually, nearly abandoned.

Outline

I. There has not always been a London.

II. During the Middle Ages, Londoners made up a pedigree for their city.

- **A.** They claimed that, long before the incarnation of Christ, King Brut (or Brutus), a descendant of Aeneas and a refugee from the Trojan Wars, founded London.
    - **1.** According to this myth, London was originally called Trinovant, or "new Troy."
    - **2.** Medieval Londoners wanted to associate their city with ancient greatness so as to claim that their rights predated (and so did not flow from) the English monarchy.
- **B.** According to one medieval chronicler, not only was London older than Rome, it "possesses the liberties, rights, and customs of the ancient city Troy and enjoys its institutions."
- **C.** But the association with Troy was also a warning of London's vulnerability; it was old and great, but it could fall.
- **D.** Unfortunately, all of this is nonsense.

III. Prehistoric and Celtic London.

- **A.** There is no evidence of any large prehistoric settlement at London's location.

B. Nor was there much settlement in London during the period of Celtic migration to Britain (800–200 B.C.E.).
   1. Because travel by water was always easier in ancient times than travel over land, the Thames estuary and river was the highway of choice into southern Britain for the waves of Celts who came from Europe.
   2. Nevertheless, given the fertility of the Thames Valley, some undoubtedly settled there.
   3. In fact, "London" is a Celtic word, not a Latin one, for "wild" or "bold."

IV. It was the Romans, not the Celts, who founded London.

A. The Romans first visited Britain under Julius Caesar in 55 B.C.E.

B. They attempted permanent conquest during the reign of Emperor Claudius in 43 C.E.
   1. In 43, he dispatched an invasion force of about 40,000 troops under the command of Aulus Plautius.
   2. They easily defeated a local tribe, the Catuvellauni, and established a base camp at Westminster.
   3. By 50, the Roman governor, Ostorius Scapula, had established a permanent trading post on the north bank of the Thames at its highest point, what is today Cornhill in the area called "the City."
   4. By 60, "Londinium" was thc largcst Roman settlement in Britain.

C. Perhaps this site was attractive because it resembles that of Rome itself.
   1. Just as Rome straddles the Tiber River in central Italy, so London straddles the Thames.
   2. Both rivers operate as east-west highways for people and commerce.
   3. Moreover, like Rome, London is situated where the river is just wide enough and deep enough for big ships from Europe to dock yet narrow enough for a bridge.
   4. The combination of an east-west river and a north-south bridge made London, like Rome, a crossroads for immigration and trade.

5. While the city developed on the hill on the north bank, the southern terminus of the bridge—the "south work," or Southwark—was important enough for the Romans to establish a garrison there.

D. Thus the Romans had established London's first major characteristic.
   1. It was a harbor and trade entrepôt.
   2. Archaeologists now know that this early version of the city consisted of the bridge, a wharf on the north side below the bridge, a market area on Cornhill, and two streets parallel to the river.

E. By this time, London also had a garrison of several hundred, forming a military choke point and thus a second component of its importance.
   1. In 60 C.E., a Celtic tribe named the Iceni, led by Queen Boudicca, slaughtered some 70,000–80,000 Roman colonists in a swath from Colchester to Londinium, burnt the latter to the ground, and nearly drove the Romans out of Britain.
   2. In response, the Romans drew upon the vast resources of their empire and superior military tactics and technology, wiping out the Iceni, leaving 80,000 dead, including Boudicca.

F. Londinium was rebuilt between 80 and 120 C.E. as a magnificent city of temples and basilicas, a forum, a fort with 1,500 soldiers, and a makeshift wall.
   1. But in the late 120s, a fire devastated about 100 acres in the center of the city.
   2. It took decades to recover, and Londinium was still a scene of devastation in 150.

G. By 200 C.E., Londinium was at its height—a great Roman town of perhaps 100,000 people and the capital of Roman Britain (the third element of its importance).
   1. Londinium once again had a forum, basilicas, and temples and now boasted a governor's palace and a regular grid street pattern.
   2. It was governed by 2 senior magistrates, 2 junior ones, and a town council of 100 property owners elected by free-born males in an annual assembly.

3. Thus London has always had an element of democracy and public involvement.

H. Archaeology has enabled us to reconstruct some aspects of city life.

1. Londinium was tied into an imperial network of distribution and consumption, but Londinium did not seem to have any exports.
2. As the Roman Empire became a Christian empire in the 2nd, 3rd, and 4th centuries, the temples were converted into churches, which established a fourth pillar of London's greatness: It became a religious center.
3. Londinium's streets were interconnected with Roman Britain via excellent Roman roads, many of which form the basis of modern roads into the countryside today.
4. Those roads were crucial to all four of Roman Londinium's functions: trade, governmental communication and religious communication from the capital to the countryside, and the movement of troops.
5. Also, to aid defense, around 200 C.E. the Romans added a substantial wall around the town. It set London's boundaries for the next 1,500 years.

V. The latest evidence indicates a measure of economic and population decline in Londinium as early as 200 C.E., probably because of the vagaries of imperial trade.

A. By the 3rd century, the whole empire began to be affected by the invasions of Germanic and other tribesmen. The Celtic military tradition was not much help in resisting these invaders, and this meant that defense would have to come from Rome.

B. Britain was always considered an outpost to the empire, and the financial burden of defense began to wreck the imperial economy. So by the late 4th century, the Roman administration had begun to pull its troops from the British garrison anyway in order to defend the heart of the empire.

C. Roman Britain was subject to repeated invasions, raids, and settlements by the Angles and Saxons, and this had a number of dire results for Londinium.

1. The governmental, religious, and commercial infrastructure that made trade possible began to fall apart.
2. As Romano-British society and culture faded, Anglo-Saxon society and culture did not, at first, take up the slack. Londinium itself was dying.

VI. As its security fell away, then its power, then its trade, Londinium, for the first and only time in its history, ceased to have a reason to exist.

A. Gradually its people seem to have fallen away as well.

1. The period 450–600 C.E. has left almost no evidence of habitation for this part of the world, so historians and archaeologists still debate whether Londinium was abandoned entirely or merely shrank to a shadow of its former self.
2. Most historians suspect that its population dwindled to perhaps 10,000.

B. At best, Londinium had become an artificial construct, a sad monument to former greatness.

C. It would take centuries for its conquerors to revive it.

Suggested Reading:

Inwood, *A History of London*, chap. 1.

Perring, *Roman London*.

Questions to Consider:

1. Why was London so attractive a site for the Romans?
2. Why was it so easy for them to give it up?

Lecture Two—Transcript

The Rise and Fall of Roman Londinium

During London's greatest crisis, the Blitz of 1940–1941, when Londoners took refuge from German bombs in underground Tube stations, they would sometimes sing songs. One of the most popular began, "There'll always be an England." Whether or not that's true, and I certainly hope so for my job prospects, there hasn't always been a London but that didn't stop Londoners from claiming otherwise.

During the Middle Ages Londoners, displaying that genius for self-promotion they have always had, made up a pedigree for their city to indicate that if it wasn't exactly eternal it was venerable. They claimed that, long before the incarnation of Christ, and in some chronicles long before the foundation of Rome, one King Brut or Brutus, a descendant of Aeneas, and a refugee from the Trojan wars, founded London.

According to this myth, London was originally called Trinovant or "new Troy." By the way, there actually was a Celtic tribe called the Trinovants when the Romans arrived, but they didn't live in cities. Now, of course, one of the foundation myths of Rome was that it, too, was a spin-off of Troy, founded by Aeneas. So, medieval Londoners wanted to associate their city with ancient greatness. Why? Well, according to one Medieval chronicler, not only was London older than Rome, it possessed the liberties, rights, and customs of the ancient city of Troy and enjoyed its institutions. So Londoners were always jockeying for position, here, I think, against the royal government. They're reasoning seems to be, if our rights and privileges predate our kings, then our kings can't take them away, but the association with Troy was also a warning of London's vulnerability. London may have been old and great, but like Troy, it could fall.

Now, unfortunately, all this is nonsense, it's no more reliable than those ancient pedigrees you can buy off the internet, I have several myself. By the way, this isn't the first London myth that we will encounter in the course of these lectures.

It was obviously hard for Londoners to imagine a time when their city did not exist, but, in fact there's no prehistoric evidence of any large settlement on this location. Just some hunter's tools dating from about 8000 B.C.E. (that is Before the Common Era, what we used to refer to as Before Christ) found near Uxbridge, to the west of London. There was a prehistoric village, also to the west, at Heathrow, long before jet noise was presumably a problem, but no big town, perhaps because the land was marshy. As you all know, the big prehistoric news was to the west, in Wiltshire, at Stonehenge. Nor was there much settlement in London during the period of Celtic migration to Britain from about 800 to 200 Before the Common Era. That is, London was, essentially, a Roman invention.

Nevertheless, because travel by water was always easier in ancient times than travel over land, the Thames Estuary and River was certainly the highway of choice into southern Britain for the waves of Celts who came from Europe. Given London's location along this popular route, prehistoric and Celtic peoples must have passed through here. Given the fertility of the Thames Valley, some undoubtedly settled here. There is one further clue that London was not entirely invented by Rome. London is not a Latin word but a Celtic one for wild or bold. Scholars have no idea if this referred to the forests which overgrew the area or some notable individual.

At least one authority states that the name "possibly means place of Londinos," the fierce one. Given London's tendency to produce wild, bold, and fierce characters, it is rather pleasant to think isn't it? That its name refers to more than the trees. Anyway, it was the Romans, not the Celts who founded London, and it was the river, not the forests which brought them there. The Romans first visited Britain under Julius Caesar in 55 B.C.E., but this was more or less a scouting trip to the edge of the Roman world. It was designed to give Caesar some good publicity back home. They didn't attempt permanent conquest until the Roman Empire was at its height, during the imperiate of Claudius, in 43 of the Common Era.

At this point the empire extended from Mesopotamia to Spain, North Africa to the shores of Western Europe. Claudius, like most Roman emperors, had come to the throne under dubious circumstances. He needed to add to those territories to demonstrate that he was a true Caesar. So, in 43, he dispatched an invasion force of about 40,000 troops under the command of Aulus Plautius. They easily defeated a local tribe, the Catuvellauni, and established a base camp at Westminster. In fact, the Romans didn't really plan on a big settlement in London at all. They'd hoped to make their main base in

Britain at Colchester, Essex, because it was on the southeast coast and so within easy reach of the Continent via the English Channel. But by 50, the Roman Governor, Ostorius Scapula, had established a permanent trading post on the north bank of the Thames at its highest point, what is today Cornhill in the City.

By 60, Londinium was the largest Roman settlement in Britain. Why was this spot so attractive? Perhaps, if you think about it, the site resembles that of Rome itself. Just as Rome straddles the Tiber River in central Italy, so London straddles the Thames. Both rivers operate as east-west highways for people and commerce. Moreover, like Rome, London is on a very particular spot on the river, where the Thames is just wide enough and deep enough for big ships from Europe to dock yet narrow enough for a bridge. In fact, according to Weinreb and Hibbert's *London Encyclopedia*, one of several bibles for this course,

> Along the whole stretch of the tidal Thames only one place exists where two spurs of high, dry and gravelly land face each other on the rivers banks on which a pair of bridgeheads could stand securely …

The combination of an east-west river and a north-south bridge made London, like Rome, a crossroads for immigration and trade. Eventually, Londinium became the meeting point for six major roads into the countryside of Roman Britain. While the city developed on the hill on the north bank, the southern terminus of the bridge, the south work or Southwark, was important too and the Romans established a garrison there to provide this entry way to the bridge.

The first Roman bridge was probably built near Westminster by about 60. There's been a London Bridge on this site ever since. In fact, London Bridge was London's only bridge across the Thames until 1750. The Romans added a large timber quay on the north side of the river by about 80. The river, of course linked with the North Sea, the English Channel and, so, easy access to the rest of the empire on the Continent.

Thus, the Romans had established London's first major characteristic. It was a harbor and trade entrepôt. According to Tacitus, by 60, Rome was already "famous for its crowd of traders and a great center of commerce." Its merchandise including glassware and pottery and jewelry which, by the way, the native

Celts loved. Archaeologists now know that this early version of the city consisted of the bridge, a wharf on the north side below the bridge, and a market area on Cornhill. There were at least two major streets parallel to the river, today following the routes of Lombard-Fenchurch streets and Cannon Street-Eastcheap.

By this time, Londinium was not only a substantial port, but a garrison of several hundred. The Romans soon figured out that whomever controlled Londinium controlled the Thames Valley and the hills now known as Cornhill and Ludgate provided a naturally defensible position. This marks London's second great significance. The second pillar of its important, if you will. It was a military choke-point. If you control this part of the Thames, you control entre to the entire west of Southern England.

Londinium's military importance was underscored as early as 60, when a Celtic tribe named the Iceni, led by Queen Boudicca, slaughtered some 70–80,000 Roman colonists in a swath from Colchester to Londinium, burnt the latter to the ground and nearly drove the Romans out of Britain.

Here's the story. Boudicca and her husband, Prasutagas, had been clients of the emperor Nero. According to Tacitus, when Prasutagas died in 60, the Roman commander annexed Icenian land, flogged Boudicca and allowed the rape of her daughters. The Iceni also complained about high taxes and the imposition of Roman religion.

They reacted by sacking Colchester and then they marched on Londinium. The Roman garrison was outnumbered. Tacitus relates the decision of the Roman commander, Suetonius Paulus, in what amounts to London's first mention in the historical records. So this is the first time we hear oh Londinium.

> [He] decided to sacrifice this one town in order to preserve the whole, the weeping, and wailing of those who besought his help did not deter him from giving the order for departure. He did allow those who were prepared to leave to accompany his formation. Those who stayed behind, because of their gender, their decrepitude or their attachment to the place were overwhelmed by the enemy. The enemy neither took captives nor bartered them nor did they observe any of the usual conventions of warfare. Instead, they massacred, hanged, burned and crucified with an energy that

> suggested they were aware that retribution would soon be visited upon them, and so hastened to exercise vengeance [while] they could.

This would not be London's last experience as a target nor Londoners' last encounter with war, nor even the last time they would be sacrificed to preserve the larger whole. And yet, as in the future, they would recover and rebuild.

As predicted, the Romans drew upon the vast resources of their empire and superior military tactics and technology, wiped out the Iceni, leaving 80,000 dead, including Queen Boudicca. In modern times, Londoners sought to make amends by putting up a dramatic statue to her on the Thames near Westminster Bridge. I never quite understood this considering how many Londoners she killed. This reminds us that controlling the city may be harder than fending off its invaders and it also reminds us that the city has always had a certain fondness for rebels and an ambiguous attitude towards authority.

Another recurring theme in this course is that London is a dangerous place. For example, it burnt down repeatedly. Londinium was rebuilt after the Iceni massacre mainly between 80 and 120 as a magnificent city of temples and basilicas with a forum and to prevent a repetition of recent history included a fort with 1,500 soldiers near modern Cripplegate. There was also a makeshift wall but in the late 120s a fire devastated about 100 acres in the center of the city. It took decades, again, to recover and Londinium was still a scene of devastation in 150.

By 200 of the Common Era, Londinium was at its height. A great Roman town of, according to one and this is an outside estimate, 100,000 people and the capital of Roman Britain. This established the third pillar of London's importance along with economy and the military government. Londinium had a forum, basilicas, temples, a governor's palace and a regular grid street pattern. It was governed by two senior magistrates and two junior ones. It also boasted a town council of 100 property owners, responsible for policing and justice, revenue collection, maintenance of buildings, roads, the water supply, etc.

Now here's why I'm excited about this. The council was elected by free born males in an annual assembly. In other words, the tradition of London democracy dates back virtually to its foundation. London has always had this element of democracy and public participation.

Archaeology has enabled us to reconstruct some aspects of the city's life. Since the 19th century, whenever a new building goes up, the archaeologists get to descend for a little while at least and dig up London's past. They've uncovered plenty of evidence of Londinium's greatness and economic reach from tiles and mosaic floors, private bath houses, an amphitheater. There's evidence of markets and products. For example, excavations on Thames Street in the late '70s and early '80s demonstrated that Londinium was tied into an imperial network of distribution and consumption. It received olive oil from Africa and Iberia, wine from the Rhineland and Mediterranean, pottery, lamps, tableware, sculpture from Italy and Gaul. All point to a thriving luxury trade.

Another one of the sub-themes of this course is that London will always drive the trade in luxury. London will always be introducing new luxuries to Britain but Londinium also needed practical things like grain from surrounding areas and fish from the Channel. At the same time Londinium itself doesn't seem to have made anything that anybody wanted, at least not yet anyway. That's always been a bit of a problem for London manufacturing. If we think ahead, the Industrial Revolution did not primarily happen in London.

Archaeologists may have discovered London's first actual business letter, and a hint of the slave trade. I'll read it now.

> Rufus, Son of Callisunus:
>
> Greetings to Epillicus and all his Colleagues. You know that I am well, I believe. [Which kind of raises the question, why he is writing.] If you have the list, please send it. [That's a business letter] Look after everything carefully and see that you turn the girl into money.

There's also lots of funerary monuments and even graffiti. This was found on a ceiling tile in Warwick Lane, "Austalis has been going off by himself every day for 13 days." For all we know, this may be the first recorded complaint about London labor. It may also be the first recorded London joke; we don't know what Austalis was doing by himself for those 13 days.

As the Roman Empire became a Christian empire in the 2nd, 3rd, and 4th centuries, the temples were converted into churches and established a fourth pillar of London's greatness. It was a great religious center. Now all of Londinium's pillars were facilitated by that fact that its streets were interconnected with Roman Britain via excellent Roman roads, many of which form the basis of modern roads into the countryside today. And so, Oxford Street and Watling Street are built on top of the old Roman roadbeds, connecting to the west and northwest, respectively via the M40 and the A5. The Colchester road heads northeast. Roman Ermine Street became Bishopsgate Street which begins at, what used to be called the Great North Road, now the A10, all the way to Yorkshire. South of the Thames, Watling St. headed east to Dover, Staines Street headed for the south-west.

This network of roads was crucial to all four of Roman Londinium's functions, trade obviously, government and religious communication from the capital to the countryside, of course and, in particular, the military, the movement of troops. As we'll see, various tribes, Picts and Scots from the north, Angles, Saxons and Jutes from across the Channel, were forever threatening Roman Britain and in particular London. There were never enough troops on the frontiers of the empire, and London's garrison was never adequate. So the way the Romans dealt with the problem was to move what troops they had swiftly to whatever trouble spot happened to present itself and so you see Roman roads. The excellence of Roman roads was crucial to that movement. Observing these roads from the air, one marvels at the straightness with which Roman surveyors were able to achieve what they did.

Also to aid defense, and perhaps maybe even more immediately important to the average Roman Londoner, around 200 the Romans added to its bridge a second great architectural feature that we'll come back to again and again. They built a wall around the town, open at the river. The Wall of London was 18 feet high and 6 to 9 feet thick. It was punctuated by a series of gates including, probably, a triumphal arch to the southwest and of course, its point was to keep out invaders. Besides the bridge, the city wall would become the most important landmark of Roman and early medieval London. In fact, the wall would define London for the next 1,500 years. It was still considered a defensive barrier right up to the Civil Wars of the 1640s. Thereafter, London's rapid development led to its piecemeal demolition but bits of the wall still stand conveniently near the Museum of London and you can walk up to it and you can marvel at its thickness and strength. It still looks like something that could keep out an invader.

Unfortunately, the Roman Empire crumbled much sooner than did its masonry. The latest evidence indicates economic decline and population decline in Londinium perhaps as early as 200, probably because of the vagaries of imperial trade. As the empire settled down, as it stopped conquering, less plunder and fewer slaves poured in, its economy begin to tighten. Worse, by the 3rd century, the whole empire began to be affected by the invasions of Germanic and other tribesmen. Now, this is a particular problem for Britain because the Celtic military tradition was not much help in resisting these invaders. The Celts had, by and large, become Romanized. Increasingly, they lived in cities trading peacefully. They weren't very warlike. This meant that defense would have to come from Rome but Britain was always considered an outpost to the empire and the empire was in trouble.

From about 180 on, the borders of the Roman Empire were increasingly penetrated by tribes from the east and west, often themselves being pushed out of the ancestral lands by other groups like the Huns. Roman emperors had the choice of either fighting the invaders or letting them settle peacefully. Now, if you let them settle peacefully, you're in effect de-Romanizing the empire but if you fight them, that's going to cost money. You either have to increase the size of the Roman army, which they did to eventually half a million men, or you have to pay off the old invaders to fight the new invaders for you.

Either way, taxes were going to go up in the Roman Empire. Worse, if you increased the size of the army you had to pull men, agricultural workers, from the countryside. Now, that meant you had fewer people to grow food. That meant less food. That meant higher food prices at a time when taxes are going up. It didn't help that the later Roman Empire and its economy also suffered from other maladies it didn't know how to cure. There's evidence that the climate got colder overall. There was the possibility of lead poisoning from Roman drinking vessels and, finally, recurring outbreaks of plague, though Londinium was spared until 664. Still, the Roman Empire was in crisis. What about Roman Britain?

Well, it turns out that the British garrison was just as likely to march off to try to make their general emperor as to defend Roman Britain against raiding tribes of warriors. For example, between 260 and 274, Roman Britain was actually part of a breakaway Gallic empire that actually seceded from the Roman Empire. Between 287 and 296, it was ruled separately by the pretender Carausius and then be his assassin, Allectus.

In 297, the Romans invaded again to try to get Britain back under Constantius Chlorus. This saved London from a plundering rebel army and it was immortalized in a medal proclaiming Constantius, "the restorer of eternal light." On the medal, the city itself was personified and kneeling, but there's also a depiction of buildings behind the personified city, these buildings look a bit like a castle. This is probably the first depiction of London in any form; the medal known as the Medallion of Arras contains this first depiction.

Early in the 4th century, Constantius's son, Flavius Valerius Constantine, used the garrison in Britain to win the imperial throne for himself, which sounds great but remember you're pulling the garrison from Britain. In fact, Londinium was never again so important. In the meantime, taxes were going up to pay for the defense of the empire and that hurt Londinium's economy.

In 406, the British garrison mutinied and decided to invade Gaul and Spain, presumably looking for plunder. In 409, the Romano-Celtic, that is the British natives, fed up with high taxes, revolted and threw out their Roman officials. By the late 4th century, the Roman administration had begun to pull its troops from the British garrison anyway in order to defend what was left of the heart of the empire.

In 410, the Emperor Honorius recalled the garrison entirely and, in a face-saving measure, gave Roman Britains the right to defend themselves. In fact, he had no power to do so. There would be no more help from Rome.

The first pillar supporting Londinium's importance had been removed. Worse, during this period, Roman Britain was subject to repeated invasions, raids, and settlements by the Angles and Saxons; 367 saw a coordinated attack by Scots, Picts, and Angles all over Britain, though this one left Londinium untouched. At this point, Londinium extended the wall to border the river, they're clearly bracing for something.

While the Romano-Celts put up a fight, theirs was, as I've indicated, a peaceful trading culture. They weren't used to war. Contrary to the 2004 Hollywood King Arthur, they generally lost the battles and the ground that had once been theirs. This had dire results for Londinium. First, the governmental, religious, and commercial infrastructure that made trade possible began to fall apart. There was no one to guard the roads or to maintain them. No troops to escort important officials or cargos. In other words, without the military pillar, the pillars of commerce, government, and religion began to collapse.

Archaeologists have also found increasing evidence that agriculture was growing within the walls. In other words, the old Roman street plan was either being grown over or being plowed over. After 420, coinage fell out of use until the 7th century. Southwark was abandoned for over 400 years. As Romano-British society and culture faded, Anglo-Saxon society and culture did not, at first, take up the slack. The invading Angles and Saxons were mobile, even nomadic warrior tribes. In the 5th century they were mostly interested in plunder. Only gradually did they become interested in farmland. They took much longer to become interested in cities and trade. For example, there's no evidence of Anglo-Saxon pottery or glassware being exchanged in London.

Some idea of their utter bewilderment at the notion that people could live in cities is conveyed by a famous fragment of an Anglo-Saxon poem written much later in the 8th century. It's called *The Ruin*. Now the poem is anonymous. In the poem, a tribesman, maybe a warrior, contemplates the vast deserted walls and buildings of an abandoned city. We don't know that it's Londinium. There's a palpable sense of a great civilization lost. He can't seem to comprehend that human beings might have built this, lived in it, and in the persons of his own ancestors probably, wrecked it.

> Wondrously wrought and fair it's wall of stone, shattered by fate. The castles rend to sunder. The work of giants moldereth away. Its roofs are breaking and falling. Its towers crumble in ruin. Plundered those walls with grated doors. Their mortar white with frost. Its battered ramparts are shorn away and ruined all undermined by eating age. The mighty men that built it departed hence, undone by death are held fast in earth's embrace. Tight is the clutch of the grave

> which, while overhead for living men, a hundred generations pass away.

Not even a sense that this happened recently on the part of the author.

> Long, this red wall, now mossy gray withstood while kingdom followed kingdom in the land unshaken neath the storms of heaven. Yet now its towering gate hath fallen. Radiant, the mead halls in the city bright; yeah, many were its baths. High rose it's wealth of horned pinnacles while loud within was heard the joyous revalry of men 'til mighty fate came with her sudden change. Wide wasting was the battle where they fell. Plague ladened days upon the city came. Death's snatched that mighty host of men. There in the olden time, full many a thing, a nobleman, shining with gold, old gloriously adorned, haughty and heart rejoiced when hot with wine. Upon him gleamed his armor and he gazed on gold and silver and all precious gems, on riches and on wealth and treasured jewels, a radiant city in a kingdom wide. There stood the courts of stone, hotly within the stream flowed with its mighty surge. The wall surrounded all with its bright bosom. There the baths stood, hot within its heart …

And at that point, the fragment of the poem fades away as London has done. Where we find evidence of Anglo-Saxon settlement at London, it's outside the walls. These people did not feel comfortable within the city. Can you imagine coming upon the buildings of London and deciding we don't want to live there, we'll camp outside. Londinium was dying.

As its security fell away, then its power, then its trade, Londinium, for the first and only time in its history, ceased to have a reason to exist. So, gradually, its people seem to have fallen away as well. The period from 450 to 600 has left almost no evidence of habitation for this part of the world. As a result, historians and archeologists still debate, hotly, whether Londinium was abandoned entirely or merely shrank to a shadow of its former self. Is it possible that the capital of Roman Britain, the future greatest city of the western world, was abandoned? Its forum silent and deserted, its walls overgrown with moss, its bridge fallen into disrepair. Its river empty, save for the occasional fisherman. Now, most historians think that its population dwindled to maybe 10,000 but this would make Londinium slightly smaller than Wimborne Minster, England, today or Hendersonville, North Carolina. At best, Londinium had become an artificial construct, a sad monument to former greatness. It would, in fact, take centuries for its conquerors to revive it. In the next lecture, we trace that revival.

Lecture Three

Medieval London's Thousand-Year Climb

Scope:

It took centuries of Anglo-Saxon rule for London to recover in size and economic activity. By the time of the Viking raids of the 8th and 9th centuries, London was once again populous, a major port—and a tempting target for raiders. The Anglo-Saxon kings did their best to protect London as a major source of loans and taxable income but took only the first steps toward making it a capital. The last king of the line, Edward the Confessor, established a monastic complex and palace at Westminster. But it was the Normans (from William the Conqueror on) who, requiring a capital on the water route to their lands in Normandy, made it London. Given London's immense wealth and crucial location, the success or failure of invasions or baronial rebellions throughout the Middle Ages often hinged on the behavior of London. As London went, so went the nation.

Outline

I. By about 500 C.E., Londinium was a shadow of its former self.

- **A.** It was cut off from the rest of Britain and the Continent.
- **B.** It was economically, and probably culturally, moribund.
- **C.** It was militarily defenseless.
- **D.** It was certainly depopulated and possibly deserted.

II. The exception was the church.

- **A.** In 597 Pope Gregory I sent Saint Augustine to Britain to convert the Anglo-Saxons.
- **B.** One of Augustine's successes was Aethelbert, King of the Saxons of Kent, who established London's first cathedral, dedicated to Saint Paul, in about 604.
- **C.** By the 8th century, London was a Christian city.
- **D.** By 1200, some 127 churches had been built within the square mile of the walls, endowed by wealthy patrons to save their souls from long sentences in Purgatory.
    1. As a result, the church ended up owning much of medieval London.

2. The church was the main provider of services like schools and hospitals.

III. The Anglo-Saxons gradually began to settle down and become farmers and even city dwellers in the 6th and 7th centuries.

A. The kings of Essex, in England's southeast, found London a convenient administrative center, which also implied military significance.

B. Between 600 and 800, the port of London began to revive.

C. Perhaps the pillar of London's significance that took longest to re-erect was that of government.

1. Basing their capital at Winchester, the Wessex line, most notably King Alfred (r. 871–899) and his descendants, would eventually unite "Angle-land" into something like what we today know as England.
2. But they faced two obstacles: The city's independent streak (because of which its citizens resisted incorporation into a Wessex empire) and the Vikings.

D. The Vikings were a group of warrior tribes.

1. Based in Scandinavia, between 700 and 1100 they became a menace to all Europe, riding their swift longboats down European rivers, across the North Sea and beyond to attack any settlement that promised plunder, such as an increasingly prosperous Anglo-Saxon London.
2. In 851 London was taken by storm and held off and on by Viking kings until 886. They were good in the long run for both the Wessex kings and their largest city.
3. Londoners realized that they needed the protection of a powerful king, and in 886 Alfred "liberated" London from the Vikings and strengthened the city's fortifications and infrastructure.

E. England continued to face Viking invasions in the 10th and 11th centuries—and as London went, so went England.

F. At the end of the Anglo-Saxon period, Edward the Confessor (r. 1042–1066) founded Westminster Abbey.

IV. The death of the childless Edward the Confessor on January 5, 1066, produced a succession crisis that would, in turn, put an end to Anglo-Saxon rule in England.

- **A.** It is generally accepted that William the Conqueror, Duke of Normandy, won the English crown when his army killed the Anglo-Saxon claimant to the throne, Harold II, and defeated his forces at the Battle of Hastings in Sussex on October 14, 1066.
- **B.** But William needed London.
  1. The surviving Anglo-Saxon leaders had rallied to yet another claimant, Edgar, who had fled to London to organize resistance.
  2. William spent the remainder of the autumn burning crops and laying waste to a wide swath of land, about 100 miles in diameter, centered on London.
  3. Then he burned Southwark.
  4. The Anglo-Saxon ruling elite capitulated.
  5. William was crowned in Westminster Abbey on Christmas Day 1066.
- **C.** William the Conqueror introduced a new, Norman dynasty and a Norman-French ruling class, who displaced the old Anglo-Saxon elite in office, titles, lands, and wealth.
  1. Not trusting his Anglo-Saxon subjects, he built a number of castles, including the Tower of London at the wall's eastern anchor point.
  2. The other major change the Norman kings brought to London was to make Westminster the capital.

V. The period of 1066–1485 was one of intermittent conflict between the king and his barons.

- **A.** Throughout the period, London was a key player because of its strategic location, wealth, and prestige.
  1. Generally, when the king was strong and successful, city authorities were happy to lend him money and support, providing troops, huge tax revenues, and—later—loans.
  2. But when the king was weak, his rule subject to question by powerful barons, London asserted its independence.

B. To win municipal support, medieval kings would often grant concessions, usually by means of a charter under the Great Seal of England.

1. Henry I granted London a charter, which in turn granted it the right to elect two sheriffs, to hold its own courts, to fix the total city tax burden at £300, for trade to be free of taxes and tolls, and not to pay the Danegeld or have troops billeted.
2. In the reign of John—when he was regent for his brother, Richard the Lionhearted—the Crown granted London a charter guaranteeing the right to govern itself.

C. Subsequent kings tried to revoke the privileges granted by John.

1. Henry III set aside the aldermen's choice for mayor 10 times between 1239 and 1257.
2. London responded in the 1260s by supporting the rebel Simon de Montfort.
3. Henry's son, Edward I, ruled the city directly in 1284–1297 but was eventually forced to relent.

D. Subsequently, when the monarch kept London's loyalty, he kept his crown.

1. Under Richard II in 1381, the lord mayor stood up to the leaders of the Peasants' Revolt, and it failed.
2. But in 1399, Londoners supported the deposition of Richard by Henry Bolingbroke, Duke of Lancaster.
3. During the Wars of the Roses (1456–1485), in 1461, Londoners opened their gates to the Duke of York, who thereby became Edward IV.
4. A quarter century later, after the Yorkist Richard III had lost his crown on Bosworth Field, London welcomed Henry Tudor, Earl of Richmond, as King Henry VII.

VI. By about 1500, as the Middle Ages ended, London had resumed its position of primacy among the cites of England. It was once again the capital and seat of government, the most important port and economic hub, the military keystone of the country, and a major religious center.

Suggested Reading:

Brooke and Keir, *London 800–1216*.

Inwood, *A History of London*, chaps. 2–3.

Questions to Consider:

1. Why was London a natural capital for England? Why did it take so long to figure this out?
2. Who was ultimately in the stronger position, the king or London?

Lecture Three—Transcript
Medieval London's Thousand-Year Climb

By about 500, Londinium was a shadow of its former self, cut-off from the rest of Britain and the Continent, economically and probably culturally moribund, militarily defenseless, certainly depopulated, possibly deserted. London, had, for the first and only time in its history, lost its reason for existence.

With one exception, that exception was the church. The Christian church had survived the fall of the Western Roman Empire and continued to exist, if not exactly flourish, in cities and monasteries. In 597, Pope Gregory I sent Saint Augustine to Britain to begin a process of reviving Christianity by converting the Anglo-Saxons. One of Saint Augustine's big ticket successes was Aethelbert, King of the Saxons of Kent, whose capital was Canterbury. To demonstrate his faith, Aethelbert established London's first cathedral, built of wood and dedicated to Saint Paul, beginning about 604. There has been a St. Paul's Cathedral on this site ever since.

By the 8th century, London was a Christian city, though as late as 1000 it had only four parishes. But by 1200, some 127 churches had been built within the square mile of the walls, their spires giving a verticality to the previously horizontal, river, bridge, wall, aspect of the city. Why so many churches?

It wasn't that Londoners were particularly religious or that its general population was so large. It was, rather, that wealthy patrons wanted to endow churches to save their souls from long sentences in Purgatory. In fact, because of this fear of Purgatory, the church ended up owning much of medieval London. Kings and commoners made frequent bequests and endowments. This was, in fact, only partly because of the link in Catholic theology between salvation and good works. It's true that lots of wealthy people were keen to leave their money to some worthy church foundation whose members would pray for their souls. But it's also because the church, not the non-existent state, was the main provider of what we would today call social services; schools, hospitals, alms houses. For example, leprosy was a big problem at the end of the Anglo-Saxon period. So leper hospitals were endowed west of the city walls at St. Giles in the Fields and at St. James's but from 1346, lepers were banned from London and from this point, the leper hospitals were mostly used for victims of syphilis.

As their interest in church building implies, the Anglo-Saxons gradually began to settle down, and became farmers and even city dwellers in the 6th and 7th centuries. The first evidence of Anglo-Saxon settlement in London comes from the late 6th century. The reason was almost certainly economic. Farmers growing more food than they ate needed markets. London's location made it convenient for shipping grain along the river or up what was left of the road system, London as a crossroads again.

As some tribes began to conquer the farmland of others, a series of great regional kings emerged in East Anglia, Essex, Kent, Mercia, Northumbria, Sussex, and Wessex in what later historians called "the heptarchy." Now, the kings of Essex, in the southeast, were subservient to those of Kent. They found London a convenient administrative center, which also implied some military significance. The fact that Mercia and Wessex also had borders near London made it a central location. And so, gradually, London began to re-erect the pillars of its former greatness. Between 600 and 800, the port of London began to revive. The Venerable Bede called the city "a market-place for many people who came by land and sea."

Indeed, the town took on a new name, Londonwic; the "wic" being Old English for a trading town. Gold coins reappear about 640. A national, even international, trading system re-emerged in which raw materials like tin, which was mined west of Angle-land or England, and wool were shipped out to the north and to Europe. Also, England was a major supplier of slaves. Finished goods like wine and metal goods were imported. Now, this amounts to a more or less colonial trading economy. England and its largest city were sideshows to the emergence of new states in Europe.

Perhaps the pillar of London's significance that took longest to re-erect was that of government. Between 600 and 900 the dominant Anglo-Saxon kingdom was never based in the southeast. Northumbria, in the far north of England was the most powerful monarchy in the 7th century; Mercia, roughly in the Midlands, in the 8th century. During the 9th century the kings of Wessex, based in the southwest, up the Thames valley from London, became the dominant power among the Anglo-Saxons.

Now London was always on the borders of some of these kingdoms. It was never in the middle and so it was not a natural capital. Basing their capital at Winchester, the Wessex line, most notably King

Alfred, or Alfred the Great, who ruled from 871–899 and his descendants, would eventually unite all of Angle-land into something like what we today know as England but they faced two obstacles, one internal, one external, in attempting to do so. The first obstacle was London itself. The city already had an independent streak and resisted incorporation into a Wessex empire, preferring, at first, to remain something of an independent city-state. The second obstacle was far greater. For just as the Anglo-Saxon monarchs began to try to consolidate their gains England began to face a terrible scourge, the Vikings.

The Vikings were a group of warrior tribes, with values and institutions not unlike those of the Anglo-Saxons in the earlier period. Though based in Scandinavia, between 700 and 1100, they became a menace to all Europe. Riding their swift longboats down European rivers and across the North Sea and beyond to attack any human settlement; city or monastery, camp or village, that promised plundered. Naturally, an increasingly prosperous Anglo-Saxon London, sitting on a river, was a very tempting target.

The short-term result of the Vikings' interest in London was nothing short of disaster. We have only fragmentary accounts of what was happening in London, but its occasional notices in sources like the *Anglo-Saxon Chronicle* are as suggestive as they are cryptic. In 839, the monks who kept the *Chronicle* recorded "a great slaughter in London." That's all they write.

In 851, London was taken by storm and held off and on by Viking kings from 886. Evidence of this period of Viking dominance can be found even today in a few London place names especially churches, interestingly enough, like St. Clement Danes on the Strand, or five different St. Olaf's. That's no accident.

The Vikings also brought their governing traditions. They established something called "the folk-moot." The folk-moot was an open air court of all citizens that met on the high ground east of St. Paul's by the 11th century about three times a year. The idea was that it would maintain order but note again, there is that example of democracy in London. So the Vikings contribute to this tradition as well. The Viking raids were, in fact, good in the long run for both the Wessex kings and their largest city. First, they forced those kings to develop institutions. For example, the fyrd, a militia. Also a regular tax called "the Danegeld" and the infrastructure to collect it which would prove indispensable as they raise money to push the Vikings back and solidified their rule in England.

Alfred and his successors eventually realized they needed an administrative center with easy communications to the rest of the country, and indeed to Europe, and that made London more attractive. They also needed funds to maintain the war effort. Here, London's wealth, taxable and lendable, was crucial. As for Londoners themselves, they realized that they needed the protection that powerful kings could afford. In 886, Alfred liberated London from the Vikings. According to the chroniclers, this was the first time that he was fully acknowledged as the English king.

This begins a pattern. To be king of England, you have to hold London. For the first time since Roman rule, London was now integrated into a larger governmental entity.

Alfred strengthened the city's fortifications and infrastructure. He cares about London. He understands London's significance. He established a new street pattern not based on the Roman one. He built quays at the water's edge, at Queenhithe and Billingsgate and Dowgate. We'll talk about these docks later on in other lectures.

In Anglo-Saxon law city merchants had to register their transactions with the king's reeve, a government official, in a great hall to facilitate their taxation. So one of the reasons that Alfred is building in London, one of the reasons he's supporting the building of docks is, he wants the tax money. Alfred's successors granted London special privileges like the right to hold a husting or an assembly which met three times a week. There's that democratic impulse again. Whenever Londoners want something, they usually want more democracy, more freedom. It was also under the Anglo-Saxon kings that the city was divided into wards, each headed by an alderman.

Though the capital remained at Winchester, London became ever more important to the running of the country. In fact, as England continued to face Viking invasions in the 10th and 11th centuries, as London went so did the nation. If London resisted successfully, as it did in 994, the invasion failed. According to one chronicler, the Danes and Norwegians "suffered more harm and injury than ever they thought any citizen would do to them."

If London capitulated, as it did to Swein and Cnut in 1013 and 1016, respectively, the country submitted to the Viking invaders. In fact,

Londoners turned this to their advantage, claiming that they had the right to name the king of England. After all, he can't be king in London unless we approve.

It was at the end of the Anglo-Saxon period that the Wessex dynasty took steps to give London more of the function of the capital. The last Wessex king, Edward the Confessor, was famously pious. More interested in religious devotion, with a name like that what else could it be, more interested in religious devotion than the usual martial pursuits of kings. Beginning in 1045, he founded a magnificent abbey to the west of the city at Thorn Ey or Thorn Island. This complex was officially a seigniorial manor nominally run by the abbot of the abbey of St. Peter's. We know it today as Westminster Abbey. Westminster would remain under the abbot's control until the Dissolution of the Monasteries under the Tudors between 1536 and 1539. It would remain a separate governmental entity from London proper, under a lord mayor, until the 19th century.

That is to say Westminster is technically a separate city from London all through the medieval and early modern periods. Now, as the king spent time there, it would also increasingly become the center of national government as well as the site of subsequent coronations and most of the burials of Edward's successors.

So, by the time of Edward's death in 1066 London was once again the greatest city, a religious center in England, as well as sharing with Winchester many of the functions of government. Above all, as that year would show, it was the military key to the country at large. For once again, as London went, so went England.

The death of the childless Edward the Confessor on the 5 of January, 1066, produced a succession crisis that would, in turn, put an end to Anglo-Saxon rule in England. Three men, the Anglo-Saxon Harold Godwinson, the Norwegian Viking Harald Hardrada, and the Norman, William, Duke of Normandy, all held viable claims to the throne of England. Godwinson, however, was the claimant on the ground, so got himself acknowledged as King Harold II in London immediately upon Edward's death. The old rule holds. He then rallied the Anglo-Saxon peerage against Hardrada, marched north to meet the invaders, and defeated the Norseman at the Battle of Stamford Bridge, Yorkshire, on the 25 of September, 1066. But just as he's celebrating his victory he learns that William is mounting an invasion on the southeast coast and so Harold then turns around and leads his troops on an exhausting 270 mile forced march south to meet Williams's invading Norman army at Hastings in Sussex.

It is generally accepted that William the Conqueror verified that title and won the English crown when his army killed Harold and defeated his forces at the Battle of Hastings, Sussex, on 14 of October, 1066. The trouble is, like most things in English history, this turns out to be wrong. As it turned out, killing the previous king and defeating the last remaining opposing army in England isn't enough. William needed London. The surviving Anglo-Saxon leaders rallied to yet another claimant, Edgar, who fled to London to organize resistance. William, needing to convince the city's leaders and the Anglo-Saxon ruling class that he meant business, spent the remainder of the autumn of 1066 burning the crops and laying waste to a wide swath about 100 miles in diameter. London was in the center. Then he marched on the city itself. He marched up from the south. He was halted temporarily at the Southwark end of London Bridge. So, in retaliation, he simply burned Southwark to the ground.

Now, you've got to imagine being a bishop, an earl, a citizen of London, you're standing on the north bank. You're looking across the river and Southwark is in flames. They got the message. Suspecting that they were next, they opened the gates to William the Conqueror. Once again, as London goes, so goes the nation. William was crowned in Westminster Abbey on Christmas Day, 1066, though not as we shall see in Lecture Five, without incident.

William the Conqueror introduced a new Norman-French ruling class who displaced the old Anglo-Saxon elite in office, titles, lands, and wealth. Naturally, he didn't trust his Anglo-Saxon subjects, so he started building castles on the north bank of the Thames. Baynard's Castle, and more famously, the Tower of London, originally called the White Tower, at its eastern anchor point on the river. Now this imposing fortress could rake the entrance to the port of London with long-bow, and eventually crossbow, and in a later age, gunfire. Its strategic location meant that it could safeguard the city from outside invaders or keep watch on its own potentially unruly inhabitants.

Now, over the course of the next millennium, the Tower would act as a fortress, a royal palace, and a notorious prison for the most prominent, accused rebels and traitors, as well as a royal refuge when the king had offended the citizenry of his own capital, but maybe its greatest impact was psychological. The Tower of London was for some time one of the tallest structures in London. When viewed from the South Bank, it formed one of two bookends along with the Westminster complex to the west, framing St. Paul's Cathedral in the middle. If the other two called Londoners to fear God, the Tower taught them to fear the king. Just in case, William the Conqueror built another famous castle at Windsor, just 25 miles upriver to the west, to reinforce the effect of the first.

The other major change the Norman kings brought to London was to make it, or rather Westminster, their capital. This made sense because of its great wealth. Kings needed to be able to confer regularly with wealthy merchants. Also, because of its proximity to Europe. Remember that the Normans were still Dukes of Normandy. They and subsequent English kings would maintain extensive holdings in France which they considered every bit as much part of their realm as say Kent or Devonshire. London's location on the Thames makes it a convenient place from which to come and go between the two halves of their possessions, much more convenient than, say, Winchester.

Now, anyone with a nodding acquaintance with the political history of medieval England knows that William and his successors needed all those castles. Through the period of 1066 to 1485 was one of intermittent conflict between the king and his barons interrupted by brief periods of stability. Throughout the period, London was a key player because of its strategic location, its wealth, and its prestige. Precisely because London could tip the balance in favor of an incumbent king or a traitorous usurper, both sides wooed it, which put London in an enviable position when it wasn't being plundered.

Generally, when the king was strong and successful, during the reigns of, for example, William the Conqueror and William II, who between them ruled from 1066 to 1100; Henry I, 1100 to 1135; Henry II, 1154 to 1189; Edward I, 1272 to 1307; Edward III, 1327 to 1377; Henry V, 1413 to 1422; and Edward IV, 1461 to 1483. During the reigns of these strong kings, the city authorities were only too happy to lend them money and support, providing troops and huge tax revenues and often loans. By the way, early in medieval London's history those loans were provided by Jewish bankers, but after their expulsion at the 13th century, Italian bankers. When the king was weak, King Stephen, 1135 to 1154; King John, 1199 to 1216—by the way, you always know a king is unsuccessful when there's no sequel. There's no Stephen II or John II, a bit like the movies—Henry III, 1216 to 1272; Edward II, 1307 to 1327; Richard II, 1377 to 1399; and Henry VI, 1422 to 1461, during the rule of these weak kings, their rule was subject to question by powerful barons, London asserted its independence, sometimes refusing to grant money unless the king made concessions, sometimes refusing money outright or even opening its gates to traitors. It did so to the rebel Jack Cade in 1450 and to Edward, Earl of York, in 1461 but shut London Bridge to Wyatt's rebels in 1554.

As this implies, London could be amazingly fickle. York became King of England in 1461 but when Cade was defeated his head was mounted on London Bride to overlook the very passage he had ridden in triumph. To win municipal support, medieval kings would grant powerful concessions, usually by means of a charter under the Great Seal of England. Now these charters would spell out that such-and-such a place was a city and that it could do certain things. For example, probably Henry I, possibly his nephew Stephen, granted London a charter, which in turn granted the right to elect two sheriffs, mainly they collected taxes, and the right to have its own courts. The right to fix the total city tax burden at no more than 300 pounds, that's a good one. The right to trade and be free of taxes and tolls and not to pay Danegeld or have troops billeted on the city.

An even better example of the pattern is provided by the reign of that famously bad medieval king, at least in the eyes of posterity, John. John served as regent for his brother, Richard the Lionhearted, before coming to the crown in 1199. During this period, to win London support for a possible succession bid, he used his power as regent to grant London a charter guaranteeing the right to, once again, govern itself. It was also during his reign that London was divided into 24 wards. After Richard's death in 1199, John did succeed despite the inconvenient existence of a better claimant, his nephew by an elder brother, Arthur of Brittany.

Now, John tried to distract his subjects from this dubious claim by launching a series of military campaigns against the old enemy, France, but these campaigns meant high taxes and city loans. Once again, John needed to grease the wheels by expanding London's rights. So in 1215, he granted its aldermen the right to elect one of their number, a mayor, annually, usually in October. Now Londoners would run with this and pretty soon they started calling their mayor "the lord mayor," as a sign of their independence. You know, give Londoners an inch, they'll take much more. Still, King John's wars disrupted trade. They increased taxes and worst of all, they were unsuccessful. He lost them.

In 1215, John returned from his wars defeated and discredited, having offended his nobles, the church, towns, and virtually every other group that mattered in England. Despite his attempts to win the city over, London opened its gates to the rebels. That crucial act gave them the base from which to extract from John the Magna Carta in June of that year at Runnymede Meadow, just a few miles outside of town.

The Magna Carta, or the Great Charter, guaranteed the rights of the barons, the church, towns, royal wards, persons accused of crimes, property holders, and many other groups. As you probably know, it represents one of the earliest attempts in post-classical western history to limit the power of rulers. And it's often thought of as the foundation for later assertions of right by the English people and others, including Americans. Once again, London's support was the crucial peace. As the city went, so went the nation and in this case, so went civilization itself. So, if you like the fact that the President can't just decree a higher tax, if you like the rights of habeas corpus, and trial by jury, thank London.

Subsequent kings tried to revoke the privileges granted by John. His son, Henry III, set aside the aldermen's choice for mayor ten times between 1239 and 1257 but London still refused to grant him taxes in 1255. They were upset at what they considered to be already high taxes, and they were upset at Henry's favor for French merchants over English ones, and his establishment of two fairs at Westminster in 1245, which of course took business away from the city. You have to remember that in 1245 Westminster, apart from the abbey and the palace, is pretty much open fields.

In 1261, sensing that he was losing the country to the rebel Simon de Montfort, Henry barricaded himself in the Tower and summoned Parliament but nobody came. In 1263, Queen Eleanor tried to escape the Tower by river but she was cannonaded with garbage from London Bridge. In the related rioting, Lord Mayor Fitz Thomas put himself at the head of the mob. So much for trying to tame London. For the next two years London gave Montfort support. In December of 1263, it opened the city gates to his army, but in 1265, Henry won back control after defeating Montfort at the Battle of Lewes. He retaliated on London by suspending the privileges of the city for two years. He imposed heavy fines on its citizens and he granted Queen Eleanor the revenues of the merchants on London Bridge. Londoners long remembered the consequences of choosing the wrong side.

Henry's son, Edward I, that's the Edward Longshanks of *Braveheart* fame, ruled the city directly between 1284 and 1297, but even he was eventually forced to relent. Still, Edward strengthened the Tower of London, adding the outer wall. He wasn't about to take any chances. He did not trust Londoners. He favored alien merchants and Italian bankers, who could lend him lots of money for his many military campaigns. He also seemed to try to build up a party in London. He broke the ruling oligarchy of families who had served as aldermen. He opened the alderman's position to fishmongers and coopers and skinners, who up to this point had never really had a look-in. In 1275, he introduced the first regular customs duties on exports of wool and leather. The customs were soon to be the most valuable taxes in the royal portfolio. He also established wool markets, staples at Dordrecht, Brabant, Malines, Antwerp. St. Omer would follow in 1313 and Calais in 1363. Now on the one hand this is good for London. It's good for the wool trade but it also increases tax revenues. It increases those customs revenues so don't think that Edward is doing this out of the goodness of his heart.

The city's privileges were only re-confirmed in the next reign when, in 1326, Roger Mortimer rebelled against the incompetent Edward II, Edward I's son. Mortimer seized the Tower, freed its prisoners and gave the keys to the citizens of London. He then used the London mob to intimidate Parliament to demand the removal of the king which happened in 1327. Because London played such a decisive role in the success or failure of a rebellion, the king had far more to lose than London did. Subsequently, when he kept Londoners' loyalty, he kept his crown. For example, under Richard II in 1381, at the time the king was merely a teenager. He's facing the Peasants' Revolt which was a revolt which began over a number of policies that the serfs on nobles' lands generally didn't like. The crucial moment in the revolt took place when the king and the lord mayor of London rode out to meet its leader, Watt Tyler. Suddenly the lord mayor grabs him, knocks Tyler down off of his horse and stabs him. That moment of London loyalty ended the Peasants' Revolt but in 1399, Londoners turned on Richard and supported his deposition by

Henry Bolingbroke, Duke of Lancaster. You can't necessarily count on Londoners' loyalty.

During the Wars of the Roses from 1456 to 1485, London tended to support whichever regime, Lancastrian or Yorkist, was in power or up on the battlefield. The lord mayor and aldermen weren't stupid, but in 1461, they do something odd. Londoners closed their gates to the ruthless leader of the Lancastrians, Queen Margaret of Anjou, despite her recent victory at Wakefield. They open them to that of the seemingly defeated Yorkist, who thereby became King Edward IV. A quarter century later, after the Yorkist Richard III had lost his crown on Bosworth Field, London welcomed Henry Tudor, Earl of Richmond.

What's my point? London usually picks winners. Both moves proved shrewd as both Edward IV and Henry VII were strong, practical, efficient monarchs who ruled effectively and frugally. That, plus their respective peace policies meant lower taxes, fewer loans, and healthier trade for London. Indeed, both Edward IV and Henry VII worked out favorable trade agreements with France and other Continental powers, which again benefited London. In doing so, both consulted London merchants and government officials on fiscal matters. If the love affair with a Yorkist proved fleeting, that with the Tudors lasted to the end of their line as we will see in a subsequent lecture.

So, by, say, 1500, as the Middle Ages ended, London had resumed its position of primacy among the cities of the British Isles, England in particular. It was once again the capital and seat of government, the most important port and economic hub, the military keystone of the country, a major religious center. Well, that's official London. Indeed that's the official history but what was it like? What did it feel like to live in London? What were its streets like? What did it smell like? What sounds would you have heard? What sights would you have seen? In the next lecture we will walk the streets of medieval London and some of its most interesting characters.

Lecture Four

Economic Life in Chaucer's London

Scope:

Chaucer's London was the most populous city in England, but at only about 30,000–45,000 people, it was still a rather modest capital for a small country on the fringes of Europe. Medieval London was still a walled town, with a few roads connecting it to the countryside. But its overseas trade brought luxury goods from Europe in exchange for raw wool. This lecture takes us on a walk through the commercial sector of medieval London, culminating in the shopping district of Cheapside, dominated by the livery companies.

Outline

I. So far, we have discussed London's importance, its foundation under the Romans, and its development of an independent streak during the Middle Ages.

- **A.** But what was London actually like to live in?
- **B.** This is the first of six lectures spread throughout the course that are designed to give you a sense of daily life in London, from the Middle Ages to the 21st century.

II. Geoffrey Chaucer, arguably the first great English poet whom we know by name, was a lifelong Londoner, so he never immigrated there, never arrived for the first time.

- **A.** Therefore, our tour of Chaucer's London will begin with one of his contemporaries, who, according to legend, came to London from the country, a poor scullery boy who rose to be lord mayor three times: Dick Whittington.
  1. In fact, historians now know that the real Whittington was not poor.
  2. He probably came to London at the traditional age of apprenticeship, 14, which would place his arrival in about 1365.
  3. He probably arrived along the Great Northern Road laid out in Roman times, and one route would have taken him down Hampstead Heath and Highgate Hill.

B. We pause, as young Whittington must have done, at the top of Highgate Hill to get our first view of the city below us about 1365.

   1. Looking south and slightly east, we spy the horizontal thread of the river, dividing the city in two. Most of the city lies on our side, the northern bank, and the two banks are connected by London Bridge, built in 1176.

   2. Across the bridge we notice a small community, Southwark, which like Westminster is outside of city control. Since Roman times, it has been the home of the Bankside stews, riverside brothels owned and regulated by the bishop of Winchester.

   3. But for most of London's history, the action has been on the north bank.

   4. London's vertical profile is dominated by the spire of St. Paul's Cathedral, which rises to nearly 550 feet.

C. We now plunge in, making our way, as Whittington probably did, down Highgate Hill, to the village of Islington, through the old city wall at Aldersgate, into Aldersgate Street.

III. Aldersgate was one of the eight gates that funneled people and goods through London's ancient wall.

A. The wall itself was about 18 feet high and 6–9 feet thick, with battlements.

B. The area within the Roman walls of the old city is today known as "the City."

   1. This area of 330 acres defines the official city of London.

   2. Because the medieval city developed haphazardly, the old Roman grid pattern was distorted by a bewildering maze of lanes, alleys, and courtyards.

   3. Because everyone wanted to live within the walls, substantial houses were narrow in the front at street level but were five and six stories high, overhanging the street, their tops almost touching.

   4. Houses of poor Londoners were built of wattle and daub and prone to collapse. They were so crowded together that they tended to burn.

IV. Walking east along London Wall, we head for the river and reach London's first great landmark, the Tower on Tower Hill.

A. Originally, as built under William the Conqueror and finished by his sons, the Tower was just the Great Keep or White Tower with its four turrets.

1. Subsequent medieval kings built additional buildings: a wall around the White Tower, the Bell Tower, the Wardrobe Tower, a moat, and an outer wall.

2. In 1235 Edward's son, Henry III, was given three leopards by the Holy Roman Emperor, the beginning of the King's Menagerie.

3. From 1303 the crown jewels were deposited here.

4. From the 13th until the 17th centuries, English monarchs spent the night before their coronation at the Tower.

5. The Tower was also a notorious prison.

B. If we move west from the Tower, we come to London's docks.

1. Many of them were named for the goods they serviced, (e.g., the Hay Wharf or Wood Quay).

2. We can't help but notice the sights, sounds, and smells of London's commerce at work.

V. From the docks we move, like the goods themselves, north up any one of a number of narrow lanes to an east-west street called Eastcheap.

A. Shopkeepers in particular trades tended to congregate in the same part of town. Because the London livery companies set prices and wages, there was no real competition, no reason to set up shop in an underserved area.

B. Moving west down Eastcheap, we note London's meat market.

C. Moving northward at the corner of Gracious (or Gracechurch) Street and Eastcheap, we look down three streets forming a wedge called the Poultry: Lombard Street, Cornhill, and Threadneedle Street.

1. Cornhill was and is the economic heart of the City. This was where the grain factors met.

2. Threadneedle Street was at this time home to the tailors.

3. Lombard Street was where the Italian bankers worked, outdoors.

4. The Poultry itself was London's market for fowl, pigs, and rabbits.

D. Moving west from the Poultry, we emerge into one of the widest and most impressive thoroughfares in central London: Cheapside.

1. This was London's chief shopping street. It was lined with shops, as well as makeshift stalls in the center.
2. Because of its length and width, Cheapside was also a grand street for tournaments and civic processions, such as the lord mayor's annual installation.
3. Because Cheapside was such a public space, it was also, during the Middle Ages, a place of exemplary punishment, especially for dishonest merchants.
4. The street is connected with other trading areas. To our right are Grocer's Lane, Ironmonger Alley, and Milk Street. To our left are Bread Street and Goldsmith's Row.

E. Nearly all of these occupational groups had their own guilds (or as they are called in London, livery companies).

1. While most towns had only one guild, London had one livery company for each trade, about 50 in all, each with its own impressive gothic hall.
2. These organizations grew out of the medieval church's hostility to certain aspects of capitalism, in particular the potential for sharp practice and social mobility.
3. They were called livery companies because, traditionally, each trade had its own distinctive uniform, or livery.
4. Specifically, a livery company was an organization of London tradesmen granted privileges by a royal charter as well as by the lord mayor and aldermen to set prices, wages, and standards of quality for all its merchants and tradesmen.
5. The fundamental fact of economic life in London in 1365, and to a declining extent well into the 19th century, was that it was organized around the livery companies.

Suggested Reading:

Inwood, *A History of London*, chap. 4.

Myers, *London in the Age of Chaucer*.

Questions to Consider:

1. Why did the myth of Dick Whittington trump his reality?
2. Why were the medieval church and its livery companies so opposed to capitalism?

Lecture Four—Transcript
Economic Life in Chaucer's London

So far we have discussed London's importance, its foundation under the Romans, and its development of an independent streak during the Middle Ages but what was London actually like to live in? What did it look like, smell like, feel like? This is the first of six lecture segments spread over the course designed to give you that sense from the Middle Ages to the 21st century. As we wander the streets of London, you might want to keep a map in front of you; you're going to need it.

Geoffrey Chaucer, arguably the first great English poet whom we know by name, the author of Romance of the Rose and The Canterbury Tales, lived from about 1343 to about 1400. He was a lifelong Londoner, born down by the river in Vintry Ward, the son of John Chaucer, a wine merchant. The name of the ward tells us that merchants of a particular type tended to congregate together. He lived through some of the most dramatic events in London's medieval history, the Black Death from 1349 to 1351, the Peasants' Revolt of 1381, but did not long survive and may have been a victim of the deposition of Richard II by Henry Bolingbroke who became Henry IV in 1399.

Chaucer was a courtier and a government official who rose to be Controller of the Customers and Master of the Works which means that he straddled both sides of medieval London and Westminster, port and capital. Unfortunately, though London figures in his writings, he didn't write very often about his own experience on the streets of London. Worse, precisely because he was born in London, he never immigrated; he never arrived as we are doing for the first time.

So, to begin our tour of Chaucer's London, I'm going to cheat and call on one of his contemporaries who, according to London's most persistent legend, came to London from the country a poor, orphaned kitchen scullion who rose to be its lord mayor three times, Dick Whittington. Now according to the story, young Dick was asked to contribute something to his master's trading voyage to North Africa. All Whittington could come up with was his cat. While the ship was away, Dick grew discouraged and he attempted to leave London by the Great Northern Road but on Highgate Hill he heard the bells of

St. Mary-le-Bow, Bow Bells, calling him. Turn again, Whittington, thrice mayor of London.

Returning, he found that the king of Morocco was so pleased with the cat's mousing abilities that young Whittington was now a rich man; the king of Morocco having paid an exorbitant amount of money for this cat. This enabled him to marry his master's daughter and become lord mayor. This became the archetype of London's story, poor boy makes good. Now, in fact, Dick Whittington was a real person who lived from about 1350 to 1423. But historians now know that he was anything but poor, he came from a minor landowning family in Gloucestershire, so London's Horatio Alger myth is every bit as believable as America's.

He probably came to London at the traditional age of apprenticeship. That would be 14 which would place his arrival in about 1365, probably along the Great Northern Road laid out in Roman times. One route would've taken him down Hampstead Heath and Highgate Hill to Islington into Aldersgate Street. Let us pause as young Whittington must have done at the top of Highgate Hill to get our first view of the city below us, circa 1365.

Looking south and slightly east, we spy the horizontal thread of the river, a silver-green snake stretching from horizon east to horizon west dividing the city in two. On closer inspection, we realize that most of the city lies on our, northern, bank. Looking up, across the river, to the South Bank, we see that the two are connected by London Bridge, the current version of which was built in 1176. The keen eyed will note that there are houses and shops on the bridge and a drawbridge to allow big ships to pass upstream. The river is dotted with those ships, mostly ocean-going carracks and barges for river traffic. They congregate near a series of docks on the north bank on either side of the bridge that gives London its wealth.

Across the bridge we notice a small community, Southwark. Like Westminster not yet part of London proper. As a place outside of city control, it's wilder than the rest of London, sort of a combat zone where Londoners go for a good or slightly illicit time. For example, since Roman times, Southwark has been of the Bankside stews, riverside brothels, owned and regulated by the reverend Bishop of Winchester. The idea was to contain vice in one place outside the city walls, just like a modern red-light district or combat zone and use the wages of sin for the good work of the church. So the good bishop drew up rules and limited opening hours. The arrangement worked quite well; South Bank prostitutes were called Winchester Geese until that famous prude, Henry VIII, closed them down.

Medieval Southwark also hosts Winchester House and Lambeth Place, the London homes of the Bishop of Winchester and the Archbishop of Canterbury, two of the wealthiest prelates in England, in Winchester's case we know why, and an impressive Gothic church, St. Mary Overie. St. Thomas' Hospital, close by, partly endowed by Whittington, was well known for treating the diseases experienced by the Winchester Geese and because Southwark is the southern and eastern entrance point for London, connecting with Watling Street and the Old Kent Road, it is also the host of lots of inns. In fact, there are 25 inns on Southwark High Street alone. The two most famous in Chaucer's time are the Tabard and the Bear at Bridge Foot and both would last into the 19th century.

It is from the Tabard, Chaucer's gentle hostelry that his pilgrims begin their famous unfinished trip to Canterbury in *The Canterbury Tales*, but for most of London's history, the action has been on the north bank. Above the city, we might notice a hazy cloud of smoke from London's many wood fires. The cloud, like the river, drifts east, as both the prevailing winds and the current flow that way. That will be crucial for London's development. Since the river also carries away London's sewage, and since nobody likes to have smoke blown onto them, London's wealthiest residents will always tend to move west, upstream and upwind. That's why the West End will always be the smart end of town. That's one reason why the East End will always, for much of London's history anyway, be considered poor and relatively undesirable, but that's in the future.

In the 14th century, there is no East End; east of the Tower is open fields. Here, Londoners graze cattle and sheep, play football and joust, practice archery, and try to avoid the evidence left behind by cattle and sheep. Below the haze, we note that London's vertical profile is dominated by one great feature, bracketed by two smaller ones. The great vertical feature is the spire of St. Paul's Cathedral which rises to the astonishing height of nearly 550 feet, the highest in England. That's about 200 feet higher than the current dome of St. Paul's. That spire, a target for lightning, would burn down in 1447 and again in 1561, the second time they wouldn't replace it. If we imagine our arrival on a sunny day, the light glints off of the steeple like a sword point. Surrounding it, the towers and spires of over 100 medieval churches, all crammed against each other in the square mile within the walls, almost like children huddling against their mother, St. Paul's.

The eastern bookend is, of course, the Tower of London. Looking west, beyond the wall, we see a narrow track hardly a road, called the Strand. It's lined with great inns and palaces owned by bishops and abbots. Some are rented out to lawyers and law students practicing in London's courts. This, the Strand, leads finally to the impressive complex of buildings at Westminster, the western bookend of the scene. There is the Abbey, minus the towers that modern visitors see. This Abbey is sort of long and low. The towers weren't erected until the 18th century. There's Westminster Hall even longer and lower, and there's Westminster Palace, narrow and vertical. Having had this overview, let us plunge in, making our way as Whittington probably did down Highgate Hill through the village of Islington, through the Old City wall at Aldersgate into Aldersgate Street.

Aldersgate was one of the eight gates that funneled people and goods through London's ancient, ancient wall. Following the wall counter-clockwise they are the Postern-gate, Aldgate, Bishopsgate, Moorgate, Cripplegate, Aldersgate, Newgate, and Ludgate. Each would give its name to the street which passed through it and the district around it. Each could be shut against invaders and was routinely shut at night. Medieval London has a curfew of 8:00 pm in winter, 9:00 pm in summer. Each had a guardhouse which, in the case of Newgate, evolved into the most notorious prison in English history, with apologies to Wormwood Scrubs. On top of these gates, the heads of less fortunate malefactors are displayed on pikes as a warning to those who dared disturb the peace of the city. On a happier note, Chaucer himself rented rooms above Aldgate between 1374 and 1386, from which he could observe a great deal of London life. The wall itself is about 18 feet high and 6 to 9 feet thick, with battlements, it is a formidable challenge to any invader or drunk out past curfew.

The area within the Roman walls of the old city is today known, with monumental self-centeredness, as the City with a capital "C." It is this area, formally within the walls today, of 330 acres which defined the official city of London because the medieval City developed haphazardly; the old Roman grid-pattern has been distorted. Some larger streets run rationally parallel to the river, like Tower Street-

Eastcheap or Cannon Street and Vintry Street, where Chaucer was born, others run perpendicular to it, like Fish Street, Gracious Street, and Bishopsgate Street but that's the last of the idea of a grid pattern. Between these streets has grown up a bewildering maze of lanes, alleys, and courtyards in no logical pattern because everyone wants to live within the walls. Substantial houses are "very narrow in the front towards the street, but are built five and six roofs high overhanging the street, their tops almost touching." This blocks out the sun. While it provides shade in summer, it makes it easier for houses to catch fire from each other. The overhangs are also responsible for one of the hazards of walking the streets of London; the custom of emptying out night-soil, human excrement and urine, from upper windows into the open street, so that it might be washed away by the rains. That's right, medieval London has no proper underground sewers. One possible explanation for the British euphemism, "loo," for the toilet is that it derives from the old warning, "Gardyloo," for "watch out below." So as we wander the streets of London we will be careful to keep our eyes peeled.

Houses of poor Londoners were built of wattle and daub. That's a fancy way of saying anything that stuck together, mud mixed with straw, animal manure, etc., with timber framing, whitewashed with lime. The house of a wealthy Londoner would be built of more substantial plaster within that timber frame. Now, these poorer houses were so ramshackle that they tended to collapse and they were so crowded together that they tended to burn. So even in 1365, London is a dangerous and, as we've seen, a messy place to live.

Walking east along London Wall, we head for the river and reach London's first great landmark, the Tower on Tower Hill. From this commanding position, the Tower dominates this part of London and the river. Now, it originally is built under William the Conqueror and finished by his sons, the Tower was just the Great Keep or White Tower with its four turrets. And the most famous bit of the Tower of London was all there was. Its four floors contained, in ascending order, first, a storehouse and later, a dungeon, the Tower's first use as a prison. This included the little ease, a cell four-foot square in which prisoner could neither lie nor stand at full length. Nice. Above that a barracks, above that a dining hall and chapel with living space for nobles, and at the top of the White Tower, the king's bed chamber and counsel chamber. Here, in embryo, are the basic components of every palace that we will visit in this course.

Subsequent medieval kings built additional buildings, a wall around the White Tower, the Bell Tower, the Wardrobe Tower. Edward I, you may remember that his relations with London were somewhat stormy, added a moat and an outer wall, 90 feet high and at its base, 15 feet thick. You think he was worried about something? In 1235, Edward's son, Henry III, was given three leopards by the Holy Roman Emperor. This was the beginning of the King's Menagerie. In the 13th century the sheriff of London was fined four pence a day to feed a polar bear and buy him a chain so that he could fish in the Thames. The menagerie was open to the public off and on until the 1830s when the animals were finally donated to the London Zoological Gardens in Regents' Park. So the London Zoo really begins life as the King's Tower Menagerie.

From 1303, the crown jewels were also deposited here. From the 13th century until the 17th, English monarchs spent the nights before their coronation at the Tower. The last monarch to do this was Charles II in 1660, but by the Tudor Period, this was virtually the only time they spent there. From this point on, the Tower was a fortress and an infamous prison housing some of England's most famous prisoners, Roger Mortimer in 1323, King David II of Scotland in 1346, and James I of Scotland in 1406, King John II of France in 1356, kings Richard II and Henry VI, both murdered here, the latter at prayer in 1471. Perhaps most famously, the two princes probably murdered by Richard III in 1483, Edward V and his younger brother, Richard, Duke of York. It was possibly their skeletons found under a staircase here in the 1670s, those skeletons have since been buried in Westminster Abbey.

Numerous Tudor and Stuart victims we will meet in later lectures spent time in the Tower of London, but also ordinary people. In 1268, 600 Jews accused of clipping coins, 267 of them were hanged. In 1345, during the Hundred Years War, 300 citizens of Caen. The first prominent execution was that of Richard II's tutor, Sir Simon de Burley, in 1386. So don't tell me that an academic is risk free. The Tower stands today as one of London's few architectural links to the Middle Ages. There isn't much of Chaucer's London left and so we have to treasure examples of it like the Tower of London.

If we move west from the Tower, we come to London's docks. Now, many of them were named for the goods they serviced. Moving east to west there was, for example, Fish wharf, perpendicular to Old Fish

Street; the Hay wharf, the Wine wharf, at the foot of Vintries Lane. The Chaucer family lived close to here on Thames Street, parallel to the river. Also on Thames Street was the steel yard. Now this is where the Hanseatic merchants from north Germany lived. They kept aloof from native Londoners and were resented for it. They also became fabulously wealthy and, at times, were granted privileges by the king that actually superseded those of native London merchants. Another reason they were resented. They imported furs and timber and iron and fish. Queenhithe was associated with goods from southern France. Billingsgate, later on, became a great fish market and Wood Quay obviously set aside for Timber.

Now, as we walk among the docks, we can't help but notice the sights, the sounds, and the smells of London's commerce at work. Fish, wine, timber, and finished cloth being unloaded from ships and then raw wool, England's chief export, being loaded in bales onto them. As we stand at the docks, we hear the hammering and the sawing of carpenters and shipwrights mingled with the music of rough speech, mostly Middle English, maybe with a broad cockney accent as well as medieval versions of Flemish, French, German, etc. We see the stitching of sail makers and observe the whole panoply of maritime activity associated with any port. Because the customs duties collected from merchants' ships are the mainstay of the royal revenue, it was very important for the king to regulate the docks and to know what ship was docking where and what its cargo was. This was especially important to Geoffrey Chaucer because he was Controller of the Customs.

So just west of us, between London Bridge and the Tower is the medieval Customs House. A structure that will burn down in 1559 and again 1666 and partially in 1714 but always be rebuilt on this same prime real estate. In fact, the Customs House is the first major structure rebuilt after the Great Fire of London in 1666. The king needs that revenue.

From the docks we move, like the goods themselves, north up any one of a number of narrow lanes. Let's say Minchin Lane, to an east-west street called Eastcheap. Here we begin to encounter retail London. In fact, the old English word "ceap" means a market. As we noted earlier, shopkeepers in particular trades tended to congregate in the same part of town because the London livery companies set prices and wages, we'll talk about that in a few minutes, there was no real competition. There was no reason to set up shop in an underserved area. Moving west down Eastcheap, we note, first of all rows of butchers; for during the Middle Ages this is London's meat market. The sights and smells of offal are horrendous, they're, well, awful. Despite being carted down to the Fleet River daily, the Fleet River is a tributary of the Thames running north-south; it eventually became a sort of open sewer.

Holding our noses, we turn northward at the corner or Gracious or Gracechurch Street and Eastcheap to take a look down three streets forming a wedge that meets at the Poultry. They are Lombard Street, Cornhill, and Threadneedle Street. Now, even in the 14th century, this is the economic heart of the city. When 21st-century Londoners refer to the City, this is still where they mean. Corn means grain in medieval and modern English and so Cornhill is where the grain factors meet. Threadneedle Street was obviously home to the tailors but in 1365, the most interesting of these streets is Lombard; for this is where the Italian bankers, the Lombards settle. Lombard Street will remain London's banking center into the 21st century. In 1365, we can actually watch the bankers at work just as easily as shipwrights and butchers. For the traditional method was to transact business in the open air while walking along the street. Trouble was, this may have worked just great in Italy but London's weather is a little more formidable. Two centuries later, John Stow noted that such meetings,

> Were unpleasant and troublesome, by reason of walking and talking in an open street, being there constrained to endure all extremes of weather, or else shelter themselves in shops.

That explains why, under Queen Elizabeth, they would move indoors. Now coming west from Cornhill all three streets meet at the Poultry. The Poultry is London's market for fowl, pigs, and rabbits and therefore for more unpleasant smells. A little further on we come to a perpendicular street called Old Juree, Old Jewry, or by the 18th century, Old Jury. The second name is the most accurate, for this is the site of the Jewish ghetto from at least the 12th century to their expulsion by Edward I in 1291. Jewish merchants have been subject to repeated persecution even before this. In 1264, the area was destroyed and over 500 Jews were murdered after a Jewish merchant was accused of charging too high an interest rate. At their expulsion, they lost all their property to the king.

Moving west from the Poultry, we emerge into one of the widest and most impressive thoroughfares in central London, Cheapside. This is London's chief shopping street. It is the Rodeo Drive of medieval England. It is lined with shops, as well as makeshift stalls in the center. It's very broad, very wide, these were really workshops with a few samples. That is, there was no stock. You couldn't go in and buy a pair of shoes. Goods were all made to order. Their proprietors lived in houses above the shop. Standing at their doors, we may spy idling apprentices, clearly not having been influenced by the story of Dick Whittington. Apprentices were young men, usually young men, there were also apprenticeships for women mainly in the clothing trade. These people were aged between 14 and 21 and their parents had bought them a place with a merchant or a tradesman. The idea was that he would train the apprentice in his or her craft. The trouble was most crafts didn't really take seven years to learn which meant that apprentices often spent more time in the devil's workshop than they did their master's.

Chaucer wrote of one such apprentice in The Cook's Tale:

> Once an apprentice dwelt within our town, learning the victuals trade. He was as brown as any berry [which meant that he got too much sun.] Blithely he'd cavort like a finch in the wood. Well-built and short, with locks coal black and very neatly kept. At dancing he so well, so blithely leapt, that he was known as Perkin Revellor. He was as full of love, this victualler, as is the beehive full of honey sweet, and lucky were the wenches he would meet. At every wedding he would sing and hop; he loved the tavern better than the shop.

Because of its length and width, Cheapside is also a grand street for tournaments and civic processions. For example, the lord mayor's annual installation, during which the conduits at either end of the street running would run with wine. How could our idle apprentice resist? Chaucer tells us,

> When there was a procession in Cheapside,
> Out of the shop immediately he hied,
> And till he'd seen it all, and took a turn
> At dancing, he would not again return.

We, on the other hand, are engaged in serious scholarly pursuits and I think, therefore, might legitimately refresh ourselves in one of Cheapside's famous taverns. There's the Bull Head or for gender equality, the Nag's Head. There's the Mitre or the Three Cranes, in fact, by 1309 there were already 354 taverns in the square mile of the City of London. Three times the number of churches to refresh its many thirsty inhabitants. Because Cheapside was such a public space it was also during the Middle Ages a place of exemplary punishment especially for dishonest merchants.

In 1382 a cook from Bread Street was put in the pillory for selling stale fish which was burnt under his nose. There was a fountain, called The Standard, which was a popular place of execution. Oddly enough, this was also the place where you generally got your drinking water. The street was connected with other trading areas as it still is. Off to our right, Grocer's Lane, Ironmonger Lane, and the dairymen in Milk Street. To our left, Bread Street and Goldsmith's Row; shoemakers on Cordwainer Street, grocers and mercers in Sopers Lane. In other words, you could get virtually any of life's necessities in Cheapside.

Now, nearly all of these occupational groups had their own guild, or as they were called in London, their own "livery companies." Most towns had only one guild but London had one livery company for each trade—about 50 in all, each with its own impressive gothic hall. Here, its masters met for deliberations and to hold feasts where the community of, say, weavers or grocers or ironmongers, could be reaffirmed. Now, these organizations grew out of the medieval church's hostility to certain aspects of capitalism, in particular the potential for sharp practice and social mobility. In other words, the church was worried that people would cheat if they could make an excessive profit, and they were worried that people would grow too rich and that would, of course, upset the social hierarchy.

They were called livery companies because traditionally, in a preliterate age, every trade has its own distinctive uniform or livery. For example, doctors could be identified by their red cloaks. We still see this occasionally in the case of, for example, hotel doorman, but what exactly was a livery company? A livery company was an organization of London tradesmen granted privileges by a royal charter as well as by the lord mayor, an alderman, to set prices, wages, and standards of quality for all of its merchants and tradesman. Let's make sure we understand that. If you a member of the livery company, you cannot undersell. You cannot over pay. You cannot produce a different kind of shoe from the shoe being produced by the shoemaker next door. Every product, every price, every wage must be the same.

Only the members of the livery company could trade within the walls. That is to say if you weren't a member of the shoemakers' guild, you couldn't sell shoes within the walls. Only members of a livery company voted in municipal elections for all sorts of local officials including London's members of Parliament. The guild also had an important social and charitable function distributing charity to the sick or unemployed members, widows and orphans, and before the Reformation it often endowed hospitals and almshouses and schools. You may be familiar with the Merchant Tailors School still thriving in London. Because trades were concentrated in particular streets, each guild had its own parish church as well as its own hall. Prior to the Reformation, guild members vied with each other to endow their church with statues, commemorative windows, etc. and so the livery company was a sort of Better Business Bureau, a trade association for standards and practices, a lobbying association, a Rotary or a Kiwanis club, and a trade union all wrapped up into one. The idea was to ensure sufficient profit for every member without letting any one member grow too rich or too poor. To ensure security for member's families, if a master became ill or died, to ensure a sufficient wage for every worker and yet no competition for labor, and to ensure a reasonable quality and price for the goods bought by each consumer.

In effect, the livery company provided a lot of the social and economic infrastructure in towns and cities that manorial society and church membership did in villages. So if you think by moving to the city you're sort of leaving a closed society, or you're going to a society which is very lonely, or in which the individual may not connect up with other individuals, well, the purpose of the livery company was to make sure that you did under a kind of umbrella of church sponsorship. The fundamental fact of economic life in London in 1365, and to a declining extent well into the 19th century, was that it was organized around the livery companies. But surely, there was more to London than economic life. In the next lecture we find out by heading west by visiting St. Paul's Cathedral, by visiting the Strand, the bishop houses along it, and the complex at Westminster.

Lecture Five

Politics and Religion in Chaucer's London

Scope:

In this lecture, we continue our walking tour of Chaucer's London with a trip to the Guildhall, London's city hall. From there we proceed to St. Paul's, not only London's cathedral but in some ways a local parish church for the entire city. This is followed by a tour of "legal London" around Fleet Street and then the Westminster complex built by Edward the Confessor and his successors, the home of the national government.

Outline

I. The guilds controlled London's economic life, but they were subject to an even higher authority.

- **A.** Heading north up Ironmonger Lane to Basinghall Street, we reach London's city hall, the Guildhall.
  1. The current Guildhall was built in 1411 and would survive the fire in 1666 and a bomb hit in 1940 to remain the official headquarters of City government into the 21st century.
  2. This is the seat of the lord mayor, the Court of Aldermen, and the Common Council, the legislative branches of London government.
  3. The lord mayor was elected annually by the citizens (i.e., guild members) of London.
  4. To assist the lord mayor in his executive functions, London had by 1365 two sheriffs, a recorder, a town clerk, and an army of subordinate officers: constables to enforce the law, scavengers to pick up trash, and criers and night watchmen at the precinct level.
  5. The key figures were London's 25 aldermen. The Court of Aldermen appointed people to subordinate offices, issued proclamations and orders regarding public health and morals, and had the right to veto any legislation passed by Common Council or Common Hall.
  6. There was much potential for conflict in this system, but it also meant that London's government was the most democratic in England.

B. Perhaps the greatest challenge facing London's government during Chaucer's lifetime was the Black Death of 1348–1349.

1. The Black Death was probably the bubonic plague (*Pasteurella pestis*) that had decimated Europe periodically through ancient times.
2. The disease was spread by the bite of a flea, carried on the back of the black rat, which rode in carts of grain or ships' holds to other cities, where crowded, unhygienic conditions allowed the rats to thrive.
3. Once you were bitten, disease onset was sudden, and your odds of survival were one in four.
4. Medieval medical science was totally baffled.
5. London's government was largely ineffective in fighting the plague, apart from attempting to clean up the filth and excrement from London's streets.
6. The plague lasted through the winter, peaking between February and Easter of 1349. The Plague returned in 1361–1362, 1368–1369, and 1407.
7. It took a century for London's population to recover, not least because the unsanitary city also faced outbreaks of tuberculosis, typhus, dysentery, smallpox, diphtheria, and measles.

II. At the west end of Cheapside sits the greatest religious building in London, St. Paul's Cathedral, subsequently known as Old St. Paul's after it burned down in 1666.

A. This was easily the greatest church in England and, as we will recall from seeing it from afar, the dominant building in London's skyline.

1. It was 585 feet long.
2. In 1365, its spire rose nearly 550 feet.

B. Along with Westminster Abbey, St. Paul's is one of two great national churches in London.

C. But St. Paul's is also a great local institution.

1. In the northeast corner of the churchyard was Paul's Cross, a freestanding pulpit from which announcements were made, citizens were summoned three times a year to the "folk-moot," and some of the most notable sermons in London were delivered.

2. Once printing was invented in the 15th century, St. Paul's churchyard would also be home to stationers, printers, and booksellers.
3. The nave of London's greatest building was a public place, and on weekdays scribes, lawyers, and government officials, even tradesmen, set up shop in the aisles.

III. Leaving St. Paul's, we head west down Ludgate Hill, through the Ludgate itself to Fleet Street.

- **A.** Fleet Street is named for the River Fleet.
  1. During the Middle Ages, cutlers, butchers, and tanners would dispose of animal carcasses and byproducts of metallurgy and leather working in the River Fleet.
  2. The river also served as a convenient open sewer, leading to frequent complaints about the stench.
- **B.** Perhaps because it was only yards from Newgate Prison, within a century or two, this area would develop a series of law schools: the famous Inns of Court.
- **C.** Carrying on down Fleet Street, we pass under Temple Bar, which represents the outermost reaches of the legal City.

IV. To the west lies Westminster.

- **A.** The principal east-west land route between the City and Westminster is an unpaved dirt track called the Strand.
- **B.** To the left or river side of the street, we view a series of stately bishops' palaces—called inns—stretching along the Thames all the way down to Westminster.
  1. These inns represent the power and wealth of the church in London.
  2. In the Middle Ages, most bishops spent most of their time in London, serving the king in high office or hanging out at court, hoping for preferment.
- **C.** On the right side of the street we see only a few shops and, just beyond them, open fields: rural London.

V. We continue down the Strand to the village of Charing.

VI. Following the river, we then turn left onto a dirt track later known as King's Street to Westminster.

- **A.** Westminster was not part of the City of London, as it lies outside of the City walls and so the lord mayor's jurisdiction.
- **B.** The religious and emotional heart of the Westminster complex is Westminster Abbey.
  1. Every English monarch since William the Conqueror has been crowned here, except Edward V and VIII, who never made it to their coronations.
  2. From 1245 to 1272, Henry III pulled down the cruciform Edwardian building and erected the present high gothic masterpiece, though the twin towers known to modern visitors would not be built until the 18th century.
  3. The present abbey is heavily influenced by French models like Amiens and Rheims.
  4. If St. Paul's is London's parish church, then Westminster Abbey is the nation's.
  5. Near here is the Chapter House, where the House of Commons met until 1547.
  6. Just outside this part of the abbey we find shops, beggars, and thieves, in part because this is a place of sanctuary.
  7. In December 1476, William Caxton will set up England's first print shop in a rented house near here at the sign of the Red Pale.
- **C.** Westminster Hall to the northeast was built in 1097 by William II as an extension of Edward the Confessor's palace.
- **D.** Westminster Palace, built by Edward the Confessor as his principal London residence, would serve as the home base of the court of England until a fire damaged it in 1512.

VII. Having seen official, governmental, and religious London, we might head down to the river to contemplate all that we have seen.

Suggested Reading:

Inwood, *A History of London*, chap. 4.

Robertson, *Chaucer's London*.

Questions to Consider:

1. Why did St. Paul's Cathedral serve as a community center as well as a church? What was the medieval attitude toward church and state?
2. What sorts of tensions might have existed between economic London to the east and governmental London to the west?

Lecture Five—Transcript
Politics and Religion in Chaucer's London

As we learned in the last lecture, the guilds controlled London's economic life but they were subject to an even higher authority, the Guildhall. If we leave Cheapside and head north up Ironmonger Lane to Basinghall Street, we arrive at the greatest of all Guild Halls, London's city hall, the Guildhall first mentioned in the early 12th century. The current Guildhall was built in 1411 and it would survive the fire in 1666, and a bomb hit in 1940, to remain the official headquarters of city government into the 21st century. This is the seat of the lord mayor where the Court of Aldermen and Common Council, the legislative branches of London government, meet.

The lord mayor was elected annually by the citizens of London meeting at the Guildhall who, because there's no secret ballot, usually took the advice of their local alderman. Later in the period, this was usually to elect the most senior alderman. At times, the king might set aside the election of someone he didn't like so, as in our own day, that appearance of democracy sometimes trumped actual choice. At least they got a show. Annually on the 29 of October, the lord mayor sponsored a magnificent procession to Westminster and back to celebrate his election.

To assist the lord mayor in his executive functions London had, by 1365, two sheriffs, a recorder, a town clerk, and an army of subordinate offices, some paid, some unpaid. Some appointed, some elected, all filled by ordinary people like constables to enforce the law, scavengers to pick up trash, criers and night watchmen at the precinct level, and later church wardens and overseers of the poor for each parish. Now, in other words, there was a great deal of participation among ordinary people in the government of London. The key figures in this equation were London's 25 aldermen.

Aldermen were elected by the existing members of the Court of Aldermen from among the wealthiest merchants and, later financers, in London. It tends to be a closed shop, they tend to elect relatives and other people of their economic rank. Each alderman was responsible for one of London's 25, after 1550, 26 wards. Taken collectively, the Court of Aldermen had immense power. They appointed to subordinate offices. They issued proclamations and orders regarding the public health. They granted ale houses licenses.

They governed London's prisons. They also had the right to veto any legislation passed by the Common Council or Common Hall. What's the Common Council?

Beginning circa the 1280s, the Common Council consisted of the lord mayor, the 25 aldermen and 210 councilors elected annually by London's tax payers on a ward-by-ward basis. The Common Council operated as a sort of House of Commons for London responsible for regulating markets and street lighting and paving and other day-to-day business. They also could inquire into city finances, but remember, the aldermen could veto any piece of legislation they came up with.

Finally, there was Common Hall. This consisted of all the freemen of the city. That is, people who had paid to become members of the Guild. That's about three quarters of the male population. That was Common Hall that elected London's four members of Parliament. So again, we see that democratic impulse operating. Finally, each ward was divided into precincts of 50 to 100 houses and also into parishes, all of which could hold their own meetings and take care of local problems. So again, there's an awful lot of self-government in London or at least local government.

Now, as we'll see, there was a lot of potential for conflict in this system but it also meant that London's government was the most democratic in England. That will have implications for us. Because after Westminster Hall, the Guildhall is the second largest hall in London, it would also in future years host state trials. The Earl of Surrey and Lady Jane Grey would be tried for treason here in 1547 and 1553, respectively, and Archbishop Crammer for heresy later in 1553. In the meantime, perhaps the greatest challenge facing London's government during Chaucer's lifetime was the Black Death.

Now, medical historians continue to debate what the Black Death actually was. The consensus is that it was almost certainly some form of plague probably bubonic, *Pasteurella pestis*, that had decimated Europe periodically during ancient times. The first outbreak of plague in London was recorded by Bede in 664. Another, made worse by famine, arrived in 1258. The Black Death of the mid-14th century came from the east. It spread along trade routes to big cities starting in Italy in 1347. In other words, the commerce that made the cities of Italy and northern Europe so wealthy, made them deadly as well.

The plague arrived in London by late September 1348. It raged in the city by November. What actually happened? Well, the disease was spread by the bite of a flea. Carried on the back of the black rat which road in carts of grain or ship's holds to other cities where crowded unhygienic conditions, remember that the street is an open sewer, allowed the rats to thrive, the fleas to migrate to human clothing which was often, in the Middle Ages, unchanged for weeks. Once bitten, onset was sudden. You could be fine at noon dying by the afternoon. Your skin would develop buboes, blackened swellings, hence the term Black Death, from internal hemorrhaging. You might then develop a high fever, a raging thirst, and delirium. Your odds of survival were about one in four. Treatment, well medieval medical science was almost completely baffled by the connection among the rats and the hygiene and the lice and the fleas. Some thought the Black Death came through the air, hence the constant burning of fires to purify it. In any city in Europe going through a plague epidemic there will always be the smell of burning.

Others thought that it was a collective punishment from God, possibly the end of the world. Londoners couldn't blame the Jews as elsewhere in Europe because if you'll remember they'd expelled them all. The Court of Aldermen were largely ineffective in this first really big plague outbreak apart from attempting to clean up the filth and excrement from London's streets. The cemeteries were overwhelmed so the city began to bury victims in Southwark and Smithfield at the rate of 200 a day. The plague lasted through the winter peaking between February and Easter 1349. Contemporaries estimated the number of deaths at between 50,000 and 100,000. That can't be right. London's population was probably no more than 45,000. A soberer modern estimate is that 15,000 people died in London because of the Black Death, but that's still 33 percent of the city's inhabitants. Whole families and religious communities were wiped out including Westminster Abbey. If you survived you probably became immune. So when the Plague returned in 1361–1362, 1368–1369, and again in 1407, that one killing, perhaps, 30,000, children were especially hard hit. It took a century for London's population to recover, not least because the unsanitary city also faced outbreaks of TB, typhus, dysentery, smallpox, diphtheria, and measles. On the other hand, the resulting labor shortage meant good times for those who survived. Higher wages, as high as 3 or 3.5 pence a day for laborers. This gave the Guilds which, remember, tried to keep a lid on wages, fits.

Now with any luck, our trip to medieval London comes between epidemics. Before leaving Cheapside, we note one last building. On the left side of the street is old St. Mary-le-Bow. A church with a distressing history of partial collapse, most notoriously in 1331, a wooden balcony containing Queen Phillippa and her ladies in waiting, who were attending a Cheapside joust to celebrate the birth of the Black Prince, collapsed on them causing a number of injuries. Saint Mary-le-Bow's tower was significant. For this church's bells rang out London's curfew. This may be the origin of the tradition that to be a true cockney you have to born within the hearing of Bow bells.

Now, having visited economic London at the docks, and on Cheapside, and military and royal London at the Tower, and civic London at the Guildhall, Bow bells remind us that it's now time to get some religion. We made the point in the last lecture that much of London is church land, names like Blackfriars and Convent Garden remind us of that. At the west end of Cheapside, we're confronted by the greatest religious building of all in London. The magnificent, gothic bulk of St. Paul's Cathedral, subsequently to be known as Old St. Paul's after it burned down in 1666.

This is easily the greatest church in England and as we will recall from seeing it from afar, the most dominant building in London. It's huge, 585 feet long. In 1365, its spire rises nearly 550 feet. It'll be struck by lightning in 1447 and then rebuilt. Struck again in 1561, it was left alone. Now the building before us is actually London's fourth St. Paul's Cathedral. According to tradition, this is the site of a Roman temple to Diana. The first cathedral was founded in 604 by Athelbert of Kent. It was built of wood and then it burnt down. Rebuilt between 675 and 685, it was destroyed by the Vikings in 961. The replacement burned down in 1087 which gave the Normans a clean slate to top their Anglo-Saxon predecessors.

The cathedral is built of white Caen stone. Apart from the spire it has great bell towers which are used as prisons. Any elevated building seems to be used as a prison in medieval London. It also has a magnificent rose window at the east end that captured Chaucer's imagination. In "The Miller's Tale," Absalon has "Powles window corven in his shoes." Along with Westminster Abbey, St. Paul's is one of the two great national churches in London. It was here, for example, that Henry V would attend a service giving thanks for the victory at Agincourt in 1415. It was here that the corpses of Richard II and Henry VI would be exhibited in 1400 and 1471, respectively, to show that there was no traction in remaining loyal to a deposed king. It was here that Prince Arthur and Catherine of Aragon would be married in 1501, but St. Paul's is also a great local institution.

Adjacent to the building is St. Paul's churchyard. Famous for two great organs of information in medieval and early-modern London. First, in the northeast corner of the churchyard was Paul's cross, a freestanding pulpit which Thomas Carlisle called "the Times newspaper of medieval England." Here kings were proclaimed, paper bulls were read, royal marriages, military victories, and ex-communications were announced. It was here that Edward IV's mistress, Jane Shore, would be forced to do penance holding a taper and it was here where citizens were summoned three times a year to attend a folk moot, a popular court.

Above all, from this pulpit were delivered some of the most notable sermons in London to crowds in the open air. Now once printing was invented in the 15th century, St. Paul's churchyard got its other great organ of information and dissemination. St. Paul's churchyard would be home to stationers and printers and book sellers, this was, sort of, the booksellers row of late-medieval and early-modern London. Nor was commerce confined to the cathedral's exterior. The name of London's greatest building was a public place, and remember there's no separation of church and state in this society, so on weekdays, scribes, lawyers, government officials, even tradesmen set up shop in the aisles of St. Paul's Cathedral. Servants hung about, there was actually one particular pillar, we're not quite sure which one, but we know servants looking for a job would hang out at this one pillar and if you were looking for a servant you went to that pillar and you could hire people. In short, if St. Paul's was a great national church, it was also in some ways London's parish church and village hall if that can be said of a city with over 100 individual parish churches. As in the early-modern village church, St. Paul's was much more than a place of worship. It was a community social and cultural center.

We're leaving St. Paul's and heading west. We go to Ludgate Hill through the Ludgate itself, through the wall onto Fleet Street. Fleet

Street is named for the River Fleet, a tributary of the Thames which flows from Hampstead south, crossing Holburn and Fleet Street, before it empties into the Thames. So this river is perpendicular to the Thames. During the Middle Ages, cutlers, butchers, and tanners used it to dispose of animal carcasses and the by-products of metallurgy and leather working. It has a lot of industrial waste because it cut right through the city but on its western border it also served as a convenient open sewer. So people complained about the stench as early as the 13th century. It had to be cleaned out repeatedly but by the mid-17th century that hadn't worked. It was now more of a Fleet ditch than it was a river.

So even in 1365, we cross Fleet Bridge holding our noses and gripping our purses. Throughout our period from the Middle Ages to the 18th century, Fleet Street was a popular staging area for apprentice riots and other youthful gangs who might accost an unsuspecting tourist. It's a dangerous area. Now ironically, perhaps because it's only yards from Newgate prison, within a century or two this area would develop a series of law schools, the famous Inns of Court. In the Middle Ages, there was already a series of Inns of Chancery, Barbard's Inn, Clifford's Inn. There are plenty of these that would later act as feeder schools to the Inns of Court. Yet far from representing law and order the law students so housed are apprentices just as much as Chaucer's Perkin Revellor was, and so may actually have contributed to the disorder of Fleet Street. You might be hit on the head by a law student, so be careful.

Carrying on down Fleet Street, we cross under yet another arch gate, Temple Bar, which lets us into the Strand. The Temple Bar was built in 1351 so it's new and par for the course it has a prison attached to it. It represents the outermost reaches of the legal city of London. That is, there's a little bit to the west along Fleet Street that is controlled by the city of London even though it's beyond the wall but once we pass Temple Bar, we're outside of that jurisdiction.

From this point, we're beyond the control of the lord mayor and Court of Aldermen. To the west lies Westminster where Chaucer felt at home. In fact, at the end of his life, he had a home here because he was a prominent courtier and government official. If the old walled city is about commerce, Westminster is about government and perhaps religion. Most people got there by boat, barge, actually. Remember that in medieval and early-modern times the easiest way to get anywhere is on the water. The principle land route between the city and Westminster, east and west, is an unpaved dirt track called "the Strand."

Now today, this is one of the busiest and most exciting thoroughfares in London. It's easily my favorite London street but in the Middle Ages it's a little more than a bridal path along the river. In fact, the word "strand" means land bordering a body of water, that's all it is. Given the horse and cart traffic and contemporary sanitary customs, we may find ourselves splattered in mud or worse. We look up from our stained hose to the left, or the river side of the street, to view a series of stately palaces called "inns." They stretch all along the Thames, all the way down to Westminster. They are, in order, the Outer Temple now leased to the Bishop of Exeter during this period, then the Inn of the Bishop of Bath and Wells, then the Inn of the Bishop of Chester, and then the Inn of the Bishop of Worcester, next comes Savoy Palace.

Now in Chaucer's time, the palace was owned by John of Gaunt, Duke of Lancaster, who was one of the sons of King Edward III. In fact it was here that Geoffrey Chaucer married the sister of Gaunt's mistress and eventual wife Katherine Swynford. Katherine Swynford and John of Gaunt are important because from them the Tudors descend. Now Gaunt wasn't popular, he was seen as trying to bring London under royal control so the palace was attacked frequently by mobs, in 1377 and again in 1381 during the Peasants' Revolt. Gaunt escaped but his doctor and sergeant-at-arms were lynched. The Great Hall was blown up. The plate and rich hangings burnt. Precious stones, owned by Gaunt, were crushed and thrown into the Thames. You see the mob hated him so much they wouldn't take any of his property. They just wanted to wreck it. The palace became an abandoned ruin and eventually sort of rookery where thieves would hang out.

Further down the Strand, Durham House for the Bishop of Durham, Norwich Place for the Bishop of Norwich, and to this we might add, just beyond Charing Cross where the river bends, York Place, the Inn of the Archbishop of York. We'll talk more about that later. These inns represented the power and wealth of the church in London. They exist because in the Middle Ages most bishops spend relatively little time in their dioceses, rather they spend it in the capital. They serve the king in high office. They sit in the House of Lords and they hang out at court hoping for a better bishopric. At the Reformation, all of these inns would be confiscated by the Crown.

We'll follow the good bishops to court but first I want to explore the right side of the street, the right of side of the Strand. We see a few shops and just beyond them, in what is today the west end, open fields, rural London. I want to remind you of the fact that once we get beyond the wall, London is mostly countryside. By the mid-1400s, these fields would house Lincoln's Inn, one of the four Inns of Court and Convent or Covent Garden owned by monks of Westminster, but beyond that, foxes were hunted on what is now Tottenham Court Road and Oxford Street. The district now known as Soho, famous for its nightlife, was named after a hunting call.

Continuing along the Strand, we reached Charing Cross. In the Middle Ages there was a separate village here known as Charing which means to turn in Old English and presumably because that's because the river turns south here. From this point, the north bank becomes the west bank. The South Bank becomes the east bank. The elaborate cross we see in 1365 which gives Charing Cross its name was the last in a series erected in 1290 by Edward I, at the spots where the coffin of his deceased Queen Eleanor rested on its sad procession from the place of her death in Nottinghamshire.

Looking just north from Charing Cross, at what would be in the 21st century Trafalgar Square, stands the Royal Mews, the royal stables. In the Middle Ages, this is where the king keeps his falcons. Among Chaucer's many non-demanding court positions, he was also Clerk of the Mews. Just beyond here, more open fields. Following the river, we turn left onto a dirt track, later on this will be known as King's Street. Still later it'll be known as Whitehall. To our left we encounter York Place, which we mentioned earlier. It was acquired in 1240 by Walter de Grey, Archbishop of York. Later on it would become famous as Whitehall Palace. We'll talk about that in a subsequent lecture.

We, carrying on, proceed towards the capital, the complex of buildings laid out in the Middle Ages as Westminster. Westminster was not technically part of the city of London. Remember it lies outside of the city walls and so the lord mayor's jurisdiction. It was the property of the chapter, the monks of Westminster, and so administered by them. It took the first step to being the capital when Edward the Confessor constructed an abbey and a palace. Now the religious and emotional heart of the Westminster complex is Westminster Abbey. As we've seen there's been a religious foundation here since Anglo-Saxon time. According to legend, the church was built in the 7th century by King Sebert of Essex on a site then known as Thorny Island. The site was chosen because St. Peter had promised good fishing to a ferryman who had kindly transported him across the river. In 785, a charter of King Offa of Mercia granted the land "to St. Peter and the needy people of God in Thorney in the terrible place which is called Westminster." We don't know why it was described as terrible. After all, there weren't politicians there yet. St. Dunstan established a Benedictine Abbey here in the 10th century upon which Edward the Confessor grafted his own expanded foundation between 1042 and 1066. He had vowed to make a pilgrimage to the tomb of St. Peter in Rome. Remember that Edward the Confessor is quite a religious fellow.

The Great Council opposed him going, leaving the country. So the Pope offered release of the vow if Edward would found or a restore a monastery to St. Peter. Now nothing remains of Edward's Norman influenced Anglo-Saxon Abbey, we'll see why in a minute. It was consecrated on the 28 of December, 1065. Eight days later, Edward died. He was buried before the high altar. This led to the succession crisis which led to the succession of William the Conqueror. On Christmas Day 1066, after overawing the Saxons, William the Conqueror was crowned here. This is the first of many coronations in Westminster Abbey but it did not go well. The Saxon citizenry outside were shouting their acclamation but the Norman nobles and knights inside thought it was an uprising and so they attacked the crowd and set fire to neighboring houses. This is why you really need an event planner. Anyway, every subsequent English monarch has been crowned here except Edward V and VIII, who never made it to their coronations.

From 1245 to 1272, Henry III, who was also a self-consciously pious king, pulled down the Edwardian building and erected the present high gothic masterpiece though the twin towers, that's known to visitors today, weren't built until the 18th century. The present Abbey is heavily influenced by French models like Amiens and Rheims. We can see this in the design of the flying buttresses, the rose windows in the transepts and the tracery of its other windows, but the single aisle design and the heavy use of Purbeck marble is English.

Subsequent kings continue to endow and add to Westminster Abbey as we'll see. If St. Paul's is London's parish church then Westminster Abbey is the nation's, and so we enter with due reverence. After our eyes adjust to the dark, we look up to note the very high nave, the tallest in England, at 103 feet. Soon we're greeted by one of the many monks of the Abbey who offers to be our guide. In all ages, this is a way for the church and its clergy to support themselves. He shows us Edward I's already ancient coronation chair. Beneath it sits the Stone of Scone, upon which Scottish kings were traditionally crowned until it was commandeered by Edward I, Edward Longshanks, in 1296. It would not be returned to its rightful owners until 1996.

English kings have always been buried in Westminster Abbey. Henry IV actually died here in 1413 after suffering a seizure while praying. It doesn't seem quite fair really. He was carried into the Jerusalem chamber and expired there, thus fulfilling a prophecy that he would die in Jerusalem. In 1365, burial in the Abbey is pretty much limited to kings, nor had Poet's Corner been established, though it would start in the south transept, in fact, if not a name, when Geoffrey Chaucer was buried here around 1400. Now he's buried here not because he was England's greatest medieval poet but because he was a government official and had that right, but later poets wanted to buried near him, hence, the creation of Poet's Corner. Near here is also the Chapter House built between 1245 and 1255. This is where the monks meet to vote on a new abbot when the old one dies. This is also where the king kept his treasury until it was robbed in 1303. Some said with the connivance of some of the said monks. And its also where the House of Commons will meet until 1547.

Just outside this part of the Abbey we find lots of shops, lots of businesses, and also lots of beggars and thieves. They're drawn to the area because of its wealth. One of the things about the west end of London is it will always have lots of poor people because there are rich people. They're also drawn here because it's a place of a sanctuary, a liberty where the king's powers of law enforcement and the city's powers of law enforcement don't necessarily operate. Hence, streets named Broad Sanctuary and Little Sanctuary and my favorite, Thieving Lane. As we walk along Thieving Lane, once again, we hang onto our purses.

Now a century after our visit, William Caxton, the first important printer in England, will rent a house near this part of the Abbey and set up England's first print shop and book store in 1476 at The Sign of the Red Pale. Caxton's shop sits on the path between the Abbey and Westminster Hall to the northeast. Westminster Hall was built in 1097 by William II, William Rufus, as an extension of Edward the Confessor's palace. At 240 feet long and 92 feet high it is the largest hall in England though Rufus thought it a mere bed chamber. We're more easily impressed by its sheer size and hammer-beam roof. If Westminster Hall was a mere bed chamber it was because it was an add-on to the main palace, Westminster Palace, built by Edward the Confessor as his principle London residence. Now, Westminster Palace would serve as the home base of the English court until damaged by fire in 1512.

Having seen official, governmental, and religious London, we might head south into more fields. There's Tothill Fields. "Tot" means a beacon. This is marshy ground between the Abbey and its mill or Millbank. Tournaments and fairs are held here. You may remember Henry III establishing a fair here that offended the officials of the City because it took business away. North and west lies another set of fields associated with St. James's leper hospital. One day this will be St. James's Park. Or we might head down to the river to contemplate all that we have seen for because of the bend at Westminster if we look east we can actually see all of it.

The South Bank is dominated by Lambeth Palace just across from us and St. Mary Overie to the east. At a distance, but directly in front of us, London Bridge piled high with precarious houses and shops. To its left, at the top of the our leftward vision, the city itself crammed into the walls gathered around St. Paul's like hordes of children about their mother. Further north, more to our left, the rows of great palaces culminating in Whitehall and the Westminster Complex from which we have just come. The scene makes little noise, just the occasional call of a bargeman, the bells of the city churches striking the hour or perhaps an occasional vote by acclamation from the commons in the Westminster Abbey Chapter House but in all that great conurbation something remarkable is happening. Her inhabitants scurry about living, dying, and above all ever becoming Londoners.

Lecture Six

London Embraces the Early Tudors

Scope:

It was under the Tudors that London came into its own as a royal city. The house of Tudor used the city as a great stage across which to process for the delight of their subjects—and the enhancement of their power. The close relationship between the city and the dynasty was forged at the very beginning of Henry VII's reign, and it survived his son Henry VIII's disastrous effect on the London economy and his confiscation of most of London's church-owned lands. Henry VIII's daughter Mary almost lost London twice: when she chose to marry Philip of Spain and when she burned nearly 300 Protestants at the stake at Smithfield.

Outline

I. On August 22, 1485, Henry Tudor, Earl of Richmond, defeated King Richard III at the Battle of Bosworth Field.

- **A.** On September 3 the new king, now known as Henry VII, entered London, greeted by trumpeters, poems in his honor, and a gift of 1,000 marks from the City.
- **B.** Thus began London's love affair with the house of Tudor that would last—with occasional tiffs—nearly until the death of Henry VII's granddaughter, Elizabeth I, in 1603.
  1. They would play to London, using it as a stage upon which to act the great drama of their rule.
  2. They would intimidate London with power.
  3. They would woo London with flattery and public appearances.

II. Henry VII (r. 1485–1509) was keen to assert his kingship rather than beg it from Parliament.

- **A.** His magnificent coronation procession was designed to emphasize his legitimacy.
- **B.** Subsequent ceremonies during his reign continued to emphasize his power and magnificence.

C. Henry VII set the tone with a vibrant court life.

1. He built the magnificent Henry VII Chapel at Westminster Abbey.
2. He also sponsored elaborate festivals at court for Christmas, Easter, and Saint George's Day.

III. Henry VIII (r. 1509–1547) staged a magnificent coronation, but after that there was not much civic pageantry in his reign.

A. He was a restless sort who did not necessarily like to stay very long in London. Rather, he traveled about the country and between his 60 palaces, houses, and hunting lodges.

1. He renovated Westminster Palace after a disastrous fire in 1512.
2. He also built a new palace down by the River Fleet, Bridewell, occupied from 1514 to 1529.
3. In 1529 he abandoned the insalubrious Bridewell, confiscating Whitehall, the former York Place, from Thomas, Cardinal Wolsey.
4. These central London houses were ringed with others, radiating from the center.

B. As a young king, Henry preferred outdoor activities like hunting in St. James's Park, tournaments, pageants, and "spontaneous" interactions with Londoners that were really carefully staged, such as his May Day excursion to Greenwich in 1515.

C. Another kind of royal "street theater" took place at the Evil May Day riots of 1517.

1. Following an incendiary Paul's Cross sermon by a Rev. Dr. Bell, there were sporadic attacks on foreigners.
2. Late on the night of April 30, an altercation in Cheapside over enforcement of curfew resulted in a riot involving 1,000 apprentices, who marched on St. Martin le Grand, an area north of St. Paul's where many resident aliens lived.
3. Henry VIII sent royal troops, arresting some 300 rioters.
4. Tradition has it that Catherine of Aragon, supported by Cardinal Wolsey, begged for their pardon on bended knee, with tears in her eyes.
5. As a result, the punishments were limited: Fourteen were hanged for treason, and May Day was suppressed for years to come.

6. Evil May Day illustrates the fragility of order in London: the destabilizing force of thousands of apprentices with little to do; the importance of street theater; the ability of the Tudors to push back with a theater of their own, emphasizing their power and mercy.

D. Henry VIII had two great effects on London.

1. Henry spent vast amounts of money on war, which drained his treasury. Also, his recoinage contributed to massive inflation, which plunged the country into an economic depression that affected London severely.
2. Henry also launched the Reformation in England, affecting London in both the short and the long term.

IV. The redistribution of land was the major initiative affecting London during Edward VI's regime (1547–1553).

A. Londoners liked his establishment of a Protestant religious settlement. Protestantism took root in London for several reasons.

1. London was a port, and so it was the first place where Protestant books and travelers alighted.
2. Protestantism emphasized literacy and individual interpretation of scripture, which appealed to a city full of literate merchants.

B. Unfortunately for Protestantism, by late 1552 Edward began a slow death from tuberculosis.

1. Since the next heir—his elder sister Mary, the daughter of Catherine of Aragon—was Catholic, he and his ministers tried to divert the succession to a Protestant relative, Lady Jane Gray.
2. At Edward's death on July 9, 1553, the Privy Council in London proclaimed Jane queen, but on July 19 Henry FitzAlan, Earl of Arundel, convinced the Privy Council to proclaim Mary.

V. Mary I's was the most tragic Tudor reign (1553–1558), in part because she misinterpreted her mandate as coming from God, rather than her people.

A. The decision to marry to Philip of Spain led to Wyatt's rebellion, in which London would, once again, hold the crucial balance.

1. In January 1554, Sir Thomas Wyatt raised a rebellion of 3,000 men in Kent and marched on London.
2. Lacking an army of her own, Mary turned to the citizens of London via an eloquent speech at the Guildhall.
3. She then rallied the royal guards and the citizenry of London, who stopped Wyatt at the Southwark end of London Bridge.
4. Afterward, Wyatt and about 90 of his followers were executed, along with Lady Jane Grey.
5. Mary's younger sister, the Protestant Princess Elizabeth, also came under suspicion and was lodged in the Tower.

B. In 1553–1554, Mary persuaded Parliament to repeal the Protestant legislation of Edward VI's reign and restore the power of the pope, the Latin mass, the seven sacraments, and the laws against heresy.

1. Devoted Protestants had two choices: flight to the Continent or martyrdom at the stake.
2. Over the next few years, Mary's regime burnt 237 men and 52 women—many of them adolescents, most of humble background—mostly at Smithfield, then London's meat market.
3. It is little wonder that, at Mary's death and Elizabeth's accession on November 17, 1558, the bells rang in London.

Suggested Reading:

Brigden, *London and the Reformation.*

Inwood, *A History of London*, chap. 5.

Questions to Consider:

1. Why did London generally like the Tudors?
2. Why did early modern people reject religious toleration?

Lecture Six—Transcript
London Embraces the Early Tudors

On the 22 of August, 1485, Henry Tudor, Earl of Richmond, defeated King Richard III at the Battle of Bosworth Field. On the 3 of September, the new king now known as Henry VII entered London from Shoreditch where he was greeted by trumpeters, palms in his honor, and all the city fathers who brought a gift of 1,000 marks. Now a cynic would say that this is just another example of London betting on the winner. Such expressions of loyalty were not to be depended on but I would point out that Londoners had not embraced every seeming winner. During The Wars of the Roses they closed the gates to Henry VI's Queen after military victory in 1461, and they'd given half-hearted acclamation of Richard III's usurpation of the two little princes in 1483. If Londoners were cynical fair-weather fans, they were also pretty prescient. As we saw in the case of William the Conqueror and throughout the Middle Ages, in the end they usually picked the winner. They certainly got this one right.

Henry VII's effective rule, which lasted from 1485 to 1509, put an end to the dynastic chaos known as the Wars of the Roses between those who supported the House of Lancaster for the throne and those who supported the House of York. It is also began the very successful rule of the Tudors. So that civic delegation of 3 September, 1485, was onto something. They started a love affair with the House of Tudor that would last, with occasional tiffs, nearly until the death of the Henry VII's granddaughter, Elizabeth I in 1603.

Over the course of the next 120 years or so, the Tudors would play to London, using it as a stage upon which to act the great drama of their rule. They would also intimidate London with power and woo London with flattery and public appearances. And only nearly lose it once during the reign of that most atypical Tudor, Mary I.

In my course on England under the Tudors and Stewarts, I take pains to show that Henry VII started his reign by asserting his kingship rather than begging Parliament or the people to grant it to him. As we've seen, immediately after the victory at Bosworth, he marched on London. Straight away he ordered the Yorkist heir, Earl of Warwick, to the Tower and the Yorkess princess, Elizabeth, whom he intended to marry, out of it. He then processed to St. Paul's where he laid banners at the altar and heard a Te Deum and he began planning his coronation before calling a Parliament.

On the 27 of October he dined at Lambeth Palace with the Archbishop of Canterbury who would preside at the coronation. Next day he processed in full magnificence to the Tower so that three days later he could process back to Westminster for his coronation accompanied by members of his household, nobility arranged in order of precedence, and Yorkist and Lancastrians, supporters of each side, paired two on a horse to indicate unity. This procession also included the newly formed Palace Guard, the Yeomen of the Guard, dressed in red livery, still the oldest palace guard in England recently instituted by Henry VII.

After the coronation he processed back to the Tower for the coronation banquet so that he could be acclaimed as king. Now medieval kings have been doing this sort of thing for centuries. The coronation ceremony itself was essentially the medieval standard. The processions were reminiscent of those of Henry V and Edward IV. The key is their timing. Henry repeatedly showed himself as king to the citizens of his capital city. He got himself crowned and acclaimed long before Parliament met on the 7 of November. Unlike Henry IV, Henry VII wanted no question that he did not owe his crown to Parliament. Once crowned, who needs ceremony? The traditional coronation tournament was postponed.

Now, in fact, Henry and subsequent Tudors would continue to use London as a stage to show that they were king and also to prove three additional things. First, their magnificence. For example, the splendid marriage of Henry's eldest son, Prince Arthur, to Catherine of Aragon, daughter of Ferdinand and Isabella. Catherine arrived at Plymouth in October 1501 where she was greeted by Henry and Arthur in great state. She made her entry in early November. She stayed at the Tower during weeks of festivities which including feasting and tournaments before being married at St. Paul's on the 14 of November. The second way they used London to display something was to display their strength. For example, the public execution of Warwick in 1499. Finally, they also used a certain amount of street theater to display their mercy, the reprieve of the Evil May Day rioters which we're going to talk about in a few minutes.

Their successors have done the same on and off ever since. The Tudors also set the tone with a vibrant court life. For one thing, they built, for example Henry VII built the magnificent Henry VII chapel at Westminster Abbey. He also sponsored elaborate festivals at court for Christmas, Easter, and St. George's Day where he made a point of wearing the crown and appearing in great state; this persisted under the most famous Tudor, this Henry's son, Henry VIII who ruled from 1509 to 1547.

Keeping with tradition and Henry VIII's flamboyant personality, I'm going to assume you've heard of him. He staged a magnificent coronation. The streets were decorated with tapestries. Goldsmith houses and Cheapside were hung with gold cloth but, in fact, after that there's not actually that much civic pageantry in this Henry's reign. Henry VIII was a restless sort who didn't necessarily like to stay very long in one place, even London. Rather he traveled about the country in between his 60 palaces, houses, and hunting lodges. So he was fickle in this as well.

He renovated Westminster Palace after a disastrous fire in 1512. He also built a new palace down by the Fleet River, a big mistake. You remember the Fleet, it's an open sewer, Bridewell in 1515. He abandoned the insalubrious Bridewell long before 1529 when he settled in his main London residence, Whitehall, which he had confiscated from Thomas, Cardinal Wolsey, this was the former York Place. But these central London houses were ringed with others radiating from the center. There was Greenwich down river, Richmond, Hampton Court, and Windsor upriver. There was Nonsuch and Oatlands and Surrey to the South. Why did Henry move around so much?

Well first, the 300 to 400 people in his entourage would tend to overwhelm the primitive waste disposal facilities at each of these palaces within a matter of weeks. That forced decampment while the palace was cleaned out. Secondly, Henry knew the value of showing his face to as many of his subjects as possible. Remember this is an age before television and newspapers. How do you know what the king looks like? You know what the king looks like by actually looking at him.

Thirdly, Henry easily grew bored and restless, not just about palaces as you probably know. In fact, as a young king he preferred outdoor activities, hunting in St. James's Park, tournaments, pageants, and spontaneous "interactions" with Londoners that were really very carefully staged. For example, in May Day, 1515, at Greenwich, we have a long eyewitness account.

> The King and Queen accompanied with many lords and ladies rode to the high ground of Shooter's Hill to take the open air and as they passed by, [and by the way this reminds us of how countrified London is, how easy it is to get out into the open air] and as they passed by the way they espied a company of tall Yeomen clothed all in green with green hoods and bows and arrows to the number of about 200. Then one of them which called himself Robin Hood came to the King desiring him to see his men shoot and the king was content. Then he whistled [just like in the Errol Flynn movie, that's not in the original] and all the 200 archers shot and loosed at once. And then he whistled again and they likewise shot again. Their arrows whistled by craft of the head so that the noise was strange and great and much pleased the King and Queen and all the company.

Now part of what's going on here is that these are traditional country skills. It was thought men had to maintain them so that they would be good soldiers for the king and there was a great deal of worry that Londoners, who were engaged in trade and didn't get out into the country that much, were losing these skills. So there's a kind of statement being made.

> All these archers were of the king's guard [Ah-ha, the whole thing was staged] and had thus appareled themselves to make solace to the King. Then Robin Hood desired the King and Queen to come into the green wood and to see how the outlaws live. [I'm sure this is going to be very accurate.] The King demanded of the Queen and her ladies that they durst adventure to go into the wood with so many outlaws. Then the Queen said if it pleased him she was content [by the way this is Catherine of Aragon still] Then the horns blew 'til they came to the wood under Shooter's Hill and there was an arbour made with bows and with a hall and a great chamber and an inner chamber, very well made, and covered with flowers and sweet birds which the king much praised. [Yeah, this is where the outlaws hang out. Part of what's going on here is a kind of a tribute to the King's mastery of nature,

> look at what his court servants can do with nature. They can, in effect, erect a palace.] Then said Robin Hood, Sir, outlaws' breakfast is venison and therefore, you must be content with such fare as we use then the King and Queen had sat down and were served with venison and wine by Robin Hood and his men to their great contentation [their great contentment].

Another kind of royal street theater took place on the same day, just two years later, during the Evil May Day riots of 1517. Now some background. Despite or perhaps because of their contact with foreigners, Londoners were famously xenophobic. Throughout the early modern period they frequently attacked foreign merchants and ambassadors in the streets, often because they'd been granted special privileges by the crown. In 1497, Andreas Franciscus, part of an Italian delegation, remarked,

> Londoners have such fierce tempers and dispositions that they not only despise the way in which Italians live but actually pursue them with uncontrolled hatred. At Bruges, we could do as we liked by day as well as by night but here they look at askance at us by day and at night they sometimes drive us off with kicks and blows of the truncheon.

The trouble seems to have begun with an incendiary Paul's Cross sermon delivered a few weeks before by a Reverend Dr. Bell who called on all "Englishmen to cherish and defend themselves and to hurt and grieve aliens for the common weal." So this is a kind of immigration issue. The next few weeks saw sporadic attacks on foreigners and the city was rife with rumors that they would be attacked en masse on May 1, May Day, which was a country festival normally associated with dancing around a maypole. At 8:30 pm on the night of 30 of April, the Court of Aldermen imposed a curfew beginning at 9:00 pm that night. A few minutes after 9:00, Alderman John Mundy was walking home from Guildhall via Cheapside. There, what should he come upon but a group of several young men, apprentices who are obviously breaking curfew; these are the descendants of Perk and Revela, right? When Mundy ordered them to remove to their homes, one of them challenged him by asking, why? When he moved to arrest that man, his compatriots attacked Mundy who fled.

This alone amounted to a breach of the public peace and social order but worse was to come. Within an hour a crowd of 1,000 apprentices had assembled in Cheapside and began to march on St. Martin le Grand, an area north of St. Paul's where lots of aliens lived. They freed prisoners arrested for previous assaults along the way. This was something London crowds often did; the mob did the same thing during the Peasants' Revolt. They would rescue prisoners. The inhabitants of St. Martin le Grand fought off their attackers, throwing stones and pouring boiling water down upon the apprentices. The apprentices responded with mass looting into the wee hours. Now according to tradition, Henry VIII was asleep at Richmond; he's awakened, he sends royal troops who arrest some 300 rioters.

Tradition also has it that Catherine of Aragon supported by Cardinal Wolsey begged for their pardon on bended knee with tears in her eyes. Now remember, they were attacking her fellow Spaniards as well as other foreigners and yet, she went down on her knees for them. As a result, the punishments were moderated, 14 were hanged for treason and May Day was suppressed for years to come.

Now as I always tell my students, a dramatic event like this should cause us to pause and look more closely. On the surface of things, the Evil May Day riots were clearly inspired by irrational xenophobia and at times the rioters behaved like the adolescents they were. But it should be noted that xenophobia would not have been considered irrational by even educated Englishmen. Moreover, the rioters could claim that they were provoked by the city authorities infringing on their just right to abroad. Londoners have never liked being told what to do. Also, the rioters may have taken inspiration from the fact that holidays, like May Day, were times when normal rules were suspended. Note, too, they limited their violence to their target as we'll see time and again. Londoners do not simply run amuck. Their riots tend to be well aimed and organized. Perhaps in response to this restraint, the government's punishment was also restrained, over 300 arrests, 14 executions, despite a terribly dangerous situation fraught with international ramifications. Finally, the intercession of the Spanish queen with the English king could only have increased their popularity. This is a classic example of the way in which the Crown threatened punishment then achieved the same ends with mercy.

Londoners would long remember the Evil May Day riots because of the sheer scale of the rioting, but it also illustrates the fragility of order in London. There was no police force, only a crew of volunteer constables. The destabilizing force of hundreds, in fact, thousands of young men, apprentices like Chaucer's Perkin with little to do, the importance of street theater, and finally the ability of the Tudors to push back with a theater of their own emphasizing power and mercy.

Street theatrical's apart; Henry had two great effects on London as he did on England. First economic, like his medieval predecessors, Henry thought warfare the proper occupation of a monarch. He fought wars against France from 1511 to 1514, 1522 to 1525, 1543 to 1546. He fought against Scotland in 1513 and again through much of the 1540s. These wars had economic consequences. The first set drained Henry VIII's treasury, the final set, in the 1540s, wrecked the economy of the country. They cost a total of $3 million pounds. Henry, to pay for this, launched a recoinage that contributed to a massive inflation. The price of food rose 85 percent over the next 10 or 15 years. The price of labor, 50 percent, this plunged the country into an economic depression that affected London severely.

The second thing Henry did to London was to launch the Reformation in England. Now the story of why he did so. He's obsession with having a male heir; his desire for a divorce from his first wife, Catherine of Aragon. He's decision to break with Rome and become supreme head of the Church of England in order to marry Anne Boleyn. That's a story told in my "History of England from the Tudors to the Stewarts" for The Teaching Company, I don't have time for it all here. Of immediate importance, this event effected London in both the short and the long term.

Short term; Catherine had been very popular with Londoners and you can see why after the Evil May Day riots. London crowds cheered her in 1529 when she appeared at Blackfriars for her divorce case. They were much less enthusiastic when the city had to mount a coronation procession for the new Queen Anne Boleyn in 1533. Anne was carried in a litter decked with damask. She wore diamonds and pearls around her neck, a robe of crimson brocade covered with jewels, a coronet of rubies. Henry did everything to present her to the populous as a fully fledged Queen but the crowd was cold.

Far more importantly for our course, between 1536 and 1553, Henry VIII and his son, Edward VI, push through Parliament a series of laws dissolving all church-run monasteries, hospitals, schools, and chantries. Chantries were small chapels endowed to pray for the souls of the dead. Several bishops also fell afoul of the regime, Cardinals Fisher and Wolsey for example, and their land was confiscated too. The result was a revolution in land ownership in London where before the church had owned most of the land in London, now the Crown acquired vast amounts of land as well as monastic buildings and all those bishops' palaces along the Strand. The greatest of these, Wolesey's York Place, would become Henry's Whitehall Palace.

The idea behind the confiscation was that the church lands would endow the monarchy and save it from Henry's debts but Henry, needing quick cash to pay for his last ruinous war with France, kept only a fraction. He or his son sold or gave away the rest. For example, the Duke of Somerset, brother of Henry's third Queen, Jane Seymour, got three bishops' palaces along the Strand which he knocked down to build Somerset House. The Russell family got lots of London land including Convent Garden (Covent Garden) for crushing a Catholic rebellion in 1549. Now the Russells will be very important for the rest of this story because they're going to develop much of the West End, think of Russell Square.

In other words, this massive transfer of land would lead to a massive rebuilding over the next century or two. The redistribution of land was the major initiative effecting London during Edward VI's reign which lasted from 1547 to 1553. Otherwise his advisors were preoccupied with three things, first, a poor economy; second, an ill advised war with Scotland which made the economic situation even worse. Both of these, by the way, were inherited from Henry VIII. And third, a Protestant religious settlement abolishing the heresy laws, the mass, and instituting an English Book of Common Prayer written by Archbishop Thomas Cranmer.

Now, these measures were far more popular in London than in the remote parts of the country to the west and the north. Protestantism took root in London during the 16th century for a lot of reasons. First, it was a port and so the first place where Protestants' books and travelers alighted. Protestantism emphasized literacy and individual interpretation of scripture. This appealed to a city full of literate merchants.

Unfortunately for Protestantism, by late 1552, Edward was beginning a slow death from tuberculosis. Now, the next heir was his elder sister, Mary, the daughter of Catherine of Aragon, who was a Catholic. So Edward and his ministers tried to divert the succession in order to save the Reformation to a Protestant relative, Lady Jane Gray. Edward died on the 6 of July, 1553, and the Privy Council in London immediately proclaimed Jane Queen but London stayed aloof. In the meantime, Mary had been alerted, sneaking out of London in the dead of night with a small group of courtiers, she escaped to Norfolk which was dominated by the Catholic Howard family. There she was proclaimed as well as Queen on the 9 of July. So both sides now had Queens. Both sides raised armies and in the most momentous game of chess in English history marched out to capture the opposing Queen.

Mary's army reached London before Jane's reached Norfolk. There Henry FitzAlan, the Earl of Arundel, convinced the Privy Council to proclaim Mary the rightful Queen on the 19. The capital rose for Mary. Jane's army disintegrated, the conspirators were imprisoned, and eventually executed. Once again, as London went, so went the nation.

Mary I's reign lasted from 1553 to 1558 and it was the most tragic of all the Tudors. In part because she misinterpreted her mandate as coming from God rather than from her people. London and the nation rallied to her because she was a Tudor, because she was the daughter of Henry VIII, not because she was Catholic and certainly not because she was half Spanish. But she thought that God, not her people, had placed her on the throne in order to strengthen England's long standing alliance with Spain and in order to return her people to the one true faith of Roman Catholicism. These two policies would test London's loyalty.

Take, for example, her decision to marry Prince Philip, the future Philip II of Spain, in 1554. As well as her decision to burn those who would not accept the return to Rome, both of these policies would, in fact, nearly lose the city for her. The decision to marry Philip led to a rebellion in which London would once again hold the crucial balance. The choice of Philip was opposed not only by Mary's Privy Council but also by many of her subjects. In January, 1554, Sir Thomas Wyatt raised a rebellion of 3,000 men in Kent and marched on London. Their goal was to prevent the Spanish marriage and maybe displace Mary in favor of the Protestant, Elizabeth, who did her best to remain aloof.

Lacking an army of her own, Mary turned to the citizens of London. She went to the Guildhall and there appealed to her subjects' loyalty in a speech as eloquent as any Elizabeth, her sister, would ever give:

> I am your Queen, to whom, at my coronation, when I was wedded to the realm and laws of the same (the spousal ring I have on my finger, which never hitherto was, nor hereafter shall be, left off), you promised your allegiance and obedience to me. … And I say to you, on the word of a Prince, I cannot tell how naturally the mother loveth the child, for I was never the mother of any [sadly this would become a tragic obsession for Mary]; but certainly, if a Prince and a Governor may as naturally and earnestly love her subjects as the mother doth love the child, then assure yourselves that I, being your lady and mistress, do as earnestly and tenderly love and favor you. And I, thus loving you, cannot but think that ye as heartedly and faithfully love me; than I doubt not but we shall give these rebels a short and speedy overthrow.

She then rallied the royal guards and the citizenry of London who stopped Wyatt at the Southwark end of London Bridge. It worked. So he went up river and he crossed at Richmond and then he marched on the city again. This time he got as far as Ludgate which was also closed to him. Note how important it is that London has a wall. It can shut the gates. He was captured at Temple Bar. Afterwards, Wyatt and about 90 of his followers were executed along with Lady Jane Gray. She was considered just too dangerous as a possible focus for rebellion to be allowed to live. Mary's younger sister, the Protestant, Princess Elizabeth, also came under suspicion and was eventually lodged in the Tower but she'd been careful to avoid overt involvement in Wyatt's plot and this eventually saved her life.

The marriage to Philip took place amidst spectacular pomp at Winchester Cathedral in July of 1554. Note it didn't take place at London. Mary wanted to avoid the city. The marriage did not prove happy. Mary loved Philip but Philip saw the alliance as primarily diplomatic. He never managed to impregnate her or give her the heir, the hope for a Catholic future, that the 38-year-old Queen depended on. Instead he merely got her to participate in an unsuccessful war with France which would eventually cost the Tudors Calais.

In the meantime, the Tudor Queen, like her predecessors, had got her way mainly because London had stayed loyal. She continued to use London as a stage. In August of 1555, she rode with Phillip from Whitehall to the Tower to dispel rumors that she was dead. By the way, that's not a good sign when there's rumors that you're dead if you're the Queen, but her next policy initiative would lose London, the burnings of Smithfield.

In 1553, 1554, Mary persuaded Parliament to repeal the Protestant legislation of Edward VI's reign. She also persuaded Parliament to restore the power of the pope, the Latin Mass and seven sacraments, the laws against heresy. Devoted Protestants had two choices. They could fly to the Continent or they could stay and be martyred at the stake. The burnings begin in February 1555 with John Rogers whose crime was to translate the Bible into English. Over the next few years, Mary's regime burnt 237 men and 52 women. Many of these people were adolescents and most were of humble background. The burnings took place mostly at Smithfield, which was then London's meat market and this may strike you as being rather odd but markets are large open air public places, they were traditional venues for exemplary punishment in front of lots of witnesses, and Mary knew that London has embraced Protestantism at a higher rate than the rest of the country. So she wanted to really send a message here.

She wanted to make a point by striking at what she regarded as the very heart and root of heresy. Now, in my Tudor Stewart course and accompanying book, I try to explain why early modern people had almost no conception of religious toleration. Why killing heretics was thought, on both sides, to be preferable to allowing them to live because, after all, in so far as they spread error, they were dragging other souls down to damnation. And after all, what's more important, the life of a body or the life of the immortal soul?

If Mary had lived longer or had an heir, England might have reverted to Catholicism and the Protestant martyrs might largely have been forgotten in the popular imagination. As the popular imagination has largely forgotten the 250 Catholics that were executed by Queen Elizabeth but instead, Mary died childless in November 1558. She was succeeded by her Protestant sister and she was branded, in the popular imagination, as Bloody Mary. That's because once her reign ended, Protestants began to write its history. In particular, John Foxe's *Actes and Monuments of these latter and perillous Dayes*, better known as *The Book of Martyrs*. This work portrayed the burning of each martyr in the most grizzly but also the most inspiring detail. Take Foxe's description of the burning of a Protestant, Bishop Hooper, in February of 1555:

> When he was black in the mouth, and his tongue swollen that he could not speak, yet his lips went till they were shrunk to the gums; and he did knock his breast with his hands until one of his arms fell off, and then knocked still with the other, what time the fat, water and blood dropped out at his fingers' ends, until by renewing of the fire his strength was gone and his hand did cleave fast in knocking to the iron upon his breast. So immediately bowing forwards, he yielded up his spirit.

With prose like that, Foxe's *Book of Martyrs* became the best selling work in English after the Bible. The Protestant martyrs sank deep into the consciousness of the English people and especially that of Londoners who would never forget the smell of the flames from Smithfield. With a reputation like that, it is little wonder that at Mary's death and Elizabeth's succession on the 17 of November, 1558, the bells rang in London.

Lecture Seven

Elizabeth I and London as a Stage

Scope:

If the early Tudors forged a successful relationship with London, the last Tudor, Elizabeth I, perfected it. She did so by deploying her instinctive common touch in frequent processions through the City. She also worked closely with the rulers of London and interest groups like the Merchant Adventurers, who kept her government supplied with loans. Toward the end of her reign, Londoners grew weary of the long, drawn-out war with Spain and the taxes that paid for it, but when the Earl of Essex tried to rally them to rebellion, they stayed loyal to the queen.

Outline

I. Looking back, it is easy to project the successes of Elizabeth's reign on its beginning and assume that everyone was thrilled at the accession of the new monarch.

- **A.** In fact, Elizabeth I came to the throne of a country beset by problems.
  - **1.** A losing war with France and trouble on the Scottish border.
  - **2.** A wrecked economy and an empty treasury.
  - **3.** A nation torn and almost literally bleeding over religion.
  - **4.** A set of cultural norms that said women could not rule effectively—seemingly confirmed by the previous reign.
- **B.** Fortunately, the new queen had many qualities that enabled her to negotiate tight corners.
  - **1.** Great native intelligence and a superb humanist education.
  - **2.** Good looks and a real sense of style.
  - **3.** An ability to play two sides against each other, which would prove especially useful in dealing with various difficulties.
    - **a.** Factions within her privy council.
    - **b.** Negotiations with France and Spain.
    - **c.** An endless array of suitors for her hand in marriage.

d. Conflicting religious factions. (The Anglican Church she established in 1559 mixed Catholic ritual and Protestant theology. This pleased all but die-hard Catholics and the most intense Protestants, who came to be known as Puritans.)

4. Most importantly for our purposes, Elizabeth had the common touch.

C. We see Elizabeth's self-command and common touch, too, in her own coronation entry into London on January 14, 1559.

1. Elizabeth was seated in a golden chariot and was wearing a blue velvet robe.
2. Accompanied by the nobility and many gentlemen in "rich attire," she passed by pageants, through elaborate arches, and amid all sorts of demonstrations, many carefully orchestrated by local notables at the instigation of the lord mayor and aldermen, anxious to demonstrate municipal loyalty.
3. On her part, she was careful to recognize civic London and work the crowd.
4. Londoners—who do not much like hierarchy—ate it up, but they also tested her with religious gifts and displays in an attempt to get her to avow that she was a good Protestant.
5. Perhaps not literally pressing the flesh, she allowed the commonest of her subjects—as the "Virgin Queen," she called them her "good husbands"—to approach her, kiss her hand, tell her about their problems, and give her advice.
6. In effect, Elizabeth turned her capital into the great stage on which she acted out the drama of Tudor monarchy, with herself as the star.

II. Elizabeth needed City support.

A. As she was chronically short of funds, she needed loans from City merchants to pay for the wars at the beginning of her reign with France and Scotland.

B. In return for their loans, she enhanced the power of the Merchant Adventurers, the most important merchants' lobbying group, in 1564 granting them a monopoly on all cloth exports.

C. She also supported raids on the Spanish empire by privateers like Hawkins and Drake that were good for London trade in the short run.

D. But in the end, the Continental wars of religion and conflicts with Spain disrupted trade.
   1. In 1568, in retaliation for English raids, Philip II closed the cloth staple at Antwerp.
   2. This led to a decline in the wool trade.

E. It is a tribute to the queen's popularity that these events did not make London grumble too much, even when they culminated in the attempted invasion by the Spanish Armada in 1588.
   1. When the armada was finally defeated, the queen proclaimed a national day of thanksgiving on November 24, 1588, and processed through crowded streets to St. Paul's.
   2. Eyewitness testimony gives plenty of evidence of the people's affection for their queen.

III. Elizabeth used her court at Whitehall, Greenwich, and Richmond to create the image of the Virgin Queen: a loving bride to her people, a pure virgin to be defended by the gentlemen of England.

A. This image eventually evolved by the 1580s into that of "Gloriana," a benevolent goddess above mere mortal desires and certainly above faction.

B. If you were a member of the elite, the way to access her was at court; here, too, she concentrated on display.
   1. She sponsored annual Accession Day pageants and tournaments on November 17th at Whitehall.
   2. She also made occasional forays into the City.

C. The court itself was mysterious and impressive, best described by a German tourist, Paul Hentzner, in 1598.

D. Elizabeth gathered at her court artists, poets, and playwrights who were urged to portray her as a semidivine being, no mere woman but a symbol of England.
   1. This trickled down into popular entertainments: She was praised as "Sweet Bessy" in ballads, and she was depicted in love songs and hymns as well.

2. Part of this image was that she was unattainable: Courtiers frequently lamented their inability to get to her, especially to obtain places.
3. In fact, Elizabeth was notoriously cheap and so tended to prefer to string artists along with hope rather than reward them with riches.
4. In paintings, she was depicted not as a human but more like a medieval saintly icon.
5. In fact, she regulated her image as carefully as any minister of propaganda in a totalitarian state.

IV. But as her reign drew to a close, Elizabeth lost some of her hold on London.

A. By 1601 the country had suffered 15 years of war and high taxes. And there were additional complications.

1. The strain of military musters.
2. A sense that they were getting a little sick of her.
3. The worst famine in over a century in the mid-1590s.
4. A wool trade in decline thanks to the war.
5. Demonstrations in London in the mid-1590s and again in 1601 at Westminster Palace, over high taxation.

B. Toward the end of her reign, two groups vied for power at court—and to be in power when the next reign started.

1. Most of the levers of government were in the hands of a group of administrators and functionaries led by Sir Robert Cecil, secretary of state.
2. The other group, filled with courtiers, soldiers, and writers, was led by the young and dashing Robert Devereaux, Earl of Essex.
3. By 1601, with the queen's reign drawing to a close, it became clear that Cecil's position was impregnable.
4. In February, Essex tried to raise a rebellion in London, but nobody came. Essex was arrested and executed within the month. The City could still depose a king, but it did not back losers.

C. Elizabeth died at about 3 am on March 23, 1603.

1. James I was proclaimed by Cecil at Whitehall Gates.
2. As for the City, security was paramount.

V. The great Tudor achievement was not the triumph over the armada but constructing a state and taming a city so well that James VI of Scotland could succeed from a distance of several hundred miles without incident.

A. The Tudors, Queen Elizabeth in particular, had wooed London, mostly successfully, for over a century.

1. She had perfected the art of Tudor public relations, and the City had more often than not stood by her.

2. But by the end of her reign, the strain of high taxes and constant war, combined with people being just a little tired of the old lady at Whitehall, meant that they received the news of her death with mixed emotions.

B. Londoners were ready for a change in 1603, and they greeted James I with cheers.

C. As we will see in subsequent lectures, they ended up regretting some of that enthusiasm.

Suggested Reading:

Inwood, *A History of London*, chap. 6.

Strong, *The Cult of Elizabeth*.

Questions to Consider:

1. What was it about Elizabeth that retained London's loyalty?
2. Why was it important for Elizabeth's propaganda campaign to portray her as superhuman? How does that fit with her well-known common touch?

Lecture Seven—Transcript

Elizabethan I and London as a Stage

Londoners rejoiced at the accession of Queen Elizabeth but that doesn't mean that they were typical of the country as a whole. Looking back, it's easy to project the successes of Elizabeth's reign on its beginning and assume that everyone was thrilled at the accession of the new monarch. In fact, Elizabeth I came to the throne of a country beset with problems, a losing war with France, and trouble on the Scottish border, a wrecked economy, and an empty treasury, a nation torn and almost literally bleeding over religion, and a set of cultural norms which said that women could not rule effectively, seemingly confirmed by the previous reign. One government official summed up the situation as follows:

> The Queen poor. The realm exhausted. The nobility poor and decayed. Want of good captains and soldiers. The people out of order. Justice not executed. All things dear. The French King bestriding the realm.

Fortunately, the new Queen had many qualities which enabled her to negotiate tight corners. She had great native intelligence and a superb humanist education. She had good looks and a real sense of style and an ability to play two sides off against each other which would prove especially useful in dealing with factions in the Privy Council, negotiations with France and Spain, an endless array of suitors for her hand in marriage, conflicting religious factions. The Anglican Church she established in 1559 mixed Catholic ritual and Protestant theology. This pleased all but die hard Catholics and the most intense Protestants who became to be known as Puritans because they wanted to purify the church of Catholic traditions.

Most importantly, for our purposes, Elizabeth had the common touch. This would be especially useful in dealing with London. This Queen always knew how to work a crowd. She frequently proved this on processions through London or from palace to palace in an open chair. On summer progresses through the Home Counties, in which she stopped, to their great cost, at the splendid homes of the nobility. She did this to show favor to her hosts, to show her face to her people, and to save money by sponging off of someone else. When abroad, she would invariably be mobbed, instead of shrinking from human contact she plunged in. According to the Spanish ambassador she ordered her carriage to be taken where the crowd seemed thickest.

We see this even before her accession in her sister's reign, when her position was precarious. When Mary ascended in 1553, Elizabeth greeted her on the outskirts of London accompanied by hundreds of armed gentlemen wearing Tudor green but when she was accused of treason during the Wyatt rebellion in 1554, she went to her interrogations wearing white indicative of virginal purity and innocence. Mary's regime was so afraid of her appearance in the streets that they sent her to the Tower by barge on Palm Sunday commanding "in all London that everyone should keep the church and carry their palms while in the mean season she might be conveyed without all recourse of people to the Tower."

This did not prevent Elizabeth from stage managing her own incarceration. According to John Foxe, when it became clear that her barge would enter at Traitor's Gate, she begged to enter by any other way. This request refused she disembarked and is said to of exclaimed,

> Here landeth as true as subject being prisoner as ever landed at these stairs … before thee, O God! do I speak it, having no other friend but thee alone. … Oh Lord, I never thought to have come in here as a prisoner; and I pray you all … bear me witness, that I come in as no traitor, but as true a woman to the Queen's Majesty as any that is now living.

Note the juxtaposition between being all alone and having all those witnesses. Then she sat down in the rain on a cold stone, in full view of her entourage and jailers. When one of them encouraged her to go in, she said, "Better sitting here than in a worse place. For God knoweth I know not wither you will bring me." With that her gentleman usher wept. Is there any doubt that Elizabeth knew full well that her words and actions would be avidly reported across the country?

We see Elizabeth's self command and common touch too in her own entry into London to start her reign. She rode from Hatfield to the Tower. Upon arrival there, she alighted, patted the ground and said, "Some have fallen from being princes of this land to be prisoners in this place. I am raised from being prisoner in this place to being Prince of the land." Again, a sense of Elizabeth, sort of starring in her own movie, taking every advantage of a situation to make it dramatic and effective.

She visited the hated Tower but once more; the night before her coronation procession. I want to take a moment to study her techniques of persuasion but also to see how Royal London tried to persuade her to back its own agenda. Now, Elizabeth's coronation entry took place on the 14 of January, 1559. She was seated in a gold chariot wearing a blue velvet robe. According to a contemporary chronicle,

> In the afternoon she passed from the Tower through the city of London to Westminster, most royally furnished both for her person and for her train knowing right well that in pompous ceremonies a secret of government doth much consist for that the people are naturally both taken and held with exterior shows.

Accompanied by the nobility and many gentlemen in rich attire, she passed by pageants, through elaborate arches, and amidst all sorts of demonstrations, evidence that Londoners had been working hard on this for several weeks. Some of these demonstrations were carefully orchestrated at the instigation of the lord mayor and the aldermen who were anxious to demonstrate municipal loyalty. Some of them were spontaneous.

On her part she was careful to recognize civic London. As she passed the companies of the city, these are the different trade guilds, standing in the liveries, she took particular knowledge of them and graced them with many witty formalities of speech. I think this is like those moments when modern politicians, you know, point to someone in the crowd or act as if they know someone in particular, a moment of connection that is, of course, intended to make it seem as if they're your friend. She worked the crowd.

> The Queen was not negligent on her part to descend to all pleasing behavior which seemed to proceed from a natural gentleness of disposition and not from any strain desire of popularity or insinuation, no, no. She gave due respect to all sorts of persons where in the quickness of her spirit did work more actively than did her eyes.

Londoners, who don't much like hierarchy, ate it up but they also tested her by offering gifts, many of them religious. Her gracious reception of them was a sign that she shared London's Protestantism.

> She diligently both observed and commended such devices, symbols, signs as were presented to her and to that end, sometimes caused her coach to stand still. Here a Bible in English, richly covered, was let down under her by a silk lace from a child that represented truth. [Now, watch how she milks this.] She kissed both her hands. With both her hands, she received it, the Bible, then she kissed it. Afterwards applied it to her breast and lastly held it up thanking the city especially for that gift and promising to be a diligent reader thereof. When any good wishes were cast forth for her virtuous and religious government, she would lift up her hands to heaven and desire the people to answer, "amen." [So she's instigating a sort of call and response with the people who are here.] When it was told her that an ancient citizen turned his head back and wept, she said, "I warrant you it is for joy" [There's her wit]; and so in very deed it was. She cheerfully received not only rich gifts from persons of worth but nosegays, flowers, rosemary branches and such like presents offered unto her from very mean, that it is poor persons. It is incredible how often she caused her coach to stay when any maid offered to approach her whether to make petition or whether to manifest their loving affections.

Perhaps not literally pressing the flesh, she allowed the most ordinary of her subjects, as the Virgin Queen, she called them her good husbands, to approach her, to kiss her hand, to tell her about their problems and to give her advice. In effect, Elizabeth, even more than her predecessors, turned her capital into the great stage upon which she acted out the drama of Tudor monarchy with herself as the star.

She took the Tudor love of pageantry and moved it beyond the court and into the streets. Her people loved her for it, for most of her reign. Again I quote the contemporary chronicler:

> Hereby the people, to whom no music is so sweet as the affability of their prince, were so strongly stirred to love and joy that all men contended how they might more effectually

> testify the same; some with plausible acclamation, some with sober prayers, many with silent and true-hearted tears, which were then seen to melt from their eyes. And afterwards, departing home. They so stretched everything to the highest strain, that they inflamed the like affections in others. …

I'm reminded of that moment in Henry V when the king talks about how, if anyone is here with me on Christmas Day years from now, he'll remember what this was like and of course, he'll exaggerate and he'll make it seem much better than it was. Now you may ask is any of this true? I mean, did she really inspire this kind of affection? A little later in the lecture, I'll give you another eyewitness account which I think suggests that she did. Good thing, too, because she needed that kind of affection, she needed her people.

First, as she was chronically short of funds, she needed loans from city merchants. For example, to pay for the wars at the beginning of her reign, wars with France ending in 1559, and over Scotland, 1560 to 1561. In return for their loans, she enhanced the power of the Merchant Adventurers. The Merchant Adventurers were founded in 1407. They were a sort of lobbying group for overseas merchants and though they're national, the vast majority of Merchant Adventurers were London merchants. These are the guys who ship wool to Europe. They're fabulously wealthy and she made them wealthier.

In 1564, she granted them a monopoly of all cloth exports. As a result, for the next 50 years, this means the Hansianic merchants can't trade anymore. This means individual members of guilds can't sell wool in Europe unless they are Merchant Adventurers. As a result for the next 50 years, the richest men in London, most of the lord mayors and the greatest aldermen, far out stripping the masters of the guilds, were Merchant Adventurers.

Elizabeth also supported raids on the Spanish empire by privateers like Hawkins and Drake. Now, in the short run, this was good for London trade. It brought in lots of profit but in the end the Continental wars of religion, and conflicts with Spain, disrupted trade. In 1568, in retaliation for English raids, Philip II closed the cloth staple at Antwerp. The subsequent Dutch revolt against Philip led to the need move the staple around. What this meant was there wasn't a good place for the Merchant Adventurers to sell their wool and the result was a decline in the wool trade.

It's a tribute to the Queen's popularity that these events didn't make London grumble too much even when they culminated in the attempted invasion by the Armada in 1588. When the Spanish Armada was finally defeated, the Queen made the most of the opportunity to link her regime to the God who had, in contemporary eyes, given England the victory. She proclaimed a national day of Thanksgiving Day on 24 of November, 1588. She and her court processed through crowded streets to St. Paul's amid the acclamations of the people. Captured Spanish banners were hung out to greet her but unfortunately we don't have a really good eyewitness account of this particular event. What we do have is a nearly contemporary account from Bishop Godfrey Goodman who remembered seeing Elizabeth leaving a council meeting at Whitehall late in 1588 when he was but a small boy.

Now, I want you to pay attention to the crowd's reaction and the eagerness to get a glimpse of the Queen and I'm going to guess that this small boy is probably, admittedly, remembering it through rose-colored glasses and there's a certain amount of romanticism but I imagine there's inaccuracy here too:

> In the year 88 I did the live at the upper end of the Strand near St. Clement's Church, when suddenly there came a report unto us, it was in December, much about five of the clock at night, very dark as it would be at that time, that the Queen was gone to council, and if you will see the Queen you must come quickly. Then we all ran; when the Court gates [so you can imagine a group of small boys running down the Strand, turning left at King's Street running into the gates of Whitehall Palace] were set open, and no man did hinder us from coming in [can you imagine this happening at Buckingham Palace or the White House today?]. There we came … and when we stayed there an hour and that the yard was full, there being a number of torches, the Queen came out in great state. Then we cried "God save your Majesty! God save your Majesty!" Then the Queen turned to us and said "God bless you all, my good people!" Then we cried again, "God save your Majesty! God Save your Majesty!" [Again she's doing the call and response thing; each side wants the other to say something and of course, they do. It works.] Then the Queen said again unto us, "You may well have a greater prince, but you hall never have a more loving

> prince," [And that's a frequent line with Elizabeth. She's always saying that] and so looking one upon another awhile the Queen departed. [So there's this moment of love where their eyes sort of meet her and her people.] This wrought such an impression upon us, for shows and pageants are best seen by torchlight, that all the way long we did nothing but talk what an admirable Queen she was, and how we would adventure our lives to do her service.

Well, there you go.

Throughout her reign, Elizabeth used her court at Whitehall, Greenwich, and Richmond to create the image of the Virgin Queen, a loving bride to her people, a pure virgin to be defended by the gentlemen of England, even that small boy. This image of a virtuous, virgin Queen leading the nation against would be ravishers eventually evolved by the 1580s into that of Gloriana, a benevolent goddess, above mere mortal desires and certainly above faction. In effect, she replaced the Catholic image of the Virgin Mary becoming a Protestant symbol of the softer, more accessible side of power.

If you were a member of the elite, the way to access her was at court. Here, too, she concentrated on display. Pageants and tournaments on the 17 of November, the anniversary of accession at Whitehall, for example, every year there was a pageant on that date. Occasional forays into the city, for example, in 1566 she stages an impromptu meeting with her then lover, the Earl of Lester, and the impromptu meeting involves hundreds of people. The court itself was mysterious and impressive as described by a German tourist, Paul Hentzner, in 1598.

> We arrived at the royal palace of Greenwich [just downriver from London]. It was here Elizabeth, the present Queen, was born, and here she generally resides, particularly in summer, for the delightfulness of the situation. We were admitted into the Presence-Chamber [today, we would call this the Throne Room], hung with rich tapestry, and the floor after the English-fashion strewed with hay, through which the Queen commonly passes on her way to chapel. [Now, that's important it's a Sunday and you know that if you station yourself in the Presence Chamber, the Queen is going to walk by you. So this is a great chance to ask her for something.] At the door stood a gentleman in velvet, with a

gold chain, whose office was to introduce the Queen to any person of distinction that came to wait on her [I think this is probably the Lord Chamberlain who was usually a great peer]. It was Sunday, when there is usually the greatest attendance of nobility. In the same hall were the Archbishop of Canterbury, the Bishop of London, a great number of counselors of state, officers of the Crown and gentlemen, who waited the Queen coming out. [Now this is one of the great things about the court. If you go to court, if you could get in pass those gates, you can see virtually the entire government. In fact, the entire ruling elite of England all assembled in one place. I don't think there's a modern equivalent. It's one of the reasons that my own research work is on the court.] Which she did [the Queen coming out] from her own apartment, when it was time to go to prayers, attended in the following manner: [So let's watch her entourage.]

First went gentlemen, barons, earls, knights of the garter, all richly dressed, and bare-headed; [because, of course, you do not wear your hat in the presence of the Queen] next came the Chancellor, bearing the seals in a red silk purse, between two, one of which carried the royal scepter, the other the sword of state, in a red scabbard, studded with golden fleur-de-lis, the points upwards. [Now note this is just to go to church. In effect what we have here is the entire social hierarchy of England personified, laid end to end.] Next came the Queen, in the sixty-fifth year of her age, as we are told, very majestic. Her face oblong, fair but wrinkled, her eyes small, yet black and pleasant, her nose a little hooked, her lips narrow and her teeth black [a defect the English seem subject to, from their too great use of sugar]. She had in the ears two pearls with very rich drops. She wore false hair and that red. [Are you starting to get the sense that she's compensating for the ravages of age?] Upon her head, she had a small crown, reputed to be made of some of the gold of the celebrated Luneburg table. Her bosom was uncovered, all English ladies have it till they marry, [So Elizabeth is calling attention to the fact that even at her relatively advanced age she is a virgin.] and she had on a necklace of exceeding fine jewels. Her hands were small, her fingers

> long and her stature neither tall nor low. Her air was stately, her manner of speaking mild and obliging. That day, she was dressed in white silk, bordered with pearls of the size of beans, and, over it, a mantle of black silk, shot with silver threads. Her train was very long. The end of it borne by a marchioness. Instead of a chain, she had an oblong collar of gold and jewels. [So note the importance of dress and how important it is to adorn her in diverting attention from her age.]
>
> As she went along in all this state and magnificence, she spoke very graciously, first to one, then to another, whether foreign ministers, or those who attended for different reasons, in English, French, or Italian [famously, Elizabeth was multilingual.] Whenever she turned her face, as she was going along, everybody fell down on their knees. [She is, after all, God's representative on earth.] The ladies of the Court followed next to her, very handsome and well shaped, and for the most part, dressed in white. She was guarded on each side by the gentlemen pensioners, [yet another Palace Guard] fifty in number, with gilt battle-axes. [This woman never walks alone.] In the ante-chapel, where we were, petitions were presented to her and she received them most graciously, which occasioned the acclamation, "Long live Queen Elizabeth." She answered it with, "I thank you, my good people." In the chapel was excellent music. As soon as it and the service were over, which scarce exceeded half an hour, the Queen returned, in the same state and order, and prepared to go to dinner. [Which is another ritual for which we don't have time.]

Elizabeth gathered at her court artists, poets, and playwrights who were urged to portray her as a semi-divine being. No mere woman but a symbol of England. She was praised in high poetical works like Spencer's *The Faerie Queen* as Diana, Belphoebe, Astraea, and of course, Gloriana. This trickled down into popular entertainments where in ballads she became Sweet Bessy. Part of this image was that she was unattainable. Courtiers frequently lamented their inability to get to her, especially to obtain places. It's no accident that the melancholy lute songs of John Dowland, the greatest songwriter of his day, who yet never received a position from Elizabeth, are always addressed to an unbending woman.

In fact, Elizabeth was notoriously cheap and tended to prefer to string artists along with hope rather than endow them with riches. In paintings, she was depicted not as a human being but more as a medieval saintly icon emerging from out of the map of England as in the Ditchely portrait or facing the future while her navy defeats the Spanish Armada in the background of the famous Armada portrait. In fact, she regulated that image carefully as any minister of propaganda would do today in a totalitarian state.

Courtiers fell or were denied patronage for writings that failed to please the Queen and in 1596, the Privy Council suppressed all unauthorized images, especially ones showing her in old age. She was always depicted as youthful but as the reign drew to a close, Elizabeth lost some of her hold on London. By 1601, the country had suffered 15 years of war against Spain and high taxes. The mid-1590s saw the worst famine in over a century, wheat prices more than doubled, people were starving in the North and West Country. The death rate rose by half. The wool trade was also in decline because of the war.

There were demonstrations in London in the mid-'90s, again in 1601 at Westminster Palace over high taxation. Finally, there's even some evidence that Londoners were getting a little sick of the old woman. Still, when they got their chance to rebel they didn't take it. Towards the end of the reign two groups vied for power at court and to be in power when the next reign started. Most of the levers of government were in the hands of a group of administrators and functionaries led by Sir Robert Cecil, Secretary of State. The other group, filled with courtiers, soldiers, and writers, was led by the young and dashing Robert Devereaux, Earl of Essex. If Cecil and his faction had the Queen's confidence and the lion's share of jobs at court, Essex had three advantages: the Queen's affection despite an age difference of 30 years, higher aristocratic birth, and popularity with the London mob.

By 1601, with the Queen's reign drawing to a close it became clear that Cecil's position was impregnable. Essex resorted to a method the Tudors had made outdated, rebellion. On the night of the 7 of February, he sponsored a performance at the Globe Theatre on the South Bank of Shakespeare Richard II which is, of course, all about deposing kings. When on the 7, the Lord Chief Justice and three other Privy Counselors arrived at Essex's house to investigate, Essex detain them. Then banking on raising the city of London, he marched into it from Essex's House, which is on the Strand, with about a 150 retainers, shouting, "For the Queen, for the Queen, the crowd of England is sold to a Spaniard. A plot is laid for my life." He was covering as many bases as he could. Now, in fact, no one seems to have cared. Instead the sheriff called for the lord mayor who trapped Essex by closing Ludgate on him. Essex was arrested and executed within the month. So the city could still depose a king as we shall see but it doesn't back losers.

Elizabeth died at about 3 am on the 23 of March, 1603. Imperious to the last, she had been reluctant to designate an heir. Historians still debate whether she actually named James VI of Scotland as that heir but he was certainly the choice of her Chief Advisor, Cecil. James I was proclaimed by Cecil at Whitehall Gates and then at Cheapside accompanied, according to one eyewitness, John Manningham, "by many noblemen, lords, spiritual and temporal, knights, five trumpets, many heralds." As for the city, security was paramount. Manningham tells us that when it became known that the Queen had died "the gates of Ludgate and Portcullis were shut and down by the lord mayor's command who is there present and the aldermen etc. and until he had a token beside promise that is some clear indication that they would proclaim the king of Scots, king of England, he would not open." London was shut down until they knew that the succession had been secured. "There was a diligent watch and ward kept at every gate and street, day and night, by householders, to prevent garboils; which God we thanked were more feared than perceived."

Elsewhere, I have argued that the great Tudor achievement was not the triumph over the Armada, crucial as that was. Rather, it was in constructing a state and taming a city so well that James VI of Scotland could succeed from a distance of several hundred miles without incident. According to Manningham, "No tumult, no contradiction, no disorder in the city; every man went about his business, as readily, as peaceably, as securely, as though there had been no change, nor any news ever heard of competitors. God be thanked, our king hath his right!" Manningham was also grateful undoubtedly that this transition involved no violence, no disruption of London life.

Well, Edward IV and Henry VII had had to win their crowns in battle, march on London, and hope it would open its gates. James VI of Scotland, now James I of England and Ireland made a leisurely progress south taking over a month to get to his capital. The Tudors, Queen Elizabeth in particularly, had wooed London pretty successfully for over a century. She had perfected the art of Tudor public relations and the city had more often than not stood by her. Admittedly, by the end of the reign, the strain of high taxes, constant war, combined with people being just a little tired of the old lady at Whitehall meant that they received the news of her death with mixed emotions. I think this is captured by Manningham:

> The proclamation [of the new king] was heard with great expectation and silent joy, no great shouting. I think the sorrow for her Majesty's departure was so deep in many hearts they could not so suddenly show any great joy, though it could not be less than exceeding great for the succession of so worthy a king [he's covering his bases too]. And at night they showed it by bonfires and ringing [of bells].

Londoners were ready for a change in 1603 and they greeted James I with cheers. As we will see, they ending up regretting some of that enthusiasm. In the meantime, it's time for another walkabout to see the London that Elizabeth and James ruled. If Elizabeth had turned the public streets into a kind of theater and her court into a high class inn, it is time to visit the real theaters, inns, and taverns that her most eloquent subject, William Shakespeare, might have known.

Lecture Eight

Life in Shakespeare's London—East

Scope:

Although he became a most successful Londoner, it is important to remember that William Shakespeare was a country boy. This lecture begins to explore London as he would have found it via a verbal walking tour, highlighting its physical and social topography. Beginning, as with Dick Whittington, on Highgate, we walk down to the river, and from there we wend our way through the Tower Hamlets and East End, down Fleet Street, to the gardens of the Middle Temple, from which we get a good view of the old City before the Great Fire destroyed it.

Outline

I. In the last lecture, we saw Queen Elizabeth I use London as a stage and cast its citizens as the extras in a drama in which she starred.

- **A.** It was during her reign that the public stage really took off in London.
- **B.** Among those attracted to the new world of the theater was a young man from Warwickshire named William Shakespeare.
- **C.** Some time between 1585 and 1592, he joined the great wave of migration to London.
    1. Between 1525 and 1600, London grew from 50,000 to 200,000 souls.
    2. We know from parish registers that the increase did not come from new births.
    3. The city was murderous due to overcrowding, disease, crime, and accidents.
    4. Therefore, for London to grow, it needed a net influx of about 6,000 migrants per year. Many were driven out of their villages by overpopulation, land hunger, and a stagnant economy and toward London's economic opportunities.
    5. The only thing unusual about Shakespeare is that he may have arrived in a company of touring actors.

II. Shakespeare might have come by water, down the Thames, possibly meeting a barge carrying grain at Oxford.

- **A.** But if he was part of an acting troop, he was far more likely to have come by land on foot, or perhaps on the back of a cart from the northwest.
- **B.** Like Whittington, he might have paused at the top of Highgate Hill and gazed at his new home.
  1. He might have noticed a darker pall of smoke than in Chaucer's day from thousands of chimneys. London's air was becoming a problem.
  2. Under the pall he could see the horizontal spectacle of the river dividing the city in two.
  3. The City's vertical profile is still dominated by two bookends and a centerpiece: the Tower of London to the east and the Westminster complex to the west, with St. Paul's in the middle.
  4. Surrounding it still are the towers and spires of over a hundred medieval churches within the walls.
  5. But the city limits have been pushed further east since our last visit, creating the East End.

III. Shakespeare might have headed down through the Aldersgate into the old walled city in search of an inn.

- **A.** London's great inns were like full-service hotels, providing accommodation, stabling, food, drink, and even occasional plays in their open courtyards.
- **B.** Typically, inns were located at the termini of major stage lines into the countryside. The link between the inn and the region it served was crucial.
  1. Often the innkeeper was an expatriate from the same region, and he might employ his fellow countrymen in the inn.
  2. Immigrants and businessmen in a strange town could make valuable business and employment contacts and receive mail and news from home.
- **C.** If Shakespeare could not afford an inn, he might have headed across the fields just north of the walled city to a little actors' community at Shoreditch.

1. This is where James Burbage built London's first purpose-built theater, called simply The Theatre, in 1576.
2. In 1577 another theater, The Curtain, opened.

IV. Setting off the next day, Shakespeare would walk down to the river, and just east of the Tower he finds the docks.

A. To maximize customs revenue, Queen Elizabeth established 17 legal docks between the bridge and the Tower on the north bank of the Thames.

B. But as London and its trade grew in the 17th century, the docks and their associated trades crept east, to Wapping, Shadwell, Rotherhythe, and beyond.

C. Perhaps from the docks he ascended St. Katherine's Street to St. Katherine's Hospital.

1. The hospital was dissolved at the Reformation, but the land remains a liberty—that is, a place outside of civic jurisdiction.
2. As a result, it attracts marginal characters, prostitutes, and the poor and is ringed with tenements and shanties.

V. The area is still dominated by the Tower of London.

A. In Shakespeare's day, the Tower was already more famous as a prison than a palace.

B. In general, royal executions (e.g., Anne Boleyn and Jane Grey) took place before a small number of witnesses within the walls on Tower Green, while noble and other traitors were dispatched before large crowds on Tower Hill outside the walls.

VI. Moving west down Tower Street, we would encounter retail London.

A. In 1590 our first notice is not visual but aural, as we hear London's famous street cries.

B. Shopkeepers in particular trades still congregate together.

C. Turning northward, we revisit the financial heart of the City at Cornhill.

1. By Shakespeare's day the bankers of Lombard Street have moved indoors into the Royal Exchange, a colonnaded piazza with shops above.

2. This was so successful that a second exchange, called the New Exchange, would be built in the 17th century along the Strand.
3. Both would become popular gathering places, not unlike shopping malls today.

D. We descend Cornhill into Cheapside, still lined with magnificent shops, still the backbone of a network of streets named for the professions that inhabit them.

E. The livery companies still control every aspect of their trades, but in 1590 their hold was starting to weaken.
1. The Reformation ended their religious functions.
2. As London grew beyond its walls, it became harder for the guild to watch out for nonliveried businessmen, especially in the suburbs.
3. The livery companies were also losing authority to the great trading lobby of overseas merchants, the Merchant Adventurers.

VII. The west end of Cheapside leads us to St. Paul's Cathedral.

A. This is still the greatest church in England and the most dominant building in London.

B. But by 1590 its decaying fabric was a national scandal.
1. In 1561 the spire had succumbed to lightning, giving the gothic cathedral a much more square and dumpy look.
2. At the Reformation most of the land owned by the dean and chapter was confiscated; revenue plummeted, and the chapter could no longer maintain the building's fabric.
3. Moreover, much of St. Paul's statuary and stained glass was destroyed as idolatrous.
4. The nave itself, known as Paul's Walk, had become a common thoroughfare for vendors of food and drink.
5. The rest of the cathedral had become another bourse, where business deals are struck, professionals are consulted, and produce and horses are sold across tombs.
6. The churchyard contained numerous bookstalls owned by the great printers of Fleet Street.

7. The northeast corner of the churchyard still contains Paul's Cross, the freestanding pulpit where public notices are announced and challenging sermons are given by the leading preachers of the day.

VIII. Continuing west down Ludgate Hill through the Ludgate itself, we encounter legal London.

A. Just north of us is the Old Bailey, built in 1539, where London's felonies are tried.

B. Next to it is the notorious Newgate Prison, already in a ruinous condition by the end of the 16th century.

C. To our left is Bridewell Prison, originally a royal palace but now a workhouse and hospital for the deserving poor and a short-term prison for minor offenders, vagrants, and sturdy beggars.

IX. We cross Fleet Bridge carefully, for this is still a popular staging area for apprentice riots and other youthful gangs.

A. It is very close to the city's most notorious liberty, a thieves' kitchen known as Alsatia.

B. Thanks to the establishment of a press here in 1500 by Wynkyn de Worde, Fleet Street is also the publishing center of England.

C. We are only steps away from London's four great law schools: the Middle Temple and Inner Temple along Fleet Street; Lincoln's Inn to the north at the end of Chancery Lane; and Grey's Inn further north still across Holborn.

X. We pause in the beautiful riverside gardens of the Middle Temple.

A. In Shakespeare's *Henry VI Part 1*, this is where the Duke of York and the Duke of Somerset pluck a white rose and a red rose, respectively, to signal their enmity, and so the start of the Wars of the Roses.

B. From here, looking east, we see the great city rise before us, capped by the ramshackle stub of St. Paul's.

Suggested Reading:

Holmes, *Elizabethan London*.

Inwood, *A History of London*, chap. 6.

Questions to Consider:

1. What might Shakespeare have learned about London and human nature walking along London's docks, in Cheapside, or in the nave of St. Paul's?
2. Why did so many people come to London if it was so dangerous?

Lecture Eight—Transcript
Life in Shakespeare's London—East

In the last lecture, we saw the Tudors use London as a stage, and cast its citizens as the extras in a drama in which they starred. Queen Elizabeth was especially adept to playing to the crowd. So it's perhaps no surprise that it was during her reign that the public stage really took off in London. During the Middle Ages, liturgical drama had long been a feature of Catholic worship. Taken outdoors, these plays became processions and festivals. On a less exalted level, strolling players put on little secular skits for the patrons of great houses. At the Reformation in the mid-16th century, the government suppressed Catholic processions and festivals and sponsored Protestant plays making fun of the pope for the country house circuit.

Over the next few decades, the "university wits" actually based mostly at the London Inns of Court, we'll talk about them later, developed full five act plays. They put them on at the Inns Christmas Rebels, Queen Elizabeth attended and liked what she saw. The Queen began to encourage the performance of plays at court. Now, because of laws on the books against roving players who were viewed very much the same as vagabonds and vagrants; she and her courtiers had to give protection to a series of companies; the Queen's Men, the Earl of Leicester's men, etc. The city authorities, in particular, hated plays. They took apprentices and other workers away from the shops. They attracted large crowds threatening health by spreading disease, and threatening stability by spreading rumor, but the Queen looked the other way when new theaters were established in the 1570s and 1580s in suburbs like Shoreditch and Southwark.

Among those attracted to the new world of the theater was a young man from Warwickshire named Shakespeare. Now in the following lecture I'm going to follow the bulk of expert opinion in assuming that there really was such a person as William Shakespeare and that he wrote the plays attributed to him. But in fact, it really doesn't matter, not for this lecture. In these lectures, Shakespeare is something of an artificial construct. He stands in for the typical late 16th-century immigrant and we know that there were plenty of those.

Admittedly, though he's better documented than most 16th-century people, we know far less about Shakespeare and his London experience than we would like. So here again we're going to have to do some imagining. We do know that William Shakespeare was born the son of a wealthy glover and alderman in the West Country at Stratford-upon-Avon, Warwickshire, in 1564. He probably received a good grammar school education. He married Anne Hathaway in 1582 and had three children. Sometime between 1585 and 1592, he joined the great wave of migration to London.

Between 1525 and 1600, London grew from 50,000 to 200,000 souls. We know from parish registers that increase did not come from new births. London was not reproducing itself. The birth rate at this time was about 34 out of a 1,000. The death rate was 39 out of a 1,000. It's not hard to figure out why. The city was murderous due to overcrowding, disease, crime, and accidents. Those waddle and daub houses could easily fall on your head. So for London to grow it needed a net, at least at the rate that we've indicated, it needed a net influx of about 6,000 migrants a year. They came driven out of the villages by over population, land hunger, and a stagnant economy. Remember the legacy of Henry VIII and subsequent wars. They came towards London for economic opportunity. The only thing unusual about Shakespeare is that he may have arrived in a company of touring actors.

So how did Shakespeare get to London? He might've come by water from the west, down the Thames, possibly on a barge carrying grain from Oxford, but if part of an acting troop he was much more likely to have come the way Dick Whittington did two centuries before. On foot or maybe on the back of a cart from the north and west down the Great North Road, through Hertfordshire to Finchley, down Hampstead Heath and Highgate Hill to Islington into Aldersgate Street. We've been here before. Like Whittington, he might have paused at the top of Highgate Hill and gazed at his new home.

For starters, he would probably have noticed a darker pall of smoke than in Chaucer's day from the thousands of chimneys. London's air was starting to become a problem. Under the pall lay the horizontal spectacle of the river, still a silver green snake stretching from horizon east to horizon west dividing the city in two. The river is still spanned only by London Bridge but it is far more crowded with ships than in 1365; a testament to London's burgeoning trade by the late 16th century.

The city's vertical profile would still be dominated by two bookends and a centerpiece. Left to right, the Tower of London to the east, the Westminster complex to the west with St. Paul's in the middle—but a lightning strike in 1561 had destroyed the magnificent spire leaving a far stubbier, boxy looking cathedral profile. Surrounding it still, the towers and spires of over a hundred medieval churches within the walls. But looking along the river in 1590, it's clear that the city limits have been pushed further east since our last visit.

In 1605, John Stowe remembered how, in his boyhood, East End lanes,

> Had on both sides fair hedgerows of Elm trees, with Bridges and easy stiles to pass over into the pleasant fields, very commodious for Citizens therein to walk, shoot, and otherwise to recreate and refresh their dulled spirits in the sweet and wholesome air, which is now within a few years made a continual building throughout, of garden houses and small Cottages.

In fact, market gardens grew food and cattle grazed where Whitechapel, Stepney, Hackney, Poplar, and Bethnal Green now stand. But by 1590, the fields east of the Tower were being filled in with houses, with workshops, and with docks as we'll see.

Shakespeare might've headed down through the Aldersgate into the old walled city in search of an inn. London's great inns were like full service hotels today. They provided accommodation, stabling, food, drink, even occasional plays in their open courtyards; another reason that Shakespeare might've spent his first London night in an inn. Now many were very old. Some began life as bishops or abbot's palaces which changed hands at the Reformation. There's that connection with the word inn. Typically an inn like The George in Borough High Street, Southwark which remains open for business in the 21st century, was located at the terminal point of a major stage line into the countryside; the line would end at the end.

In a previous lecture, we learned how the Tabard in Southwark linked to the Dover Road East. Bishopsgate Street and Holborn were filled with inns to accommodate visitors from the north and the west like Will Shakespeare. J. A. Chartres has argued in an important article that the link between the inn and the region it served was crucial. Often the innkeeper was an expatriate from the very same region and he might employ his fellow countrymen in the inn. Immigrants and businessmen in a strange town must have found it comforting and helpful to hear familiar accents from home and make connections with people from their own country. Here, one could make valuable business and employment contacts and receive mail and news from home. In the 17th century, some inns even sponsored annual feasts for the London expatriates from a particular county. Not unlike college and school reunions today.

If Will couldn't have afford an inn, he might've headed across the fields just north of the walled city to a little actors community at Shortditch. Here in the shadows of the ancient Church of St. Leonard's, outside the jurisdiction of the city fathers, is where the prostitutes went after Henry VII shut down the Bankside stews in 1546. Thirty years later, this is where James Burbage built London's first purpose-built theater called, appropriately enough, "The Theater" in 1576. In 1577, it was joined by The Curtain.

Eventually Shakespeare settled in the parish of St. Helen's, Bishopsgate. Now, wherever he spent his first night, let us assume that bright and early one morning he sets off to see the city. Walking down to the river just east of the Tower, he finds the docks near St. Catherine's Hospital. Here, as in Chaucer's day, he could watch the commerce of England at work as raw wool was loaded onto barges for transport out to the big ships or wine and finished cloth from those ships was unloaded. He, too, as we did in 1365, would hear the hammering and the sawing of carpenters and shipwrights mingled with the music of cockney speech but the whole operation was much more organized now.

To aide in customs collection, Elizabeth's regime had established 17 legal docks between the Bridge and the Tower but as London and its trade grew in the 17th century, the docks and their associated trades would creep further east to Wapping, to Shadwell, to Rotherhythe, and beyond. Perhaps from the docks he ascended St. Catherine's Street to St. Catherine's Hospital.

Now the hospital was a medieval foundation that was dissolved at the Reformation but the land remains a liberty. A liberty, like a sanctuary, is a place outside of civic jurisdiction. It isn't that the laws don't apply, it's that law enforcement can't go there. As a result, liberties tend to attract marginal characters and the poor. The area is also known for prostitution. By 1590, the hospital is ringed with tenements and shanties.

The East End is a traditional arrival point for immigrants along the river and even in 1590 was already thought of as one of the poorest, least desirable parts of London. You'll also remember that the smoke and the sewage also tends to drift east but it was also among the most colorful and industrious. It would've been here that Shakespeare might've heard his first cockney accent or learnt the hard headed practicality, any effrontery of working-class Londoners. Think of the opening lines of *Julius Caesar*. When asked their trades, the smart-alecky workers reply in puns and thus a cobbler says, "A trade, sir, that I hope I may do with a safe conscious which is indeed, sir, a mender of bad soles."

The area is still dominated, of course, by the Tower of London. Kings no longer live here. Instead, it's given over to animals and prisoners. Under James I, the menagerie grew to include 11 lions, two leopards, three eagles, two owls, 23 mountain lions and a jackal. James liked to watch the animals fight each other and built a gallery for this purpose.

In Shakespeare's day, The Tower was already more famous as a prison. The prisoner list under the later Tudors and early Stewarts is a veritable Who's Who, Sir Thomas Moore and Bishop Fisher, Queens Anne Boleyn and Catherine Howard, Thomas Cromwell, various Dukes of Norfolk and Somerset, Lady Jane Gray, Archbishop Crammer, Princess Elizabeth as we saw in a previous lecture, the Earl of Essex after his failed rebellion in 1601 and Sir Walter Raleigh in 1592 after his seduction of Elizabeth Throgmorten.

In 1603, he returned to The Tower for trying to place Arabella Stewart on the throne. He practically set up house in the upper floors of the Bloody Tower with his wife and son. He set-up a laboratory for experiments. He wrote *A History of the World*. He was visited by Henry, Prince of Wales. He was allowed out in 1617 to lead a gold-hunting expedition to South America but upon his return without any gold, he was finally executed.

In general, royal executions took place before a small number of witnesses within the walls on Tower Green. Anne Boleyn and Jane Grey are good examples, and you can still see the scaffold at the

Tower of London today, but noble and other traitors were generally dispatched outside of the walls before huge crowds on Tower Hill. This not being an execution day, we make our way around the castle, through the Postern Gate to the north and so enter the city within the walls.

Moving west, down Tower Street, we encounter retail London. In 1590, our first notice is not visual but oral as we hear London famous street cries. In the early 17th century a number of prominent musicians like Orlando Gibbons and Thomas Weelkes would actually set these words in motets which became famous. I won't try and do the motet because I don't have six voices but I can least give you some sense of what the cry sounded like:

> God, give you good morrow.
> New muscles, new lily white muscles
> New fresh herrings, new thornback new
> Hot mutton pies hot, rosemary and
> Bayes, quick and gentle,
> Ripe walnuts ripe, [etc., etc.]

While the criers were generally, actually I don't think they cried, etc. While the criers were generally mobile, shopkeepers in particular trades still congregate in the same part of town and so, we can still buy a nice roast in Eastcheap but the main meat market has moved further west, just outside the walls at Smithfield. We might stop for a drink at the Boar's Head Tavern, soon to be immortalized just a few years hence as the hangout of Falstaff and his band in the *Henry IV* plays.

From here, we might head to Billingsgate Fish Market. Londoners were intelligent shoppers and believed in testing the goods as Thomas Platter, a foreign visitor, relates in 1599:

> And I noticed that each of these fishermen and fishwives kept a copper or brass needle and thread in the tub, with a sharp knife. And when the purchasers desired a pike the salesman and saleswomen slit open its belly at their bidding, placing the guts in their hands to show whether the pike was sufficiently fat, and then sewed it up again: if the pike proved fat enough, then the purchaser took it, but if the guts looked thin and poor the fishmonger kept it, throwing it back

> into the basin, among the tenches … all this I witnessed in London with my own eyes, nor is it otherwise.

I don't know why we would doubt him. Having no need of fish, we turn northward at the corner of Gracious or Gracechurch Street and Eastcheap to revisit the financial heart of the city at Cornhill. Recall that, during the Middle Ages, we could watch the bankers at work in open air in Lombard Street, but by Shakespeare's day they had moved indoors. They finally got enough sense to get in out of the rain. At Christmas 1565, the city warned 45 householders, living on Cornhill, nice of them to do it at Christmas, mostly cloth workers and drapers, to move. A consortium led by Sir Thomas Gresham had purchased the site between Cornhill and Threadneedle to build the Royal Exchange.

The Royal Exchange is a colonnaded piazza with shops above, modeled on the Bourse at Antwerp. Platter described its appearance and function in 1599:

> The Exchange is a great square place like the one in Antwerp where all kinds of fine goods are on show; and since the city is very large and extensive, merchants having to deal with one another agree to meet together in this palace, where several hundred may be found assembled twice daily, before lunch at eleven, and again after their meal at six o'clock, buying, selling, bearing news, and doing business generally.

So you can see this is a great place to go to hear the news, catch up on the events of the day. Gresham's venture was so successful that a second, New Exchange, would be built in the 17th century along the Strand. Both would become popular gathering places, places to do business and also places to shop. Businessmen struck deals but this was also a place where any respectable man or woman could go shopping, and indeed interact with each other in public in ways not tolerated elsewhere in society. At the Royal Exchange, they might encounter the latest exotic luxury goods that were beginning to arrive from the Continent, from Asia, and from the Americas in ever increasing numbers. So again, this is an engine for the creation of a kind of luxury trade in London and it also creates a new kind of culture of shopping.

We descend Cornhill, through the Poultry into Cheapside, still lined with magnificent shops. Still the backbone to a network of streets named for the professions that inhabit them. We'll remember that to our right is Grocer's Lane and Ironmonger Lane, to our left Bread Street and Goldsmith's Row, etc. Now, in theory, the livery companies still control every aspect of this trade but in 1590, their hold is starting to weaken.

First, the Reformation ended their religious functions and, as a result, the guilds are no longer donating a lot to the parish church. They're no longer making large bequests. The emphasis on good works has declined with the change in theology. Perhaps, more importantly, as London grew it became harder and harder for the guild to control any individual trade because all a tradesman had to do, who didn't want to pay money to the guild, was set up a shop outside the walls. Now think about it, if you're a guildsman and you want to stop people from doing that, you've got to shut up your shop and go looking for these kinds of black market sellers.

By 1590, there was also a kind of separation between two kinds of guild. The Common Council was increasingly dominated by member of the twelve great companies. These were the Mercers, the Grocers, the Drapers, the Fishmongers, the Goldsmiths, the Skinners, the Merchant Taylors, the Haberdashers, the Salters, the Ironmongers, the Vintners, and the Clothmakers. Now, if you paid attention to that long list you'll note that these are essentially retail trades. It was the retailers who were doing better than the craft trades. The trades that made something like the shoemakers or the coopers, who made barrels. Increasingly, it would be these great companies which would sort of run things in London. Even they were losing authority to the great trading lobby of overseas merchants, the Merchant Adventurers, who generally outweighed them in wealth and outranked them as mayors and aldermen. So even if the Grocers decided on something in Common Council, they might very well get it vetoed by the Merchant Adventurer aldermen who were looking out for their own interests.

As in 1365, the west end of Cheapside leads us to St. Paul's Cathedral. This is still the greatest church in England. The site of Elizabeth's Great Armada Thanksgiving in 1588. Still, the most dominant building in London but anyone who could recall its appearance in 1365 would be shocked at its decay by 1590. Of course, there's no one alive who can do that. In 1561 the spire had succumbed to lightning, as we've said, giving the Gothic cathedral a much more square and really rather dumpy look, but it was the Reformation that really caused the cathedral to go into eclipse. Most of the land owned by the Dean and chapter was confiscated. Revenue plummeted. The chapter could no longer maintain the building's fabric. Moreover, much of Paul's statuary and stained glass was destroyed as idolatrous by Protestant reformers. Its high altar replaced with a communion table, and indeed the nave itself, known as Paul's Walk, became a common thoroughfare between Carter Lane and Paternoster Row for vendors with vessels of ale and beer, baskets of bread, fish, flesh, and fruit, and men leading mules, horses, and other beasts.

By the 17th century only the choir and the crypt, known as St. Faith's Chapel underneath, remained for services. The choir would be the bit at the east end. The rest of the cathedral became another bourse, where business deals were struck, professionals were consulted, produce and horses were sold across tombs, and the baptismal font came to be commandeered as a counter. The churchyard contained numerous bookstalls owned, and this is rather more optimistic I think, owned by the great printers on Fleet Street and patronized by literate Londoners, possibly Shakespeare, certainly Samuel Pepys in the 17th century. Whenever he wanted a book, would go to Paul's Yard.

The northeast corner of the churchyard still contained Paul's Cross, the free-standing pulpit where official announcements were made and challenging sermons delivered by the likes of Hugh Latimer, John Donne, and William Laud. Not all of these men were safe. Afraid of its power, Parliament ordered it destroyed in 1643. So St. Paul's Cathedral was, even more than before, a community center but by the early 17th century, the decaying fabric of St. Paul's was also a national scandal.

In 1628, Charles I commissioned Inigo Jones to do something. He renovated the interior and designed a new, if rather an incongruous, classical portico for the West Front but during the Civil Wars of the 1640s Parliamentarian troops used the cathedral as a barracks. Jones's portico was given over to petty tradesmen and beggars. These groups inflicted further damage to the cathedral and the roof fell in. Thus, Old St. Paul's was in terminal decline when, in 1663, the Dean and Chapter asked Sir Christopher Wren, a young, up-and-coming architect, to survey the building. He concluded that it wasn't worth saving, but they insisted. The Great Fire of 1666 would put an end to the argument.

Continuing west down Ludgate through the Ludgate itself, we encounter legal London. That is, just north of us is The Old Bailey, built in 1539, where London's felonies are tried. It is located conveniently next to the notorious Newgate Prison. Now in those days I should explain that prisons were mostly temporary holding pens, while criminals awaited trial or the execution of sentence. You were almost never sentenced to a prison for a term of years. The one exception was debtors, who, if they couldn't escape to a liberty like St. Katherine's or The Mint in Southwark, they might find themselves forever incarcerated because there was just no way to work off their debt while they were in prison.

Newgate was already in a ruinous condition by the end of the 16th century. The water supply was inadequate. The ventilation was poor and the crowding such that prisoners were subject to a malady called "gaol fever" which often carried them off before the hangman did. Sometimes it even infected the judges and the lawyers in The Old Bailey. We turn sadly away, holding our noses because of the stench, and look along Fleet Street to our left.

Here we see another remarkable testament to the fear of disorder, Bridewell Prison. The area started out far more optimistically. It's named for a holy well dedicated to St. Bride. In 1514, the king's palace at Westminster suffered a serious fire. Needing new digs, Henry VIII built Bridewell Palace at the intersection of the Fleet and Thames Rivers between 1515 and 1520. Now unfortunately, you will recall that the Fleet was an open sewer flowing south into the Thames and the king soon decided that he didn't very much like his rather smelly palace.

In 1553, Edward VI generously bestowed the insalubrious palace on the city to house vagrants and orphans and to punish those guilty of misdemeanors. Now to understand this piece of the correctional puzzle, remember that the economy was in trouble, in part thanks to Henry VIII's inflationary policies, in part thanks to a decline in the wool trade. Henry had made things worse by dissolving the monasteries and almshouses that normally took care of the unemployed and this had a direct bearing on London, whose officials complained in 1539 of "the poor, sick, blind, aged and impotent persons … lying in the street, offending every clean person passing by with their filthy and nasty savours."

Henry's government did take some responsibility for the poor via The Poor Law of 1536, but assistance was confined to the impotent poor, the lame, the halt, the sick, women and children who were thought not to be able to help it because there was no modern understanding of economics or unemployment. Able bodied men, characterized as sturdy beggars, were assumed to be deliberately idle and so deserving of punishment. So Bridewell was designed to preserve London's impotent poor and punish the sturdy beggars. That is, it was a workhouse and a hospital for the deserving poor, a short-term prison for minor offenders, vagrants and sturdy beggars who were publicly whipped once a week.

The idea was that the poor would partially pay for their support and avoid idleness by spinning hemp and splitting stones. Above all, do anything to avoid incarceration in Bridewell because it was so unpleasant. The city's orphans were housed here as well, dressed in blue coats which they received every year at Easter.

Having made a note to avoid incarceration in this social experiment, we cross Fleet Street, holding our noses and gripping our swords. This is still a popular staging area for apprentice riots and other youthful gangs who might accost an unsuspecting tourist. According to one contemporary account "the street-boys and apprentices collect together in immense crowds and strike to the right and left unmercifully without regard to person; and because they are strongest, one is obliged to put up with the insult as well as the injury."

This area is very close to the city's most notorious liberty, a veritable thief's kitchen known as Alsatia. Arguably more edifying is the fact that, since the establishment of a press here in 1500 "at the sign of the Sun" by Wynkyn de Worde, Fleet Street has been the publishing center of England. In fact, the words "Fleet Street" are still shorthand in England for the gentlemen and now women of the press. Although, in fact most of the newspapers have since moved elsewhere.

Legal booksellers thrived here because we are only steps away from London's four great law schools, the Inns of Court, the Middle Temple and Inner Temple along Fleet Street, to the north at the end of Chancery Lane, Lincoln's Inn and further north still across Holborn, Grey's Inn on the lane named after it. All had been established by the 1470s, typically instruction comprised seven or eight years of lectures by practicing barristers but dancing, music, and history were also taught as a way of preparing students to move among gentlemen, yet another way in which London afforded social mobility.

That's why the Christmas revels at the Inns of Court, lasting from All Saints Day, November 1, to Candlemas, February 2, were famous, and sometimes attended by royalty. The magnificent Middle Temple Hall, built in 1573, will be the site of the premier of Shakespeare's *Twelfth Night* in 1601. Since London doesn't have a university, the four Inns of Court also provide the greatest concentration of young people in the city.

Let us pause for a moment in the beautiful riverside gardens of the Middle Temple. In Shakespeare's *Henry VI*, Part One, this is where the Dukes of York and Somerset pluck a white rose and a red rose, respectively, to signal their enmity, and so the start of the Wars of the Roses. From here, looking east, we see the great city rise before us, capped by the ramshackle stub of St. Paul's. Looking west, we are enticed by the irregular buildings of what will soon be the West End.

Lecture Nine
Life in Shakespeare's London—West

Scope:

We continue our tour of Shakespeare's London down Fleet Street, past mighty noble palaces on the Strand, to the center of court and government at Whitehall and Westminster. Whitehall Palace, originally York Place, was renovated by Cardinal Wolsey, confiscated by Henry VIII, and improved by subsequent monarchs. It became the headquarters of a vibrant court life, where not only politicians but scholars, writers, and entertainers got their start. Westminster Palace became the home of Parliament. Finally, if Queen Elizabeth turned London into free theater, it was in her reign that playwrights, actors, and above all theater managers began to turn public theater into a paying proposition. This lecture concludes with the experience of attending theaters like the Rose and the Globe on the South Bank.

Outline

I. Up to this point, the city we have explored was still largely the medieval town Chaucer knew, albeit somewhat more secular thanks to the Reformation.

II. But once we return to Fleet Street and head west through Temple Bar onto the Strand, we begin to see signs of a new, bigger, and more vibrant London.

- **A.** Temple Bar represents the outermost reaches of the legal City of London.
- **B.** The Strand is the principal land connection between the City and Westminster.
    - **1.** On its south side, to our left we see the same series of stately palaces stretching down to Westminster that we saw two centuries ago, except now they are named for powerful aristocrats, not bishops.
    - **2.** If we look right, we see rows of shops, and beyond them to the north, open fields.
    - **3.** But between 1600 and 1750, the West End would all be filled in, moving the center of London's gravity beyond the walls, to the west.

4. That process began in 1627 with the creation of London's first square, Covent Garden, designed by Inigo Jones on properties owned by the Russell family.

III. Following the river, we turn at Charing Cross onto King's Street, later known as Whitehall Street, and get a good view of Westminster and the complex of buildings that form the heart of English government.

A. Walking toward them, we encounter, straddling the street, the rambling series of buildings that comprise Whitehall Palace.

1. Whitehall sits on the site of the original York Place, the ancient palace of the Archbishop of York.
2. It was confiscated from Thomas, Cardinal Wolsey, by Henry VIII in 1529.

B. We continue down King's Street to the heart of the capital, the complex of buildings laid out in the Middle Ages as Westminster.

1. As before, the religious and emotional heart of the Westminster complex is Westminster Abbey.
2. Westminster Hall, built in 1097 by William II (William Rufus), is now divided into various law courts: King's Bench, Chancery, Exchequer, and Common Pleas.
3. Westminster Palace had served as the home base of the court of England until a fire damaged it in 1512. Henry VIII abandoned it, giving it to Parliament.
4. Westminster is also full of lodging houses for members of Parliament and courtiers.
5. As in the Middle Ages, because the rich congregate here, so do the poor, which means that crime and begging remain a local hazard.

IV. At the end of our long hike through London, it is time for a little entertainment.

A. Southwark consists of five manors, three of which were purchased by the City in 1550, forming London's 26th ward, Bridge Ward Without.

1. But because it developed across the river, outside of the jurisdiction of the lord mayor and Court of Aldermen, Southwark was a place where activities slightly disreputable, even dangerous, could flourish.

2. By 1590 Southwark had also developed a theater district, and from our vantage point at Westminster we see a flag flying at the Rose—a sure sign of a play this afternoon.

B. The obvious way to cross the river is to head back into the City and take London Bridge, the only land route across the river until 1750.
   1. The bridge here in 1590 dated back to 1176, a replacement for structures previously burned.
   2. Because London real estate was at a premium, the bridge was completely covered by houses and shops.
   3. London Bridge was a perennial traffic jam.

C. In part to avoid this traffic, we hail a barge instead.
   1. Both the north and south banks have numerous stairs and water gates leading down to the river.
   2. The greatest inhabitants of London—the king, the lord mayor, etc., have their own elaborately decorated barges.
   3. Along the riverbank, we find watermen advertizing their trade in time-honored London fashion, by calling out "Oars! Oars!"
   4. We land at Stangate Stairs, Lambeth. Looking to our left, across Lambeth Marsh, we see the former St. Mary Overie—renamed St. Savior's after the dissolution—from the steeple of which we might get a bird's-eye view of London.
   5. Having a play to see, we strike off down the riverside path known as Narrow Wall.

D. Heading east, we come to Paris Garden, London's first pleasure garden, a sort of amusement park for grown-ups on the South Bank where the thick foliage covered all sorts of nocturnal activities.
   1. We stop here for a preplay drink.
   2. Next we come to the Bankside Bear Garden. From at least 1546, bears and other wild animals were tormented by dogs for the entertainment of jaded Londoners.

E. Two generations later, the Bear Garden was joined by London's first outdoor theaters: the Rose (1577), the Swan (1596), and the Globe (1598).
   1. In such theaters, all of London—or at least 3,000 of them—could come together in the afternoon to see the latest play.

2. But even here, hierarchy obtained: The wealthy sat in upper boxes for three pence; the middling orders below them on benches for two pence; and ordinary people stood in the pit for a penny—hence their designation as "groundlings."
3. These were open-air circular theaters of three stories, the galleries roofed with thatch.
4. The stage itself jutted into the pit, giving a ground's-eye view to the groundlings. The stage had a trap door, leading down to "hell." Above the rear of the stage was a platform called "heaven." At the back of the stage were three doors for entrances and exits from the "tiring house," where players costumed and awaited their entrances.
5. Theaters like the Globe represented a new form of patronage: that of the paying public.
6. Still, to be performed at all, that play had to get past the Lord Chamberlain's Office, which might forbid or censor it.
7. The theater companies all gave command performances at court. All still required a royal or noble patron to stay on the good side of the civic authorities.

V. Though we have walked but three miles, the variety and bustle of London is already such in 1590 that it has been an exhausting day.

Suggested Reading:

Gurr, *Playgoing in Shakespeare's London.*

Inwood, *A History of London*, chap 7.

Questions to Consider:

1. How did London's economic growth spur the patronage of new entertainment possibilities?
2. How significant was the social mixing that took place in a London theater?

Lecture Nine—Transcript

Life in Shakespeare's London—West

Up to this point, the city we've been exploring was still largely the medieval town Chaucer knew, albeit somewhat more secular thanks to the Reformation. But once we return to Fleet Street and head west through Temple Bar into the Strand we begin to see signs of a new, bigger, and more vibrant London.

Temple Bar represents the outermost reaches of the legal city of London. And it's a tribute to the longstanding independence of the city that, beginning with Elizabeth's procession to celebrate the Armada victory at St. Paul's in 1588, even the monarch must ask permission to cross this line when traveling east. On state occasions the royal party stops here to ask entry of the lord mayor, who always grants it and submits the city sword as a mark of loyalty. The sword is then returned to him so that he may carry it before the sovereign in procession. Since we are moving west and are far less threatening than a Tudor monarch, we proceed without incident, if not necessarily without trouble. Even without the interest of the lord mayor, Temple Bar forms a choke-point for east-west traffic. As you recall, the Strand is the principal land connection between the City and Westminster. This is a street we'll return to again and again. In some ways its changing personality mirrors that of London itself.

Starting as a bridle path along the river, until its paving in 1532, the Strand was "full of pits and sloughs; very perilous and noisome," to use a contemporary quote. Noisome means smelly. Given the horse and cart traffic and sanitary conditions of the time, even in 1590 we may still find ourselves splattered with mud or worse. Looking to our left we see more or less the same series of stately palaces stretching all the way down to Westminster that we saw two centuries ago, except now they're named for powerful aristocrats not bishops. They are, in order from east to west: Essex House, Arundel House, Somerset House, The Savoy Palace which is still a ruin, Durham House, Norwich Place, York House, Suffolk House, and finally the former York Place, now Whitehall Palace.

Most have changed ownership repeatedly since our last visit. To take just one example, Durham House was periodically confiscated by the Crown and given to Anne Boleyn in 1529, Princess Elizabeth in 1550, the Duke of Northumberland, who married his son Guildford to Jane Grey here in 1553, the Earl of Leicester in 1566, Sir Henry

Sidney in 1567, the Earl of Essex in 1572, and Sir Walter Raleigh in 1583. There's a lot of English history in that list. Most of these notables died young, several at the block, and each time the property would find its way back to the bishop.

There's plenty of English history in the other houses too. It was from Essex House that the Earl of Essex launched his ill-fated rebellion in 1601. During the 17th century, Arundel House was owned by the 21st Earl of Arundel, a friend of Charles I and the greatest noble art connoisseur of his day. He filled Arundel House with one of the great art collections in England. He patronized the engraver Wenceslaus Hollar and the painter Van Dyke and all sorts of other notables. Hollar stood on the terrace of Arundel House to engrave one of the most important views of London, showing the squat Gothic form of St. Paul's, he's looking east, and the crowded city within the walls 20 years before the fire would consume them all.

In 1550, to take another house, Edward VI's favorite, the Duke of Somerset demolished the palaces of the bishops of Chester and Worcester, an inn of Chancery, and a church to build Somerset House. But at Somerset's execution in 1552, the magnificent House reverted to the Crown.

During the 17th century it was traditionally the residence of the Queen's Consort. Now it just so happens that all Stuart Queen's Consorts were Catholics, and since Catholic princesses always secured the right in their marriage contracts to attend their own liturgy served by their own priests, Somerset House became a hotbed of Catholic intrigue in a virulently Protestant country. Further down the Strand, York House was awarded by James I to his principal favorite, George Villiers, Duke of Buckingham. He built a magnificent watergate. Now, remember the smartest way to travel up and down, from east to west, west to east, is by barge. This is the only part of the house to survive its demolition in 1672. If you go to the Victoria Embankment Gardens you can see where the river originally ran because, of course, the embankment filled in down to the river and you can see this wonderful watergate. It's virtually the only relic of these splendid palaces.

Walking along the Strand we have so far, naturally, looked steadily left, because that's where the palaces are and that's where the river is. That is where our eye is left but if we look right, we see rows of shops, as we would expect along the street, but if we look just beyond them to the north, the buildings of the city trail off and we see the Royal Mews, or stables, and then open fields. According to John Stow, on May Day, Londoners "would walk into the sweet meadows and green woods, there to rejoice their spirits with the beauty and savor of sweet flowers, and with the harmony of birds, praising God in their kind." You may remember in previous lectures, I've emphasized the fact that London stops pretty clearly and then you've got open country. You can go out. You can hunt. You can walk in the fields, but between 1600 and 1750, this area of London, the West End will all be filled in, moving the center of London's gravity beyond the walls, and towards the west.

That process began thanks to the Dissolution of the Monasteries. One of the beneficiaries of the Dissolution was the Russell family. They were avid Protestants and supporters of Henry VIII and Edward VI. The resulting Russell estate in London is vast. It includes the former Convent Garden once owned by the monks of Westminster Abbey. This western land became valuable because members of the elite wanted to be close to the court which is at Westminster and Whitehall, and remember they wanted to be upwind and upriver from city smells and sewage. You'll recall that both the prevailing winds and the river tend to flow east.

So, in 1627 Francis Russell, fourth Earl of Bedford, commissioned Inigo Jones to design a number of houses "fit for the habitation of Gentlemen and men of ability" at Convent Garden, just north of the Strand. Jones was heavily influenced by Italian Palladian architecture and by the need to provide accommodation which was airy yet secure from the street. The result was London's first planned housing development and the first square with three sides of tall terraced houses, completed on the west side by St. Paul's parish church not to be confused with St. Paul's Cathedral which is fronted by impressive columns. The security of the piazza was derived first by the high rents of 150 pounds a year and the fact that entrance and egress could be controlled at narrow checkpoints. Some of this exclusivity would be traded for convenience around 1650, when a market was added to the center of the square and we'll talk about Convent Garden Market quite a bit in subsequent lectures.

Let's follow the courtiers down the Strand to Charing Cross. Following the river, we turn onto King's Street, later known as Whitehall Street, and we get a good view of Westminster and the complex of buildings which form the heart of English government, but first, walking towards them, we encounter, mostly on our left side but also parts which straddle the street to our right, a rambling series of buildings which comprise her majesty's Palace of Whitehall.

Whitehall sits on the site of the original York Place, the ancient palace of the Archbishop of York. The most famous recent inhabitant of York Place, Thomas, Cardinal Wolsey, had used his immense wealth he received from multiple bishoprics and government offices to expand York Place into a palace surpassing anything the king had at Bridewell or Westminster. This was a mistake, for Wolsey worked for the covetous Henry VIII. At Wolsey's fall in 1529, Henry confiscated the palace, renamed it Whitehall, and expanded it across King's Street, adding Holbein Gate astride the road, a cockpit, tennis courts, and a tiltyard for tournaments. All of which should remind us that the king was far more physically vigorous than his cardinal. The tiltyard is now the site of Horse Guards parade. The result was, like Henry himself, exuberant but undisciplined, an assemblage of impressive structures that seemed to have little to do with each other and no plan apart from following the curve of the river, nothing like the Louvre in Paris. There was some attempt in the early 17th century by the Stewarts to regularize Whitehall. That resulted in Inigo Jones banqueting house, commissioned by James I, a magnificent structure, but Whitehall remained a sort of hodgepodge.

Across St. James's Park is St. James's Palace. It was originally a leper hospital. It was confiscated at the Reformation, Henry VIII is all heart, and rebuilt as a hunting lodge for the king. He also added a bowling alley. If we stroll into the Park we might actually encounter the royal retinue on a hunt. This is another example of the free entertainment provided to Londoners by royalty. Turning away from St. James's Park we continue down King's Street, to the heart of the capital, the complex of buildings laid out in the Middle Ages as Westminster.

As before, the religious and emotional heart of the Westminster complex is Westminster Abbey. The major addition since our last visit is the magnificent Henry VII Chapel built in perpendicular style between 1503 and 1519. This chapel houses the bones of most of Henry VII's Tudor, Stewart, and early Hanoverian descendants—they stopped burying here after 1760—under elaborate fan-vaulting, in the words of Washington Irving, "stone seems, by the winning labor of the chisel, to have been robbed of its weight and density, suspended aloft and the fretted roof achieved with wonderful minuteness and the airy security of a cobweb."

Though great statesmen are not yet buried at Westminster Abbey in 1590, Poet's Corner is established in the south transept. Chaucer lies here, as does Spenser. At Spenser's funeral in 1599, it is said that his fellow poets threw manuscript works into the grave after him. When Ben Jonson asked to be buried in the Abbey, he quite modestly requested that "two feet by two feet will do for all I want." So, at his death in 1637, he was buried standing up.

During the Civil Wars, Cromwell's New Model Army would use the church as a barracks and a stable. They're Puritans and have no love for such high church fodderal; thus demonstrating their disdain for high church sensibilities. According to one account they, "broke down the communion rails before the Table and burnt them in the very place in the heat of July but wretchedly profaned the very table itself by setting it about with their tobacco all before them."

A short distance away, we find William Rufus' Westminster Hall. It's now divided into various law courts which meet here: King's Bench, Chancery, Exchequer, and Common Pleas. The Hall also contains numerous shops and stalls to entice or refresh those waiting for a case or a verdict. On court days it is thronged with litigants and spectators especially when the weather is bad, for this is a good place to get in out of the rain. It may be here that Shakespeare learned what he knew of lawyers.

But the Hall assumes its full magnificence when the law courts are cleared for a great state trial, as occurred here in 1535 for Sir Thomas More and Bishop Fisher, 1536 for Anne Boleyn, 1552 for the Duke of Somerset, 1606 for Guy Fawkes and the Gunpowder Plotters, 1641 for the Earl of Strafford and, most spectacularly of all, in January, 1649, for the trial of the king himself, Charles I. We'll talk about that in the next lecture.

More happily, the king's coronation banquet traditionally takes place here. At the center of the banquet is a great moment when a member of the Dymoke family rides in on horseback and throws down the gauntlet and challenges anyone to challenge the title of the king. Of course, everybody stops eating but presumably no one has ever been so foolish as to challenge the king's title in his own mess hall. Among the many guests at a coronation banquet would be peers and members of Parliament. In 1590, when not dining together, they met in Westminster Palace.

Now this was Edward the Confessor's palace and it had served as the home base of the court of England until a fire damaged it in 1512. Henry VIII abandoned it, first for Bridewell and then permanently for Whitehall. What to do with a half-burnt royal palace on prime real estate? Give it to Parliament. The result was very much an ad hoc arrangement. The House of Lords met in the White Chamber. It was the undercroft to this part of the building that Guy Fox and his fellow Catholic conspirators rented in 1605 and filled with barrels of gunpowder in the hope of blowing up the king and political elite at the state opening of Parliament on November 5th of that year. They were upset that James I had not granted a toleration to Catholics and they thought that the way to get England to tolerate Catholics was to blow up the king and the Houses of Parliament. It's really a rather stupid plan and they were all caught and eventually hanged, drawn, and quartered.

The House of Commons met wherever they could be housed; the Abbey's Chapter House or Refectory and then, after it was secularized at the Reformation in 1547, in St. Stephens Chapel. These locations were in fact too small for the full membership. If everybody showed up there wasn't room for everybody; this lead to a hot-house atmosphere in which members crowd together shoulder to shoulder on the former choir benches. That crowding together, that hot house atmosphere, I think, explains a lot of English history and the current nature of Question Time. Worse, the building was in constant disrepair but you've got to remember that in the 16th century Parliament was not a regular institution of the government. It was more of a periodic and brief occurrence, usually called and dismissed as quickly as possible. So no one thought that Parliament needed a splendid permanent home.

Westminster Palace must have seemed perfectly adequate in 1590 for these occasional meetings. Finally, circa 1590, Westminster is full of lodging houses for members of Parliament and courtiers. As in the Middle Ages, because the rich congregate here, so do the poor, which means that crime and begging remain a local hazard. One of the interesting demographic facts about London is that while the East

End contains almost no rich people the West End which does, also has lots of poor people.

At the end of long hike through London, it is time for a little entertainment. The place to get it is on the South Bank, at Southwark. Southwark consists of five manors three of which were purchased by the city in 1550, forming London's 26th and final ward, Bridge Ward Without. Still, because it developed across the river, outside of the jurisdiction of the lord mayor and Court of Aldermen, Southwark was a place where activities slightly disreputable, even dangerous, could be found. It's a bit of a combat zone. We've already noted the Bankside stews shut down by Henry VIII. By 1590 Southwark had also developed a theater district and from our vantage point at Westminster we see a flag flying at the Rows—the Globe isn't built until 1598, so we're eight years too early—a sure sign of a play this afternoon but first we have to cross the river.

The obvious way to do that would seem to be to head back into the City and take London Bridge, the only land route across the river until 1750. The bridge current in 1590 is still the one built in 1176. It consisted of 19 small arches and a drawbridge and gate on the Southwark side. Those arches created two pools in the river, the Upper Pool above London Bridge to the west, the Lower Pool, below it to the east.

Despite the drawbridge, most of the big ships moored and unloaded their cargoes in the Lower Pool but you can see big ships west of that, as well. William Camden, writing in 1586, was astounded at the number of ships in the river, a sign of London's prosperity.

> A man would say, seeing the shipping there, that it is, as it were, a very good wood of trees disbranched to make glades and let in light, so shaded it is with masts and sails.

Between the pools, the Bridge's 19 arches created rapids which were extremely dangerous to shoot even at ebb tide; professional London watermen would generally refuse. Lay attempts were viewed as suicidal. If you rented a barge and took it out yourself and attempted to shoot those rapids, and if you didn't make it, you would be listed as a suicide in the Bills of Mortality. Because London real estate was at a premium, the bridge is still covered with houses and shops. Another medieval custom rendered the Bridge gruesome at the end of the 16th century.

Beginning in 1305, the severed heads of traitors were mounted on pikes at the battlements of the Southwark Gate to warn anyone entering London of the severity of royal justice. This is where the heads of both Sir Thomas More and Bishop Fisher ended up and, five years later, with poetic justice, they were joined by that of their nemesis, Thomas Cromwell, Earl of Essex. The heads don't seem to have deterred many; London Bridge was a perennial traffic jam.

Now in part to avoid this traffic and in part because we want to sample a method of travel more characteristic of London, like Will Shakespeare in Tom Stoppard's *Shakespeare in Love*, we hail a barge instead. Both the north and south banks have lots of stairs and watergates leading down to the river. The greatest inhabitants of London, the king, the lord mayor, bishops, nobles own magnificent, elaborately decorated barges to transport them along the river. Witnessing the royal barge, banners flying, trumpets playing while he processes up river to Hampton Court or down river to Greenwich is another one of those free entertainments to be had just by the fact of living in London. But being poor scholars we have to hire.

Along the riverbank, we find watermen advertizing their trade in time-honored London fashion, by calling out "Oars! Oars!" Apparently young ladies, just up from the country and used to dropping their "h" sometimes misheard this as some sort of an accusation. Not being so offended, we book passage at Whitehall steps and head across the river. As we embark, we try to avoid the thick mud as we step into the boat. We settle in, and we proceed in a stately fashion. Even up-river from the bridge we thread our way among the big ships and the 2000 wherries counted by William Harrison in 1577, and the swans, which are all the personal property of the Queen. To injure one of them is a felony, potentially subject to death.

Approaching one merchantman after another, we hear the different languages and accents of traders from France, Germany, from the Low Countries, Sweden, Denmark, and assorted coastal regions of the British Isles reminding us that London is a great international port. If the Thames is an aural delight, its sights and smells are not all that pleasant. It will not be until the 19th century that London constructs a modern underground sewer system. In the meantime, the run-off from London's garbage and night soil, night soil being a very fancy word for human excrement, empties into London's streets and is carried by frequent rain into gullies and small streams like the Fleet River and then down, ultimately, into the Thames.

So once more holding our noses, we land at Stangate Stairs, Lambeth. Looking to our left, across Lambeth Marsh and essentially east, down river, we see the former St. Mary Overie, after the Dissolution of the Monasteries, it's renamed St. Savior's. This is a magnificent church on the South Bank, but we don't have time, the steeple of this church still gives the best view of London and it's from the steeple that two famous panoramas were drawn; one by Claudios Vischer in 1616 and the other by Wenceslaus Hollar in 1647. Having a play to see, instead we strike off down the riverside path known as The Narrow Wall.

Heading east, we come to about 100 acres of marshy riverbank known as Paris Garden. Paris Garden was confiscated by Henry VIII and eventually awarded to the bailiff of Southwark, William Basele. He, rather enterprisingly, opened it to his fellow Londoners for bowling and gambling. Over the next two centuries, it would develop into London's first pleasure garden. A pleasure garden is a sort of amusement park for grown-ups, on the South Bank, where the thick foliage covered all sorts of nocturnal activities. We'll visit a pleasure garden later in this course. We stop here for a moment for a pre-play drink.

Turning back to the river, we come to the Bankside Bear Garden. From at least 1546, when Henry VIII himself paid a visit, bears and other wild animals were tormented here by dogs for the sport of jaded Londoners. A German visitor remembered his 1584 visit thus:

> There is a round building three stories high, in which are kept about a hundred large English dogs, with separate wooden kennels for each of them. The dogs were made to fight singly and with three bears, the second bear being larger than the first, and the third larger than the second. After this a horse was brought in and chased by the dogs and at last a bull who defended himself bravely. The next was, that a number of men and women came forward from a separate compartment, dancing, conversing, and fighting with each other; also a man who threw some white bread among the crowd, who scrambled for it. Right over the middle of the place a rose was fixed, [probably a Tudor rose] this rose being set on fire by a rocket. Suddenly lots of

apples and pears fell out of it down upon the people standing below. Whilst the people were scrambling for the apples, some rockets were made to fall down upon them out of the rose, which caused a great fright but amused the spectators. After this, rockets and other fireworks came flying out of all corners, and this was the end of the play.

Such was this the sophistication of London entertainment before the arrival of the public theater. Two generations later, the Bear Garden was joined on the South Bank by London's first outdoor theaters, The Rose in 1587, The Swan actually in Paris Garden in 1596, and The Globe built in 1598. Now in the following visit, we're going to be visiting The Rose but most of our archaeological knowledge comes from attempts to reconstruct The Globe, so I'm going to fudge back and forth a bit.

In such theaters all Londoners, or at least 3,000 of them, could come together in the afternoon to see the latest play, but even here, hierarchy obtained. The wealthy sat in upper boxes for three pence, the middling orders below them on benches for two pence, and ordinary people stood in the pit, the large open area on the ground level for a penny, hence their designation as groundlings and by the way, they would stand; you're not allowed to sit.

Particularly privileged individuals, for example, young aristocrats, desperate to be seen, might actually demand to sit on the stage or the gallery overlooking it. These were open air circular theaters with three stories, the galleries roofed with thatch. That helps to explain why, in 1613, during a performance of Shakespeare's *Henry VIII*, one of the special effects, a firing cannon, set the thatch on fire, burning The Globe to the ground. The stage itself jutted into the pit, giving a ground's eye view to the groundlings. That stage had a trap door, leading down to "hell" from which Banquo's ghost in *Macbeth* could suddenly appear on stage. Above the rear of the stage was a platform called "heaven," above which was a balcony from which Juliet could await her Romeo, defenders of towns in the *Henry VI* plays could shout imprecations at rebels, musicians could play before curtain time and a powerful aristocrat could claim the best seats; he could actually be sitting up there so that everyone could get a look at him.

At the back of the stage were three doors for entrances and exits from the tiring house, where the all male cast costumed and awaited their entrances. Thomas Platter describes the experience in 1599:

> On September 21st after lunch, about two o'clock, I and my party crossed the water, and there in the house with the thatched roof witnessed an excellent performance of the tragedy of the first Emperor Julius Caesar with a cast of some fifteen people; when the play was over, they danced marvelously and gracefully together as is their wont, two dressed as men and two as women.

Theaters like The Globe, or The Rose, clearly represented a new form of patronage, that of the paying public. It was public taste, not that of the court or the church, which dictated whether a new play succeeded or failed. Think about it, before the Reformation that option isn't really available for much in the way of art. Still, to be performed at all, that play had to get past the Lord Chamberlain's Office which might forbid or censor it if it dealt with a sensitive political topic, for example. The theater companies all gave command performances at court and all still required a royal or noble patron to stay on the good side of the civic authorities. And so you get the Earl of Worcester's Men, the Admiral's Men, etc.

The Globe was home base of the Lord Chamberlain's Men. At least six actors were shareholders in this company and the theater itself, with the builders Cuthbert and Richard Burbage holding double shares. Actors not only took on many parts, but were expected to write as well, if necessary. Among the playwright-player-shareholders in the Lord Chamberlain's Men was our young immigrant to London from Stratford-upon-Avon, William Shakespeare. The miracles of *Hamlet*, *Lear*, *Richard III*, *A Midsummer Night's Dream*, and *The Tempest* would not have been possible without certain developments at the end of the 16th century.

First, the royal protection gave Shakespeare and other playwrights and actors the freedom to mount their plays. Second, the courage and ruthlessness of impresarios like the Burbages, who drove their authors and players very hard in order to scrape together a profit. Third, the rise of a popular London audience with some disposable income and an interest in being entertained. Finally, and I think most miraculously, the development of the English language to a point of sufficient refinement and versatility by the end of the Tudor century, that it could be deployed by those playwrights to such great effect, and yet still be understandable to people of all social ranks including our friends, the groundlings.

Though we have walked but three miles, the variety and bustle of London is already such, in 1590, that it has been an exhausting day. No wonder Donald Lupton wrote of the city in 1632, "she's certainly a great world, there are so many little worlds in her." Soon after those words were written, that world would seem to come apart. In the next lecture, London would be forced to choose sides in a terrible civil war and it would once again prove the old adage, that as London went, so went the country. In the next lecture, London under the early Stewarts and the English Civil Wars.

Lecture Ten
London Rejects the Early Stuarts

Scope:

The early Stuarts, James I and Charles I, cultivated a refined court life and assembled one of the great art collections in Europe. But they rarely showed themselves to London, and the inhabitants of the capital objected—increasingly vocally and en masse—to what they perceived as their inclinations to Catholicism, high taxation, and arbitrary power. In the late 1630s and early 1640s, apprentice boys and tradesmen's wives signed petitions against the power of the bishops, ordinary citizens demonstrated outside of Whitehall Palace, and London's mayor and aldermen began to refuse to loan the king money. In 1642 the king was forced to leave the capital to raise an army against Parliament. London's wealth proved decisive in Parliament's subsequent victory in the British Civil Wars. The king would only return to it for his trial and execution in January 1649. After experimentation with a republic and a military dictatorship, Parliament restored the monarchy, at the insistence of Londoners, in May 1660. Once again, as London went, so went the nation.

Outline

I. The Stuarts ruled in England from 1603 to 1714, during which period the most dramatic event in British history—the Civil Wars of the mid-17th century—happened.

- **A.** London played a crucial role in bringing those wars to fruition, ensuring that Parliament won them, and then ensuring that the king won the peace.
- **B.** Though the lord mayor and aldermen relied on the king for their privileges and supported him with money and troops, they had their issues with the Stuarts.
  - **1.** James I and Charles I had a very high notion of their prerogative and occasionally clashed with Parliament.
  - **2.** They were spendthrifts on favorites and art.

3. Their foreign policy was pacifist at a time when many Protestants wanted to get involved in the Thirty Years' War (1618–1648).
4. In religion, James steered a middle path between Catholics and Puritans, only persecuting those who were disloyal.
5. Charles I embraced a "high church" theology and ritual; he left Catholics alone but persecuted Puritans who did not want high church ritual.
6. Many came to feel that Charles I in particular was flouting the constitution.

II. The City had its own issues at the beginning of the 17th century.

A. By 1600 London had grown to about 200,000 people; by the end of the 17th century, it would reach over half a million.

1. London's phenomenal expansion served as a demographic safety valve, because England's agricultural economy could not otherwise absorb its growing population.
2. In fact, early modern London needed between 6,000 and 8,000 immigrants every year to grow at this rate, since its death rate was higher than its birth rate.
3. According to historian E. A. Wrigley, these facts had a profound effect on England as a whole.
4. The London experience must have had profound social, cultural, and psychological effects on all immigrants.

B. The last years of Queen Elizabeth had seen a seemingly endless war with Spain, high taxes, bad harvests, high unemployment, and a stagnant wool trade.

C. There was a widespread perception that crime was on the rise.

D. Puritans were Protestants who thought that the Church of England retained too many Catholic structures (bishops, for example) and ceremonies.

1. Most London parish priests were chosen by the government or church, so they were safely Anglican.
2. But where the vestry or parish could choose its own clergyman, that parish was often Puritan.

III. Though London's rich City elite, headed by the lord mayor and Court of Aldermen, were closely allied with the Tudor and early Stuart monarchs, both kings and aldermen had to worry about the Common Council and Common Hall—the London liverymen and those free of the guild who voted for members of Parliament.

- **A.** They leaned toward Puritanism and saw the Stuart court as favoring popery and arbitrary government.
- **B.** As national tensions grew more strained between the Stuarts and Parliament in the 1630s, the City's elite and its citizenry began to take sides.
  1. One of the first large demonstrations by ordinary Londoners came in 1637 when William Prynne, John Bastwick, and Henry Burton had their ears cropped for writings critical of the bishops and the queen.
  2. In 1640 Charles I was forced by a rebellion in Scotland to call a Parliament.
  3. As the Parliament sat, Londoners of all ages frequently crowded Old Palace Yard, between Westminster Palace and Westminster Hall, demanding abolition of the bishops and the execution of Charles's right-hand man, the Earl of Strafford.
  4. Royal authority over the City was breaking. By early 1642, City funds for the king dried up, and London began to prepare to defend itself against its own sovereign.
  5. From this point, the City authorities threw their weight behind Parliament, and once the war started in August, they threw money as well.

IV. The English portion of the British Civil Wars, which began in August 1642, should have been well matched.

- **A.** Most social groups split evenly between the king's supporters (or Cavaliers) and Parliament's supporters (the Roundheads).
  1. The crucial difference was London, which supported Parliament.
  2. London had the apparatus of government, especially taxation.
  3. London had the wealth to loan Parliament vast sums of money.
  4. London had most of the country's manufacturing base.

5. London had the trained bands, the closest thing to a professional military force in England.

B. The king failed to capture his capital early in 1643.

1. From this point, it was a war of attrition, which Parliament won.
2. In 1646, after the decisive Battle of Naseby in Oxfordshire, the last Royalist army in England surrendered and the king was taken prisoner.

C. Parliament, the Scots, even the army now negotiated with the king to return as a constitutional monarch.

1. But Charles I never negotiated in good faith. After the king started a second civil war in 1648, the most radical elements in the army, led by General Oliver Cromwell, ordered Parliament purged of all but the most radical members.
2. The following month, January 1649, the resulting "rump" of a Parliament tried Charles I in Westminster Hall on a charge of high treason against the people of England. The king's execution took place at the Banqueting House at Whitehall on January 30, 1649.
3. Within weeks, the Rump Parliament abolished the monarchy and the House of Lords.
4. England was now, for the first and only time in its history, a republic.

V. Having abolished the monarchy, the Puritan Rump Parliament also abolished the court, selling off much of the king's artwork, disbanding the royal musicians, etc.

A. But if the Puritan regime was hard on the visual and performing arts, it was terrific for the literary arts, having abolished censorship in 1641.

B. The Commonwealth, as the republic called itself, was never popular, and in 1653 the army shut down the Rump Parliament and named Cromwell Lord Protector of England.

1. His regime was efficient, militarily successful, and expensive, necessitating higher taxes than Charles I had ever demanded.
2. The regime was also intrusive, suppressing drunkenness, adultery, Maypole dancing, and Christmas celebrations as nonbiblical.

3. Once again, Londoners balked at such strong control.

VI. In October 1658, Oliver Cromwell died from overwork.

A. There followed a succession of provisional governments.

B. Finally, at the instigation of, among others, the London apprentices, the Convention Parliament of 1660 invited Charles I's eldest son to return as King Charles II.

Suggested Reading:

Inwood, *A History of London*, chap. 8.

Pearl, *London and the Outbreak of the Puritan Revolution*.

Questions to Consider:

1. Why were the Stuarts so ineffective in wooing London in comparison to their Tudor predecessors?
2. Why did London tend toward Puritanism and not Royalism?

Lecture Ten—Transcript

London Rejects the Early Stuarts

The Stuarts ruled in England from 1603 to 1714. Histories of the British Isles during this period have a lot of trouble avoiding that fact that the most dramatic event in British history, The Civil Wars of the mid-17th century happened on their watch. Histories of London are not immune, for London played a crucial role in bringing those wars to fruition, in making sure that Parliament won them, but then making sure that the king won the peace.

It used to be that historians had no trouble explaining this connection. The British Civil Wars were about the English, Scots, and Irish seeking freedom from Stuart absolutism. London, as the freest place in the British Isles, was bound to spur and support that fight. Unfortunately for this simple interpretation, historians know a lot more now. It turns out that nobody in the British Isles necessarily wanted to rebel against the king, let alone depose him. Rather, they wanted all their kings, Tudor and Stuart, to rule as Protestants and within the laws.

The authorities in London were especially tied to the Stuart regime. They depended on royal charters to guarantee their own governmental power, trading privileges—remember The Merchant Adventurers. Tudor and Stuart kings depended on London for troops. The London militia or trained bands formed at least 10 percent of nearly every royal land force in every war during this period. And of course, they relied on the city fathers for loans of that immense wealth generated by trade which could be of great use to a king about to fight a war.

Now it's true, the lord mayor and aldermen might have had their issues with the Stuarts. James I, who ruled from 1603 to 1625 and Charles I who ruled from 1625 to 1649, had a very high notion of their prerogative, and occasionally clashed with Parliament. They were also spendthrifts. James spent money on his favorites, Charles on his art collection at Whitehall, and of course, that money was tax money.

Their foreign policy was pacifist at a time when many Protestants wanted to get involved in the Thirty Years' War, 1618 to 1648, on the Protestant side. In religion, James steered a middle path between Catholics and Puritans, only persecuting those who were disloyal, but Charles I was more rigid. He embraced a high church theology and ritual for the Church of England. He left Catholics alone. This included his unpopular French Queen, Henrietta Maria, and her many Catholic courtiers at Somerset House. But he persecuted Puritans who did not want high church ritual. Many came to feel that Charles I, in particular, was flouting the constitution. Between 1629 and 1640 he ruled without Parliament in what came to be known as "the Personal Rule."

During this period, he imposed taxes, including new Customs rates, without parliamentary permission; a no-no since the Middle Ages. He violated the right of habeas corpus and in 1637 he attempted to impose the Anglican prayer book on Scotland, leading to a disastrous civil war there. But even that did not yet mean that Londoners were anxious to rebel.

The city had its own issues at the beginning of the 17th century. Remember, first of all, that London was growing rapidly. By 1600 it had grown to about 200,000 people. By the end of the 17th century, it would reach over half a million. This was twice the rate of growth being experienced in the rest of the country. No wonder that James I complained that "with time England will only be London and the whole country be left waste." In fact, London's phenomenal expansion served as a demographic safety valve.

England's agricultural economy was not flexible enough to create jobs for all these new bodies to do. Remember England is growing as well. London absorbed them. It also absorbed foreign refugees from the Wars of Religion, especially Dutch and French Protestants. London also provided opportunities for younger sons and apprentices to make their fortunes; remember the Dick Whittington story; while the landed elite could come to court and sample its cultural and intellectual life.

The Stuarts, by the way, hated all of this. They repeatedly ordered the aristocracy back to their country estates where they could keep an eye on the people. Nevertheless, London absorbed all these people who wanted jobs or freedom or fun. In fact, early modern London needed these immigrants to grow, for, as we have seen, its death rate was higher than its birth rate. In order to grow as it did, London needed between 6,000 and 8,000 immigrants a year. According to the historian E. A. Wrigley, these facts had a profound effect, not only on the history of London, but on the history of England as a whole.

First, the growing city had to be fed. As a result, farms in Essex and Kent were forced to improve production rates and grain merchants had to improve distribution. Cattle were driven from as far away as Wales. In the years following 1600, a true market economy developed and England's transportation system was forced to keep up via the dredging of rivers, and better roads, carriages, wagons, and carrying services. The English shipping industry also had to expand, not only to cover London's foreign trade, but also to supply the crucial coastal trade that kept London in fish and sea coal. Sea coal wasn't mined at sea, it came from Newcastle as you would expect, but it came via the sea into the Thames.

From the late 16th century new trading companies arose to challenge the monopoly of The Merchant Adventurers. In most cases, they existed to export wool and import luxury goods to far-flung locations. There was the Muscovy Company, for Russia, founded in 1555, the Spanish Company in 1577, the Eastland Company, for the Baltic, in 1579, the Turkey, later the Levant, Company in 1581, the Senegal Adventurers, later the Royal Africa Company in 1588, the East India Company in 1600, the Virginia Company in 1606, and the Massachusetts Bay Company in 1629. In most cases, the idea was that the English would sell wool to these far flung destinations but, of course, the Indians, for example, weren't terribly interested in English wool and eventually these companies made their profits mostly on the import of luxuries. The one exception is the Royal Africa Company which eventually dealt in slaves.

The East India Company was a stock company, allowing investors to share the risk. So there's another sign of London's modernity. By 1700 sophisticated credit facilities, bonds and bills of exchange, a penny post, and newspapers would arise, in part to facilitate trade and communication between capital and countryside and capital and world. In the meantime, the London experience must have had profound social, cultural, and psychological effects on these new immigrants. Imagine having grown up in the countryside, in a small and relatively quiet village, with its own calendar and traditions. Everyone knows everyone else. Now imagine arriving in London to find more people crowded into one place than you'd ever experienced in your life. The sights, the noise, the smells would've been nearly overwhelming. Many people complained of London's stink and filth.

In 1606 Thomas Dekker was more concerned with noise and crowding:

> In every street, carts and coaches make such a thundering as if the world ran upon wheels: at every corner, men, women, and children meet in such shoals, that posts are set up, of purpose, to strengthen the houses, lest with jostling one another they should shoulder them down. Besides, hammers are beating in one place, tubs hooping in another, pots clinking in a third, water tankards running at tilt in a fourth.

Unlike the narrow world of the village, here you would encounter people from every part of England and many parts of Europe, with different accents and, perhaps, even different religious and social traditions from yours. Your own customs will soon be left behind as more or less irrelevant. Who cares what you did in Shropshire? Where, in the village, the sun and agricultural seasons, spring for planting, fall for harvest, determined time, now your day ran according to your master's watch; your job as a servant or a tradesman carried on irrespective of the season. Didn't matter what the weather was outside. You still had to produce the same number of shoes. Disease and sudden death would have been even more prevalent than in the village. This, plus changing economic opportunities, meant that your relationships would be made and broken far more quickly, far more casually, and far more often than in the village. You would get to know many more people but those relationships might not run nearly as deep as the ones that you had had back home. Now, all of this may have been good for London's long-term economic growth. In fact, Rigley argues that it's all necessary to happen before there can be an Industrial Revolution, but it threatened the social and mental stability of Londoners.

Remember, too, that the last years of Queen Elizabeth had not been happy; there was an endless war with Spain, it took James to work out of peace in 1604, high taxes, bad harvests, high unemployment, a stagnant wool trade from which London had not yet really fully recovered. Worse, there was a widespread perception that because of the economic crisis crime was rising. That perception was fed by city dramas like Decker and Middleton's *The Roaring Girl* of 1611. City dramas were about the life of the city. They were about apprentices. They were about merchants and tradesmen. This particular play depicted the career of a famous London pick-pocket, Mary Frith, better known as Moll Cutpurse. Moll unnerved those who embraced the traditional order, not just because she picked pockets, she wore disguises, often male, to do so. At a performance of the play at London's Fortune Theater she appeared in man's apparel and in her boots and with a sword by her side. She played upon a lute. She sang a song and said to the audience "that she thought many of them were of opinion that she was a man but if any of them would come to her lodging they should find that she was a woman." No wonder the civil authorities hated the theater and worried about loose women. The lord mayor and aldermen were convinced that their city was awash with crime. Listen to William Fleetwood, London's Recorder, reporting to Lord Burleigh in 1583.

> Upon Friday last we sat at the Justice Hall at Newgate from 7 in the morning until 7 at night, where were condemned certain horse stealers, cutpurses, and such like, to the number of 10, whereof 9 were executed, and the tenth stayed by a means from the court. These were executed upon Saturday in the morning [quick justice]. There was a shoemaker also condemned for willful murder committed in Blackfriars, who was executed upon Monday in the morning. Amongst our travails this one matter tumbled out by the way, that one Wotton, a gentleman born, and sometime a merchant man of good credit, who, falling by time into decay, kept an alehouse at Smarts Key near Billingsgate, [Another reoccurring theme of this course is you can rise and you can fall in London, you can become very wealthy, you can become very poor, very fast] and after … some misdemeanor being put down, he reared up a new trade of life, did this Wotton and in the same house he procured all the cutpurses about this city to repair to his said house. There, was a schoolhouse set up to learn young boys to cut purses. There were hung up two devices, the one was a pocket, the other was a purse. The pocket had in it certain counters [counterfeit coins] and was hung about with hawks bells, and over the top did hang a little sacring-bell [this is the bell that's rung as mass at the elevation of the host]; and he that could take out a counter without any noise, was allowed to be a public foister; and he that could take a piece of silver out of the purse without the noise of any of the bells, he was adjudged a judicial nipper. [Note that a foister

is a pickpocket, and a nipper is termed a pickpurse, or a cutpurse.]

In other words, two and a half centuries before Charles Dickens's Fagin, London already has a school and slang for crime. Nor was London orthodox. London was a hotbed of Puritan sympathy. You'll recall that Puritans were Protestants who thought that the Church of England retained too many Catholic structures, bishops, for example, and ceremonies. Now, most parish priests in London were chosen by the government or the bishops of the Church of England, so they were safely Anglican. But where the vestry or parish could choose its own clergyman, that parish was often Puritan, for example, St. Anne's Blackfriars or St. Stephens' Coleman Street, a notoriously Puritan parish. The city was also studded with Puritan lectureships, that is, sermons, regular sermons, sponsored by wealthy Puritan merchants. That reminds us that there were Puritans at all social levels, including some aldermen. These men could not have been happy with royal policy as the 1630s wore into the 1640s.

Now as we've seen, London's rich city elite, headed by the lord mayor and Court of Aldermen, were closely allied with the Tudor and early Stuart monarchs, from whom they received trading privileges and other concessions but both kings and aldermen had to worry about Common Council and Common Hall. This was the London liverymen and also those who were free of the guild, that is if you didn't want to become a full liverymen you could just pay a small annual fee called "quarterage" and that allowed you to trade in London. These people are free of the guild and therefore they're known as "freemen." These peoples had numbers on their side and also a vote for members of Parliament. They leaned towards Puritanism and they saw the Stuart court as favoring Popery—remember Henrietta Marie and her Catholic court—and arbitrary government. As national tensions grew more strained between the Stuarts and Parliament, the city's elite and its citizens began to take sides.

One of the first large demonstrations came in 1637 following the condemnation in Star Chamber of William Prynne, John Bastwick, and Henry Burton for writings critical of the bishops and the Queen. Their punishment was to have their ears cropped in Westminster Palace Yard. On the day, a great crowd cheered them to the place of punishment and afterwards, in a show of support, many spectators dipped their handkerchiefs into the "martyrs" blood. This should have reminded Charles I of the London crowds' reaction to the burnings under Bloody Mary. It should have told him that he was in danger of losing the capital. Later that year, the Scots rebelled rather than accept the imposition of an Anglican-style prayer book, we've already referred to this; because the king had no money for an army to suppress the rebellion, he had to call a Parliament—later to be called "the Long Parliament" because it would sit in one form or another until 1653.

Opposition leaders like John Pym used this opportunity to pass legislation limiting the king's and the church's power. Now what they said of the king is, yeah, we'll give you money for an army but first we want to pass laws limiting your ability to dissolve us, limiting your ability to do some of the things you've been doing. Ordinary Londoners, egged on by Puritan preachers, egged Pym on in a series of monster petitions, some with as many as 10,000 signatures.

As the Long Parliament sat, Londoners of all ages crowded Old Palace Yard, between Westminster Palace and Westminster Hall, demanding redress of grievances, and especially the abolition of the bishops and the execution of Charles's right-hand man and chief advisor, the Earl of Strafford. The power of the mob is perhaps most obvious in the case of Strafford.

In the spring of 1641, Parliament agonized over a motion for his attainder for high treason, that is, a vote as to whether he had committed treason. Ten thousand Londoners signed yet another petition for his execution. When Strafford's bill of attainder was finally brought to Whitehall for the royal signature, the parliamentary delegation was accompanied by a mob which surrounded the palace for a week, shouting for the Earl's blood. They knew the king was reluctant to condemn a loyal servant who had only done his bidding but with these shouts ringing in his ears, Charles caved in, conceding control of the Tower of London to Parliament and signing Strafford's warrant of execution. He was beheaded before a crowd of 100,000 on Tower Hill on the 12 of May, 1641, many of those people must have felt satisfaction that they, London, had bent the king himself to their will.

Now, I don't want to leave you with the impression that all Londoners, or even the London crowd, were all against the king.

During the fall of 1641, as Pym's program to limit royal power grew more radical with every piece of legislation, he's hampering the king more. The city authorities began to re-think their support. That autumn, a Royalist was elected lord mayor in a hard fought election. And when the king returned from a progress to Scotland on 25th November he was greeted by cheering crowds, and he behaved at his entrance with an Elizabethan graciousness. He, too, had a London constituency and he could play to it but the king would soon lose this support as he lost command of London as a political stage.

On the 29 of November, a crowd, equipped with swords and staves, surrounded Westminster Palace, once again demanding the abolition of the bishops. The Earl of Dorset, commander of the trained bands guarding Parliament and a Royalist, actually gave the order to open fire on the demonstrators, but the London militia refused the order. They were not going to fire on their relatives and friends. Royal authority over the city was breaking down. In early December, London received word, vastly exaggerated, of a rebellion in Ireland. The report was that 200,000 Protestant landowners had been murdered by Catholics in their beds. The death toll was actually closer to 9,000, but either way, Protestant London, again egged on by Puritan preachers, panicked that Catholics, encouraged by the king, might rise up and murder London's Protestants in their beds.

It was in this climate, in December, that 15,000 substantial citizens and 30,000 apprentices put their names to two more monster petitions again demanding abolition of the bishops. Again, you may wonder about why do they care about the bishops? Well, the bishops were the ones who were seen as imposing high church ritual, that is, Catholic ritual in Puritan eyes on Puritan congregations. So this is really an attempt to prevent the religion of the country from going, in the eyes of the crowd, Catholic. Between 27 and 29 December, the December Days, huge crowds malingered outside the Houses of Parliament demanding the same, abolition of the bishops and threatening to attack Westminster Abbey.

Once again the king ordered the lord mayor to tell the trained bands to shoot to kill but once again, the order was ignored. From this point, city funds for the king dried up and London began to prepare to defend itself against its own sovereign. Something it hadn't done since the Middle Ages. Citizens organized in augmentation of the trained bands; chains were put across city streets. By early January

1642, Charles I no longer felt his family safe in London, they all left by spring. From this point, the city authorities threw their weight behind Parliament and, once the war started in August, they threw money as well.

The English portion of the British Civil Wars, which began in August of 1642, should have been well matched. Most social groups split evenly between the king's supporters, the Cavaliers, and Parliament's supporters, the Roundheads. The crucial difference was London. London supported Parliament and London, after all, had the apparatus of government, especially taxation. It had the wealth to loan Parliament vast sums of money. It had the country's manufacturing base and that meant muskets and uniforms. It had the trained bands, the closest thing to a professional military force in England. Since the king had all the best generals at first, the English Civil Wars would, a bit like the American, be a race to see if the best generals could win a decisive blow before London's wealth proved decisive.

Now capturing London would've been a decisive blow. The king made an attempt in November, 1642, the City strengthened the walls and built a perimeter in the suburbs and sent the trained bands out to stop the royal forces at Turnham Green, which they did. After one more attempt in the summer of 1643, both sides settle down into a war of attrition which Parliament won, thanks to the wealth of London. Parliament can always keep raising armies and supplying them with muskets and uniforms.

In 1645, after the decisive Battle of Naseby, in North Hamptonshire, the last Royalist army in England surrendered and the king was taken prisoner, but this didn't exactly end the war. Parliament, the Scots, even the army negotiated with the king to return as a constitutional monarch but Charles I never negotiated in good faith. He was convinced that to give up one shred of his prerogative was a sin against the crown God had given him. Instead, he continually asked to go to London. He thought that if he could play to the crowd there, he might get his crown back with all of its power. But after the king started a second civil war in 1648, the most radical elements in the army, led by General Oliver Cromwell, concluded that there would be no peace in England until the king was dead.

On the 6 of December, 1648, a detachment of the army led by Colonel Thomas Pride marched on Parliament and purged all but the most radical members, the ones likely to vote the king guilty of treason. This became known as "Pride's Purge." The following month, January, 1649, the resulting rump of a Parliament, called "the Rump Parliament," brought Charles I up on a charge of high treason against the people of England. The dramatic trial took place in Westminster Hall and is described in detail in my lectures on England under the Tudors and Stuarts, but perhaps, for a moment, we can imagine the scene. The greatest hall in all England filled to the rafters with people, held back by redcoats. In the center of the room in a box the magnetic object of all eyes, the king dressed in black wearing the Star–in-Garter. He actually refused to plea because he didn't recognize the court. All courts are the king's courts, how could any court bring the king up on a charge of treason? All treason is against the king, how could the king be guilty of treason? And that's why Parliament said that he'd been guilty of committing treason against the people of England, a new constitutional principle.

The verdict of guilty a foregone conclusion, the king's execution took place at Inigo Jones' Banqueting House at Whitehall, the part of the palace which still survives today, on the crisp morning of the 30 of January, 1649. It is said that when the henchmen raised the head, he did not say, "behold the head of the traitor" because he didn't want his voice recognized. The crowd groaned.

Within weeks, the Rump Parliament abolished the monarchy and the House of Lords. And England was now, for the first and only time in its history, a Republic. Having abolished the monarchy, the Puritan Rump Parliament also abolished the court, selling off much of the king's artwork, disbanding the royal musicians, etc. In 1642, it had already closed the theaters and banned elaborate church music and organs but if the Puritan regime was hard on the visual and performing arts, it was terrific for the literary arts.

You see, in 1641 the Long Parliament had also abolished censorship. Between that year and 1660 at least 20,000 pamphlets and newspapers were printed. They reported the news of the war. They debated how to give England peace. By the way, this did not necessarily make London any more important. With the end of censorship you could set-up a printing press anywhere in the country. It could be argued that these measures actually diminished London's significance for awhile. London itself would continue to prove unruly.

The city government remained in Puritan hands but London's apprentices failed to follow orders. Londoners had protected Puritanism when it was persecuted, but they protested Puritan moves to suppress Christmas celebrations and stage plays, often they snuck off to attend secret performances of both. Moreover, London Royalism never quite died out. Remember, London was always a bit of royal city even if it liked rebels too. In 1648, there were bonfires on the anniversary of the king's accession on 27 March. On 9 April, a group of young people rioted to shouts of "Now for King Charles." After Charles I's execution, the new lord mayor was sent to the Tower for refusing to proclaim the abolition of the monarchy.

The Commonwealth, as The Republic called itself, was never popular and by the early 1650s, the country was yearning for more traditional structures. In 1653, the army, under Oliver Cromwell, shut down the Rump Parliament and after a brief interval named Cromwell "Lord Protector of England." His regime was efficient, militarily successful in Ireland, Scotland, and the Caribbean, and expensive, necessitating higher taxes than Charles I had ever demanded. It was also intrusive. Cromwell's Puritan major generals suppressed drunkenness, adultery, Maypole dancing, and even Christmas celebrations as non-Biblical. Once again, Londoners balked at such strong control.

In September 1658, Oliver Cromwell died more or less from overwork. There followed a succession of provisional governments. In early December, 1659, the London apprentices planned to march on Parliament with yet another petition, this time demanding the restoration of the Stuarts. They're nothing if not fickle. Later, at the Royal Exchange, they beat off a detachment of the army sent to suppress them as London householders threw stones at the soldiers from their open windows. So London is never easy to control. In short, by this time, the Protectoral regime had lost London.

Now at this point, General George Monck, the ranking commander in Scotland, began to march south with the only fully paid army in the British Isles. He reached London in February of 1660 and restored the Rump Parliament on the understanding that it could dissolve itself and call for new elections. Londoners celebrated by lighting bonfires and roasting rump steaks in the streets that night. Everybody understood that the new Parliament would invite Charles I's eldest son, also named Charles, to return as king.

On the 29 of May, 1660, coincidentally the anniversary of his birth, Charles II entered London accompanied by Monck, newly named Duke of Albemarle, as well as a host of aristocratic supporters, both old and new. John Evelyn, a contemporary direst of the time, records the scene:

> This day came in his Majesty, Charles the 2nd to London, after a sad, and long Exile, and calamitous suffering both of the King and Church, being 17 years. This was also his Birthday, and with a Triumph of above 20,000 horse and foot, brandishing their swords and shouting with unexpressable joy. They wayes strewed with flowers, the bells ringing, the streets hung with Tapestry, fountains running with wine: the Mayor, Aldermen, and all the Companies in their liveries, Chains of Gold, banners; Lords and nobles, Cloth of Silver, gold and velvet every body clad in, the windows and balconies all set with Ladies, Trumpets, Music, and myriads of people flocking the streets and was as far as Rochester [which is on the coast], so as they were seven hours in passing the City, even from two in the afternoon 'til nine at night.

If you stop and think about, this is, in effect, the old pre-Civil War hierarchy restored, laid out in person, end to end, from Rochester to London in all its glory. No wonder that Evelyn, a devout member of the Church of England, a landed gentlemen who'd lost a lot during the Revolution wrote, "I stood in the strand, and beheld it, and blessed God."

With The Restoration, city government returned into the hands of conservative Royalists and this restored the old tension between a Royalist Court of Aldermen and a Puritan or Parliamentary Common Council, Common Hall, and Citizenry. Now, for a while in the 1660s those tensions would be obscured by events, for London was about to experience two of the greatest crises of its history. Those crises were about to be recorded by its most observant citizen, one Samuel Pepys, esquire.

Lecture Eleven

Life in Samuel Pepys's 17th-Century London

Scope:

Samuel Pepys was a native Londoner, educated at Cambridge, who returned and made good. Unlike Chaucer and Shakespeare, he left a diary of his wide-ranging experiences and innermost thoughts. Using Pepys as our guide, we will explore the streets of 17th-century London, from the refined galleries of the court at Whitehall to the pleasure gardens, dockyards, taverns, and back alleys where London life was lived raw.

Outline

I. The restoration of the monarchy was an opportunity for new men like Samuel Pepys.

II. Pepys was born in London, the son of a tailor, in Salisbury Court off Fleet Street on February 23, 1633.

- **A.** He was educated nearby at St. Paul's School before going up to Magdalene College, Cambridge.
- **B.** Returning to London in 1654, he would have taken a coach down the old northern road and had his first glimpse of the city he had left four years before.
  1. In 1654 central London looked very much like Shakespeare's city, with its three great landmarks, including stubby St. Paul's.
  2. But it had spread further east from the Tower as new East End suburbs had been filled in.
  3. Looking right, the West End was also beginning to fill in at Covent Garden and Lincoln's Inn Fields.
  4. London had by now grown to perhaps 400,000 souls—with the sewage and air quality problems that implies.
- **C.** Pepys's cousin Edward Montagu got Pepys a job as clerk to the Exchequer (in effect, the state's bank), where he worked from 1659 to 1660.
  1. In 1660 Montagu won Pepys a job as Clerk of the Acts of the Navy Board.

2. In 1673 Pepys was named Secretary of the Admiralty and was elected a member of Parliament, serving 1673–1679 and 1685–1688.
3. He was made a fellow of the Royal Society in 1665 and its president from 1684 to 1686.
4. Closely associated with the king's brother—James, Duke of York, who as James II would be overthrown in the revolution of 1688–1689—Pepys fell with his master, resigning from the Admiralty in 1689.
5. He spent the rest of his life as a leisured London gentleman pursuing scientific and artistic hobbies.
6. The diary he kept from 1660 to 1669 recreates 17th-century London in all of its quirky glory.
7. In this lecture we use his diary to accompany a 17th-century Londoner on a typical day.

III. Samuel Pepys was an early riser, often at the Navy Office by 6.

A. Servants were expected to arise at least as early to help their master dress and cook him a breakfast.

B. The Navy Office was in Crutched Friars, on Tower Hill, just northwest of the Tower itself.

1. Pepys's tenure there is important, for he helped lay the foundations for the logistical support of the Royal Navy.
2. Pepys worked hard at his job. He was happy to save the king money but also to make a little for himself—or even take a bribe outright, but always discreetly.

IV. Pepys spent a lot of time inspecting the king's various dockyards at Deptford, Chatham, and Portsmouth.

A. The Royal Dockyards were fast becoming the largest single employer of English workers in one place.

B. The historian who follows Pepys closely gets to watch, firsthand, a complex preindustrial process—the building and supplying of a ship of the line.

C. Admittedly, an awful lot of navy business was done at taverns and coffeehouses.

V. Inns, taverns, coffeehouses, and clubs were a crucial part of the social and business scene of Pepys's London.

A. Inns and taverns were old and upscale.

1. Pepys went to the George Inn, which survives today as a pub in Southwark.

2. Taverns, Pepys's favorite haunts, offered drink of all kinds (wine, spirits, beer, cider, and perry), food, and private rooms to rent.

3. Alehouses offered only home-brewed beer and a lower-class clientele. The authorities tried to shut them down as places where stolen goods were fenced, prostitutes solicited, and free (and thus dangerous) speech reigned.

B. The coffeehouse arose as a result of England's growing Mediterranean trade.

1. Coffee was introduced to England about 1652 when a Turkish émigré, Pasqua Roscee, opened the first coffeehouse in London on Cornhill, in the business district.

2. The coffee was very strong, and Englishmen liked the narcotic effect. They also liked the fact that the newspapers of the day were distributed at the coffeehouse. And they liked the conviviality and social mixing.

3. For these reasons, the government tried to shut them down via a royal proclamation of 1675, but people went anyway and the proclamation was soon withdrawn.

4. Coffeehouses drew clientele from the businesses in the neighborhood.

C. Some aristocrats did not like the social mixing of the coffeehouse, and they preferred the club.

VI. The greatest club of all was the court at Whitehall.

A. The king's household was not merely the seat of government but the social and cultural center of England as well.

1. Politicians, writers, painters, composers, and even scientists rose and fell by their access to the sovereign.

2. Even if you lacked ambition yourself, this was the place to go to see the latest plays and art, hear the greatest preachers and musicians, catch the latest news and gossip, and chart the changes in the political world.

B. The alfresco spectacle of the court was readily available to Londoners, though the Stuarts went out a lot less than the Tudors had.

C. Once inside, the gentry could sample a variety of activities.
   1. Nearly anyone could attend the regular services in the Chapel Royal.
   2. There were frequent balls; Pepys got carried to one on New Year's Eve 1662.
   3. Members of the elite could also attend twice- or thrice-weekly informal gatherings called "drawing rooms."
   4. Those with more private business to transact with the king could go up the back stairs and converse with him in his private office or closet.

VII. Pepys loved the theater, and fortunately so did his master.

A. At the Restoration, Charles II granted charters for two companies: the King's Company and the Duke's Company.

B. A new theater district was established in the West End in locations like Drury Lane off Covent Garden, Lincoln's Inn Fields, and the Haymarket.

C. The second thing the Merry Monarch did was demand for the first time that actresses appear on stage beginning January 3, 1661.

VIII. If that wasn't enough pleasure for Pepys, he could always cross the river into Southwark, and specifically to Vauxhall Pleasure Garden.

A. A pleasure garden was an early modern version of an amusement park—for adults.
   1. Patrons meandered down walks behind high hedges.
   2. They strolled beautifully manicured gardens.
   3. They retreated to secluded booths where they could order dinner and drinks.
   4. They listened to the latest music.

B. Above all, this was a perfect location for amorous intrigue.

IX. "And so home to bed." Few Londoners could have rested with so much content at night as Samuel Pepys. But Pepys's contented dreams would be disturbed in the mid-1660s by a succession of nightmares: the Great Plague and the Great Fire.

Suggested Reading:

Pepys, *The Illustrated Pepys*.

Tomalin, *Samuel Pepys*.

Questions to Consider:

1. Why do historians tend to view Samuel Pepys as an essentially "modern" figure? Do you agree with this view?
2. Consider the entertainment possibilities of 17th-century London. Why do you suppose so many new possibilities were appearing in Pepys's day?

Lecture Eleven—Transcript
Life in Samuel Pepys's 17th-Century London

The restoration of the monarchy was a major political, social, and religious watershed. It was also an opportunity for new men like Samuel Pepys. Samuel Pepys was born in London, the son of a tailor in Salisbury Court, off Fleet Street, on the 23 of February, 1633. He was educated nearby at St. Paul's School before going up to Magdalene College, Cambridge. Returning to London in 1654, I suppose we can just about imagine him taking coach down the old northern road and getting his first glimpse of the city he'd left four years before.

In 1654, Central London looked very much like Shakespeare's City with its three great landmarks, including stubby St. Paul's in the middle, but it had spread, further east from the Tower as new East End suburbs had been filled in, Shadwell, Ratcliffe, Whitechapel on the North Bank Deptford, Rotherhithe, pronounced Redriff, and Bermondsey on the South Bank. Looking right, the West End between Temple Bar and Whitehall, connected by the Strand, was also beginning to fill in; Covent Garden and Lincoln's Inn fields to its north for example. As this implies, London had by now grown to perhaps 400,000 souls with a sewage and air quality problems that implies.

Like many successful people, Pepys had a connection and a knack for being in the right place at the right time. His cousin was Edward Montagu, General at Sea under Oliver Cromwell. Montagu got Pepys a job as Clerk to the Exchequer, in effect the state's bank, from 1659 to 1660. Pepys was able to rent a house in Axe Yard, Westminster with his wife, Elizabeth, and take a servant. He was moving up in the world.

Montagu commanded the fleet that fetched Charles II home at the Restoration in 1660 and he took Sam with him. Sam had the knack at being at the right place at the right time. This won Montagu the title "Lord Sandwich"; it won Pepys a job as Clerk of the Acts of the Navy Board. In 1673 Pepys was named Secretary of the Admiralty. That year he was also elected MP, Member of Parliament, serving from 1673 to 1679, he was re-elected in 1685, he was also a Fellow of the Royal Society beginning in 1665 and its president from 1684 to 1686.

Samuel Pepys was closely associated with the king's brother, the Lord High Admiral James Duke of York, who as King James II would be overthrown in the Revolution of 1688–1689. This put an end to Pepys's public career; he fell with his master and resigned from the Admiralty in 1689. He spent the rest of his life as a leisured London gentleman, pursuing scientific and artistic pursuits and maintaining a fascinating correspondence with his friend John Evelyn.

Now obviously with a resume like this, Samuel Pepys would have made any contemporary "Who's Who," in fact one of the great mysteries of history is why he was not knighted. But it is the diary he kept between the years 1660 and 1669 that makes him indispensable. In this remarkable document, 17th-century London lives again in all of its quirky glory, from the splendid corridors of Whitehall to the seediest alehouses in Deptford. As we'll see, Sam Pepys tells us everything. One reason is he never expected anyone to be able to read the diary, it is written in shorthand, very difficult to figure out; and as a result we experience the interior life as well as the exterior life of a 17th-century Londoner, very, very fully. What I propose to do in this lecture is walk with Samuel Pepys on a typical day.

Sam Pepys was an early riser, often at the Navy Office by 6:00. That did not mean that he foraged in his house alone, servants were expected to a rise at least as early to help their master dress and cook him a breakfast. If she was smart, Pepys's long-suffering wife Elizabeth would get up, too, just to keep an eye on him; otherwise he might engage in some dalliance with their servant girl Deb Willet as he did one Sunday morning in December, 1667, when Elizabeth was ill. "Up, thither come to me Willet with an errand from her mistress, and this time I first did give her a little kiss, she being a very pretty humored girl, and so one that I do love mightily."

Deb probably didn't have much choice in the matter; masters of households had absolute command over their servants living under their roofs. In theory this meant paternal care, but a man as flexible in his morals as Sam Pepys could take advantage of the situation. Eventually Mrs. Pepys figured it out and Deb Willet had to go. It is entirely characteristic of a man that after this little Sunday morning thrill, three days before Christmas, he went to church where he heard "a dull sermon" and then he went to the office.

The Navy Office was in Crutched Friars on Tower Hill, just northwest of the Tower of London itself. Pepys's tenure there is important for he helped lay the foundations for the logistical support of the Royal Navy. Moreover, he was, in some ways, a new kind of administrator. Up until this point in English history, there was no notion of a civil service or even of dedication in the service of the king. Appointment was by patronage, the aristocratic holder of an office was expected to do no work, as befit a gentleman. He privately hired clerks to do that. Since they were paid little, they were expected to charge fees for services, take bribes, and exploit perquisites, like leftover wood, etc.

Now in comparison, Pepys worked hard at his job. He arrived at the office early and stayed late, sometimes past midnight, as he did on the 17 of February, 1664.

> Sir W. Rider came and stayed with me till about 12 at night, about understanding the measuring of Mr. Woods masts … yet I am ashamed I understand it no better, and do hope yet, whatever be thought of me, to save the King some more money, and out of an impatience to break up with my head full of confused confounded notions, but nothing brought to a clear comprehension, I was resolved to sit up and did till now it is ready to strike 4 clock, all alone, cold, and my candle not enough left to light me to my own house, and so, with my business however brought to some good understanding, and set it down pretty clear, I went home to bed with my mind at good quiet, and the girl sitting up for me, the rest all a-bed. I eat and drank a little, and to bed, weary, sleepy, cold, and my head aching.

Anyone who has ever stayed late at the office for the good of the company can identify with this, right?

Pepys was happy to save the king money, but also to make a little bit of money for himself or even take a bribe outright, but always discretely.

> 2 February, 1664: Off to the Sun Taverne with Sir W. Warren, and with him discoursed long, and had good advice, and hints from him. And among other things he did give me a pair of gloves for my wife wrapped in paper, which I would not open, feeling it hard, but did tell him that

> my wife should thank him, and so went on in discourse. When I came home Lord in what pain I was to get my wife out of the room without bidding her go, that I might see what these gloves were. And by and by, she being gone, it proves a pair of white gloves for her and 40 pieces in good gold which did so cheer my heart that I could eat no vitals almost for dinner for joy, to think how God do bless us every day more and more. After dinner to the office where doing infinite of business till past 2:00 at night to the comfort of my mind, and so home with joy to supper and to bed.

So Pepys has a rather flexible idea of his responsibility to the king, he is perfectly happy to save the king money and he does a good job, but he's going to cover himself as well. Nor was he above the occasional sexual dalliance with a desperate wife wanting to get her husband out of a bad ship into a good one in time of war.

As a part of the process of overseeing the supply and building of the Navy, Pepys spent a lot of time inspecting the king's various dockyards at Deptford, Chatham, and Portsmouth.

> 15 January 1661: Up and down the yard all the morning and seeing seamen exercise, which they do already very handsomely, then to dinner at Mr. Ackworth where there also dined with us one Captain Bethell, a friend of the Comptrollers; a good dinner and very handsome. After that and taking our leaves of the officers of the yard, we walked to the waterside and in our way walked into the rope-yard, where I do look into the tar-houses and other places, and took great notice of all the several works belonging to the making of a cable.

Now, I want to remind you here that Pepys would consider himself a gentleman. He doesn't know how any of this stuff works, he's got to learn so he goes and he looks and he's a good quick study.

> So after a cup of burnt wine at the tavern there, we took barge and went to Blackwall and viewed the dock and the new Wet dock, which is newly made there, and a brave new merchantman which is to be launched shortly, and they say to be called the *Royal Oak*. Hence, we walked to Dick-Shore, and thence to the Tower and so home.

Now this, apart from the Tavern visits, may all sound pretty dull but it is eyewitness testimony of what was fast becoming the largest single employer of English workers in any one place, the royal dockyards and more generally, the London docks. The historian who follows Pepys closely gets to watch, firsthand, a complex pre-industrial process, the building and supplying of a ship of the line involving raw materials drawn from far afield. For example, Epping Forest for the wood for the ship, or the Baltic and even Russia for rope and tar, and it was Pepys's job to make sure that all those things were there. He also gets to see, the historian does, the skills and hard work of hundreds of men: ship designers like Phineas Pett; carpenters, sail makers, victuallers. After all, how do you field a vast fleet of over a hundred ships as the English, the French, the Dutch, and the Spanish routinely did in the 17th century without the wonders of modern technology?

You'll also realize as you read this stuff that an awful lot of navy business is done at taverns and coffeehouses. Inns, taverns, coffeehouses, and clubs were a crucial part of the social and business scene of Pepys's London. Now, two of these institutions were quite old and upscale; Pepys went to the George Inn which survives today as a pub in Southwark. Taverns, Pepys's favorite haunts, were nearly as grand. The Swan at Dowgate or the King's Head in Chancery Lane, both frequented by Pepys, dated back to Tudor times.

A tavern offered lots of services, drink of all kinds, wine, spirits, beer, cider, and perry, perry is fermented from pears. It offered food and a few private rooms to rent; political plots were always made in taverns.

Alehouses were much more informal. They only offered home-brewed beer and a lower-class clientele. So an alehouse would be a far more ad hock arrangement. The authorities routinely tried to shut down alehouses as "nests of Satan" because this is where stolen goods were supposed to be fenced, prostitutes solicited, and free and dangerous speech reigned. In other words, alehouses were full of ordinary people up to no good. But because the beer was home-brewed and an alehouse is essentially somebody's house, public house, turned over to the use of the public; it was easy to move them and so very, very hard to constrain them.

Ordinaries were restaurants, they served food with drink on the side. The big one in Pepys's day was Chantelle's, a popular French restaurant off the Strand. The lunch lines were out the door, so Londoner's have as much difficulty getting lunch then as they do today.

Pepys's London saw the rise of two new kinds of watering hole. The coffeehouse is the first. It was the result of England's growing trade, especially the Levant Trade. Coffee was introduced to England around 1652 when a Turkish émigré named Pasqua Roscee opened the first coffeehouse in London on Cornhill, in the business district, smart man, in 1652. The coffee was very strong and Englishmen liked the narcotic effect. They also liked the fact that newspapers of the day were distributed at the coffeehouse and they liked the conviviality and social mixing. For a penny anybody could rub shoulders with anyone else. You could be standing in the coffeehouse or sitting at a table next to a duke.

For these very reasons, the government hated them. Coffeehouses had more unsupervised speech, and who needs to read those newspapers? In a royal proclamation of 1675, the government tried to shut them down. But you might as well try to stop the rain from falling as keep Londoner's from a good time. People went anyway and the proclamation was soon ignominiously withdrawn.

Now Pepys doesn't go very often in the 1660s to the coffeehouse, maybe because he's a government official and doesn't want to be seen there, but he does go at least once. He makes a famous visit to Will's in Covent Garden.

> In Covent Garden tonight, going to fetch home my wife, I stopped at the great Coffee-house there, where I never was before—where Dryden the poet, I knew at Cambridge, and all the wits of the town, … and had I had time then, or could at other times, it will be good coming thither, for there I perceive is very witty and pleasant discourse. But I could not tarry and it was late.

Will's drew writers because it was located in Covent Garden near the post-Restoration theater district; famously John Dryden used to hold court by the fire, ever-ready to listen to the work of young poets. So if you'd just written some poetry, you went to Will's and you handed Dryden, who was Poet laureate of England, your poems and he would evaluate them for you.

Coffeehouses drew their clientele from the neighborhood, and also the businesses in the neighborhood, and as a result certain coffeehouses became associated with certain businesses. For example, Lloyd's and Garroways were in the financial district on Cornhill, so they drew merchants and stockbrokers. In fact, Lloyd's, as I'm sure you know, eventually evolved into the famous insurance company. The St. James's near the court drew politicians.

Now some aristocrats didn't much like the social mixing of the coffeehouse, they didn't actually want to sit next to Sam Pepys. They preferred another kind of institution new to Pepys's London, the club. Sometimes clubs evolved out of coffeehouses. White's began as a coffeehouse and then became famous as an aristocratic gambling club. It is still accepting members and turning non-members away to this very day.

The Grecian, on the Strand, was where scholars and scientists met after the free lectures at Gresham College; you may remember Sir Thomas Gresham as the man who founded the Royal Exchange. Well, at his death he left money for a series of free lectures; they are still free, by the way. Well, after these meetings they would adjourn to the Grecian and from those meetings evolved the Royal Society, founded in 1663, of which Pepys was eventually President.

The Royal Society mixed serious scientists like Sir Isaac Newton and Sir Edmund Halley with gentlemen amateurs like Pepys and Evelyn who, by the way, could bank roll their experiments, so it was a nice combination.

Towards the end of a day at the dockyards, and after lunch at a tavern, Pepys might take a barge (he much preferred this to walking or taking a hackney coach down the Strand) and head for the greatest club of all, the court at Whitehall.

In an age when monarchs still mattered, the court was the center of the world. We might be tempted to think of the court as the equivalent of the White House or Buckingham Palace but it was much more than that. The king's household was not merely the seat of government, but the social and cultural center of England as well. It was Bloomsbury and Carnegie Hall, the corner of Hollywood and Vine, *People Magazine*, and American Idol, the round table of the Algonquin Hotel, and one long continuous frat party. Not just politicians, but writers, painters, composers, even scientists rose and fell by their access to the sovereign. And where did they get that access? They went to court.

Even if you lacked ambition yourself, this was the place to go to see the most glorious interiors in the kingdom. The greatest art collection in the British Isles, the latest plays, this is where you heard musicians of international stature, the latest poetry and the best preachers. This is also the place where we talked about how the court gathers the movers and shakers together, this is the place to catch the latest news and gossip and chart the changes in the winds of politics.

So who could go to court? We've already seen that the alfresco spectacle of the court was pretty much available to any Londoner, though the Stuarts went out a lot less than the Tudors did. Outdoors there was remarkably little security surrounding a British monarch, just a few guards and courtiers with swords. The parks, in particular St. James's and Hyde Park, were open spaces as well as being royal spaces. And so Charles II could, in theory, be approached by any passerby as he sauntered about St. James's or Hyde Park. And so for example on the 17 of February, 1667, Pepys records, "Attended the king and Duke of York round the Park, and was asked several questions by both; but I was in pain, lest they should ask me what I could not answer." Again, who in the business world, you know, hasn't had this feeling, the boss asks you a question and you freeze up.

Admittedly, Pepys was a high government official, ordinary Londoners would have had a lot more trouble getting past the throng of courtiers attending the king as he walked. Still, the king being outdoors like this was a security nightmare. In 1682 and again in 1696, there were plots to assassinate the king while out riding. Less dangerously in January, 1678, a lunatic named Richard Harris was committed to Bedlam after throwing an orange at Charles II in St. James's Park. We know he was a lunatic because he thereby wasted a perfectly good 17th-century orange. I mean, how many of those could there have been?

What about indoors? Porters at the gate of palaces, the yeomen of the guard, and the servants of the public rooms were repeatedly ordered to prevent the entry of unsuitable persons to the court. But, in fact, these officers were far more afraid of keeping someone important out than letting someone unimportant in. In my experience as a historian of the court, they only get fired if they keep out the drunken son of the Duke of Queensbury; so they let you in if you look halfway decent. Whitehall's ground plan is in any case open to river and park and it is so disorganized that practically anyone who looked like a gentleman or a lady could get in. This is the "if it walks like a duck" school of security. That explains why Pepys and his friend John Evelyn could walk freely in the Privy Gallery at Whitehall for hours "talking to this man and to that," waiting for ministers to emerge from a meeting or just out of idle curiosity to observe the king's art collection.

Nearly anyone could attend the regular services of the Chapel Royal, as you can today by the way, though then we might have to bribe the groom of the vestry to get in. This explains how Thomas Allen, a baker, could have had his pocket picked by James Burke, a vagrant, during a service in 1686, that's from my own research.

Some people, John Evelyn in particular, came for the sermons by the best preachers in England, many of them future bishops. Pepys was drawn by the latest musical compositions of composers like Matthew Locke, Pelham Humfrey, and Henry Purcell, performed by the greatest choral establishment in England, the choir of the king's Chapel Royal. You could even try out Catholic services, as Pepys did on Christmas Eve, 1667. You could catch them at the Queen's Chapels at Somerset House and at St. James's and many people snuck off to do so.

There were frequent balls, Pepys got carried to one on New Year's Eve 1662:

> Mr. Povy and I to White Hall. He carry me thither on purpose to carry me into the ball this night before the King. He brought me into the room where the ball was to be, crammed with fine ladies, the greatest of the Court. By and by comes the King and Queen, the Duke and Duchess, [that is the Duke and Duchess of York; the Kings brother and sister-in-law] and all the great ones. And after seating themselves, the King takes out the Duchess of York; and the Duke, the Duchess of Buckingham; the Duke of Monmouth, my Lady Castlemaine; and so other lords other ladies: and they danced the Bransle; very noble it was and a great pleasure to see. Then to country dances; the King leading the first, which he called for; which was, says he, Cuckolds all awry, the old dance of England.

It's a rather pointed comment considering how many men at court Charles II had cuckolded in the course of fostering something like twelve illegitimate children.

> The manner was, when the King dances, all the ladies in the room, and the Queen herself, stand up and indeed he dances rarely, and much better that the Duke of York. Having stayed here as long as I thought fit, to my infinite content, it being the greatest pleasure I could wish now to see at Court, I went out, leaving them dancing.

Now again what I want to point out to you is how open the court is, this is a monarchy that aspires to be absolute and yet anyone dressed respectably could get in to see this. We, for the most part, live in democracies, but when was the last time you dropped in on a State dinner at the White House and were welcomed?

Members of the elite could also go to court two or three times a week during the court season; generally in the afternoon or early evening, to attend relatively informal gatherings called "drawing rooms." Oddly enough these were not held in the drawing room. Generally, they were usually hosted by the Queen in her Presence Chamber. This might be the point to tell you, by the way, if you happen to have a drawing room in your house that it is not for drawing it's for withdrawing, "drawing room" is a shortened version of "withdrawing room." There in the drawing room or the presence chamber you might see the whole royal family as Pepys did on the 7 of September, 1662.

> Meeting Mr. Pierce, the surgeon, he took me into Somerset House and there carried me into the Queen-Mother's, that's Henrietta Maria, presence-chamber, where she was with our own Queen Catherine of Braganza sitting on her left hand whom I did never see before. Here I also saw Madam Castlemaine, a lady in waiting to the Queen, and also the King's favorite mistress, and which pleased me most, Mr. Crofts, the King's bastard, a most pretty spark of about 15 years old. By and by in comes the King, and anon the Duke of York, the King's brother and his Duchess; so that, they being all together, was such a sight as I could never almost have happened to see with so much ease and leisure.

Sounds like a happy family doesn't it? Indeed. Remember how under Elizabeth the court was the place to see everybody who mattered, and in the next century Jonathan Swift noted how at a drawing room you could see all the royal ministers, foreigners, and persons of quality. In fact, Jonathan Swift will go to court under Queen Ann and just by watching the faces of the people there he can tell how the army is doing in the war of the Spanish Succession. It's better than the stock market as a barometer of the political temperature.

But what if we had more private business to transact with the king? We can do this privately because we can up the backstairs. We go to the backstairs, we find a page on the backstairs, we tell him we need to see the king, he runs up, knocks on the door, and if the gentlemen of the bed chamber in waiting agrees, we actually get to have a private conversation with the Sovereign of England in his office, or as it would have been known, his closet.

Now having finished his business at court, Samuel Pepys might very well inquire whether there was a play tonight in the Cockpit Theater at Whitehall. Pepys loved the theater and, fortunately, so did his master. At the Restoration, Charles II did two important things to re-establish the theater. You'll remember that it had been closed down by Parliament in 1642. First, he granted charters for two companies; the King's Company managed by the Master of the Revels, Thomas Killigrew, and the Duke's Company managed by Sir William Davenant, who claimed to be Shakespeare's illegitimate offspring, and he wasn't.

These men and their successors established a new theater district in the West End in locations like Drury Lane off Covenant Garden, Lincoln's Inn Field to the north, and the Haymarket, somewhat west of that near what is today Fogger's Square. These were indoor theaters with lots of mechanics for spectacular effects. Those effects were expensive so to pay for them they charged high prices which kept the groundlings out. Restoration Theater is a lot less democratic than its Elizabethan counterpart. Plays were also performed at court. In short, the Restoration Theater was an upper- and middle-class pursuit.

Repertory was mostly new, except for the occasional revival of Shakespeare, and that repertory tended to reflect the pre-occupations of the court. For example, Restoration audiences liked aristocratic heroic drama on classical themes. Dryden wrote lots of these and even some aristocrats, for example the 2nd Duke of Buckingham. They also liked the comedy of manners by writers like Wycherley and Etherage which reflected the modes of speech and indeed the social interaction that tended to take place at court.

The second thing the Merry Monarch did to promote the theater was to demand for the first time that actresses appear on the stage. If you haven't figured this out, Charles II particularly liked women, and so beginning on the 3 of January, 1661, we get the first stage actresses. No wonder Pepys, who also liked women, loved to go to a play and go back stage to talk to the actors. On May Day, 1667, he wasn't backstage, he was actually on the street, he was happy to see the pretty comic actress and royal mistress Nell Gwynn:

> At her lodgings' door in Drury-lane in her smock sleeves and bodice, looking upon one: she seemed a mighty pretty creature.

Pepys loved to go to a play; but he tended to watch the play very critically, for example on the 29 of September, 1662:

> To the King's theatre, where we saw *A Midsummer Night's Dream*, which I had never seen before, nor shall ever again, for it is the most insipid, ridiculous play that I ever saw in my life. I saw, I confess, some good dancing and some handsome women, which was all my pleasure.

If that wasn't enough pleasure for Sam Pepys, he could always venture across the river into Southwark and specifically to Vauxhall Pleasure Garden. A pleasure garden was an early modern version of an amusement park for adults. Patrons could saunter along endless meandering walks behind high hedges, stroll beautifully manicured gardens, retreat to secluded booths where they could order dinner and drinks, listen to the latest music, and delight to the fires of numerous small lamps as the twilight descended. Above all, this was a perfect location for amorous intrigue. Because the pleasure gardens were such mazes, even "the most experienced mothers often lost themselves in looking for their daughters."

Our diarist recounts the pleasures of Vauxhall on a May night in 1667:

> By water to Fox-hall, and there walked in Spring Garden. A great deal of company, and the weather and garden pleasant:

> that it is very pleasant and cheap going thither, for a man may go to spend what he will, or nothing, all is one. But to hear the nightingale and other birds, and here fiddles, and there a harp, and here a Jew's trump, and here laughing, and there fine people walking, is mighty divertising. Among others, there were two pretty women alone, that walked a great while, which being discovered by some idle gentlemen, they would needs take them up [I think today we would say pick them up]; but to see the poor ladies how they were put to it to run from them, and they after them, and sometimes the ladies put themselves along with other company, and then the other drew back; at last, the ladies did get off out of the house, and took boat and away. I was troubled to see them abused so; and could have found in my heart, as little desire of fighting as I have, to have protected the ladies.

Readers of the *Diary* will have an idea of precisely what sort of protection Samuel would have afforded them. Few Londoners could have rested with so much content that night as Samuel Pepys. But Pepys's contented dreams would be disturbed in the mid-1660s by a succession of nightmares. In the next lecture, London in crisis: "Plague and Fire."

Lecture Twelve

Plague and Fire

Scope:

Between the spring of 1665 and the autumn of 1666, London experienced two great disasters: the Great Plague and the Great Fire. London's overcrowded and ramshackle housing, its continuous contact with the outside world, its strategic location, and a complete lack of modern scientific medical knowledge had made it prey to disease and fire throughout its history. Periodic epidemics routinely killed off a quarter of the population, and periodic fires routinely destroyed whole districts. Yet Londoners went about or resumed their business and London survived.

Outline

I. In the years 1665 and 1666, London was struck by two disasters that threatened its very existence: the Great Plague of 1665 and the Great Fire of 1666.

- **A.** The 1660s were the decade of Restoration, and Londoners celebrated that event with abandon.
  - **1.** This period saw an explosion of scientific progress and the beginning of the turnaround of the English economy.
  - **2.** But generally, people were optimistic out of nostalgia for the old rather than anticipation of the new.
- **B.** Puritan preachers said that London was ripe for God's punishment.

II. Some time after Christmas 1664, the first symptoms of plague appeared.

- **A.** By the spring of 1665, parish clerks and the compilers of the Bills of Mortality began to notice a spike in burials and that most of those were from plague.
- **B.** It is generally agreed, though not without dissent, that from 1347 through the 1720s western Europe was subjected to repeated visitations of the same disease.
  - **1.** Though medieval Europeans called it "the Black Death," by the 17th century they referred to it simply as plague.

2. There are two types of plague—bubonic and pneumonic, both enterobacteria. One passes through flea bites, the other through the air, but contemporary Europeans did not understand this pathology.
3. Symptoms appear within 3–7 days of exposure. They include fever, diarrhea, headaches, swelling of the armpits and groin (infected lymph nodes), and rampaging internal bleeding, leading to black blotches on the skin, hence "Black Death."
4. Popular remedies included rosemary, cakes of arsenic under the armpits, charms and amulets, and the maintaining of open fires to "burn" the plague out of the air.
5. The death rate ranged from 30 to 70 percent.

C. Parish officials and Londoners generally were no strangers to the plague.
1. London's first visitation came in 664 C.E.
2. There was another round in 1265 and then the infamous Black Death of 1348–1349, when 15,000 died out of a total population of perhaps 45,000 (33 percent of London's populace).
3. In 1563, 1603, 1625, and perhaps 1665, London lost one-fifth to one-quarter of its population.

D. The plague's effects on London and Londoners were dramatic.
1. In the long term, demographic effects were few, as London replenished itself rapidly; but the short term was devastating, and by mid-August the city streets were deserted.
2. Economic London ground to a halt.
3. The political effects varied: Charles II and his court fled to Windsor, then Oxford; following tradition, the lord mayor and aldermen stayed on the job.
4. Community broke down.
5. The greatest effect of the plague epidemics may have been psychological.

E. Londoners did not get a full reprieve until spring.
1. Nobody knows why the plague went away.
2. The plague of 1665 was the last major plague epidemic in England.

III. Once again, the Great Fire, which began on September 2, 1666, was nothing unusual.

A. London was continually subject to fires, beginning in 60 C.E.

1. London burned so readily because it was made of wood.

2. Many industries, like smithies and bakeshops, used open flame.

B. The Great Fire began on the morning of September 2, just after midnight in the house and bakery of Thomas Farriner, the king's baker, in Pudding Lane, just north of the river.

1. Neighbors tried to fight the fire, but Londoners had few tools with which to do so.

2. London's dryness and high winds overwhelmed their efforts.

3. In contrast to the plague, local government ignored the matter at first.

4. By midmorning, people gave up trying to fight the fire and tried to save their belongings.

5. Samuel Pepys went to Whitehall to break the news to the king and the Duke of York.

C. On Monday, September 3, the flames pushed north, west, and south.

1. Rumors began of foul play on the part of Catholic foreigners; French shops and men were openly attacked in the streets.

2. By this time, the lord mayor had fled.

3. Charles II, hoping to recover from the charge of abandoning his capital to the plague, put the Duke of York in charge of fire-fighting efforts.

D. Tuesday, September 4, saw the worst destruction.

1. The fire leapt over firebreaks at Fleet Street and Cheapside, heading east, north, and west toward Whitehall Palace and the Tower of London, with its gunpowder stores.

2. It surrounded and devoured St. Paul's.

E. On Wednesday, September 5, the winds died down and the firebreaks worked to stop the Fire at Pye Corner.

F. The fire destroyed 13,200 houses, 87 parish churches, St. Paul's Cathedral, and virtually all of the City within the walls.
   1. Remarkably, it is thought to have killed fewer than 10 people, though historian Neil Hansen suggests that poor people and vagrants were probably not reported.
   2. Hundreds more may have died that winter from poor nutrition and exposure.
   3. The fire made homeless 70,000 out of a population of 460,000 (15 percent), who camped out at Moorfields.

G. The government immediately blamed Catholics.
   1. This explanation was inscribed on The Monument, erected by Wren and finished in 1677.
   2. Puritan preachers thundered that London and the Restoration court were being punished for their sins.

IV. But London did not drop to its knees after plague and fire. Instead, it rebuilt.

Suggested Reading:

Hansen, *The Great Fire of London.*

Moote and Moote, *The Great Plague.*

Questions to Consider:

1. Why did the government of London perform so well during the plague, so poorly during the fire?
2. Which do you suppose had the greater psychological impact on Londoners, plague or fire?

Lecture Twelve—Transcript

Plague and Fire

In the mid 1660s, Samuel Pepys's hometown was struck by two disasters that threatened its very existence, the Great Plague of 1665 and the Great Fire of 1666. What happened? Well, remember that the 1660s were the decade of Restoration; you will recall that Londoners celebrated that event with abandon. This period saw the foundation of the Royal Society in 1663 and an explosion of scientific progress, and the beginnings of the turnaround in the English economy, national population growth began to slow down allowing for fuller employment, a Commercial Revolution, based on foreign and colonial trade was just beginning to enrich the country and its chief port. But generally, people were optimistic, not out of anticipation of the new, but out of nostalgia for the old. The Stuarts had been restored in springtime, Puritanism and rule by the major generals had been sent packing, fun was back in at court, the theater, music was back, so were Christmas celebrations.

Not that the Puritans went quietly; in January of 1661, a London cooper (a barrel maker) and Fifth Monarchist, that is a Puritan who wanted to usher in the reign of King Jesus, named Thomas Venner tried to raise a rebellion in London, but only about 50 people showed up. Puritan preachers said that England, and that Sin City London, were ripe for God's punishment, it came in 1665.

Sometime after Christmas in 1664, Dr. Nathaniel Hodges was "called to a young man in a fever, who had two risings about the bigness of a nutmeg broke out, one on each thigh." The young man survived, but he was the first harbinger of London's last, and most notorious, outbreak of the plague.

The spring of 1665 was unusually warm, and parish clerks and the compilers of the Bills of Mortality, a weekly list of deaths, began to notice that they were recording more burials, and that most of those were from plague. The Parish of St. Giles in the Fields reported the week ending 30 of May, 9 plague deaths; 6 of June, 31 plague deaths; 18 of June, 68; 20 of June, 101; and the week ending the 27 of June, 143 people had died of the plague. You'll note the element of modernity here. London had been compiling the Bills of Mortality ever since a previous outbreak in 1592 but Pepys also noted that such statistics were not always to be trusted. Parish clerks wanted to avoid panic and so they under-reported, and sometimes they missed the poor entirely. Puritan dissenters lived and died outside the parish structure so they wouldn't be recorded either.

The diarist really knew that something was amiss by early June:

> This day, much against my Will, I did in Drury-lane see two or three houses marked with a red cross upon the doors, and "Lord have mercy upon us" writ there which was a sad sight to me, being the first of that kind that to my remembrance I ever saw. It put me into an ill conception of myself and my smell, so that I was forced to buy some roll tobacco to smell and to chew which took away the apprehension.

What was Pepys so afraid of? It's generally agreed, though not without dissent, that from 1347 through the 1720s Western Europe was subjected to repeated visitations of the same disease. Though medieval Europeans called it the Black Death, not the Black Plague as careless students sometimes do today, by the 17th century they referred to it simply as the plague. What was the plague?

There are two types, bubonic and pneumonic, both enterobacteria. Pneumonic plague is less common and is passed through air. Bubonic plague ensues from the bite of a flea, carried on the European Black Rat, *rattus rattus*, which traveled in carts engaged in trade. Contemporary Europeans did not understand this pathology. If breathed upon or bitten, symptoms appear within three to seven days, they include fever, diarrhea, headaches, a swelling of the armpits and groin, infected lymph nodes, and rampaging internal bleeding leading to black blotches on the skin, hence the term Black Death. There was little people could do. Popular remedies included rosemary, cakes of arsenic under the armpits, charms and amulets, the maintaining of open fires to burn the plague out of the air. One Dr. Hodges, who stayed at his post through the plague epidemic, "drank sack, [that's Spanish white wine] … to dissipate any lodgment of the infection," probably about as good a method as any. Despite these measures, the death rate would range anywhere from 30 to 70 percent.

One of the most frightening aspects of the disease was its suddenness; one could be fine one minute, dying the next. Thus Pepys's coachman:

> June 17, 1665: It stroke me very deep this afternoon, going with a Hackney-coach from my Lord Treasurer's down

> Holborne the coachman I found to drive easily and easily; at last stood still, and come down hardly able to stand; and told me he was suddenly struck very sick and almost blind, he could not see. So I light and went into another coach, with a sad heart for the poor man and trouble for myself, lest he should have been stroke with the plague being at that end of the town that I took him up. But God have mercy upon us all.

In fact, parish officials and Londoners generally were no strangers to the plague. London's first visitation came in 664. There was another round in 1258 and then the infamous Black Death of 1348–1349. Here are some numbers:

In 1348–1349, something like 15,000 people died out of a total population of maybe 45,000, that's 33 percent of the population of London. Plague returned in 1361–1362, and there were 11 outbreaks between 1407 and 1479. In 1563, 17,404 died, [20.5] percent of a population of 85,000. In 1593, 10,675 died, [8.5] percent out of maybe 125,000. In 1603, 23,045 or [16.3] percent out of 141,000, James I had to postpone his coronation. In 1625, another coronation year, more bad luck for the Stuarts, 26,350 people die out of a little over 200,000, so that's about [12.8] percent. In 1665, we know that at least 55,797 deaths out of 459,000, about [12.2] percent of the population, but some contemporary estimates of the death toll which go through 1666 put it at between 70,000 and 100,000 people.

So, when was the Great Plague? In absolute terms, 1665, but proportionally 1348–1349 killed more people then 1563, 1603, and 1625, in each of these latter cases London lost one-fifth to one-fourth of its population. Let's stop and think about that for a moment …

On average, every 40 years or so, early modern London saw one-fourth of its population simply wiped out, the worst months were in summer. In contrast to modern urban dwellers, who tend to dread winter, early modern people hated summer because disease seemed to thrive in the warmer months. By July, 1665, 1,000 were dying per week. In the third week of September, the Bills of Mortality report 8,297 deaths. The French ambassador thought this was an underestimate and the real figure was 14,000.

So what effect did this have on London and Londoners? Demographically, in the long term, the demographic effects were few in the sense that London replenished itself rapidly. But the short term was devastating. Pepys faithfully records the rising death toll over the summer, but more poignant are his personal losses …

> 31 July: Proctor the vintner of the Miter in Woodstreet, and his son, is dead this morning there of the plague.
>
> 8 of August: And poor Will that used to sell us ale at the Halldoor, his wife and three children dead, all I think in a day.
>
> By mid-August, the city streets were deserted and London began to take on the atmosphere of one of those deserted cities in a science-fiction epic.
>
> 16 of August: Lord, how sad a sight it is to see the streets empty of people, and very few upon the Change jealous of every door that one sees shut up, lest it should be the plague and about us, two shops in three, if not more, generally shut up.

As this implies, economic London ground to a halt. Shopkeepers fled or went bankrupt, people avoided taverns, theaters, large gatherings.

On 22 July, Pepys records, "I to Fox-hall, where to the Spring-garden, but I do not see one guest there the town being so empty of anybody to come thither."

Long distance trade became impossible because nobody wanted anything that came from London. Politically, Charles II and his court fled, first to Windsor, and then to Oxford. Now this is what rich people did, when there was plague in town you left; but it was seen as cowardly.

Following tradition, the lord mayor and aldermen stayed on the job, they always did this during a plague epidemic and they issued orders. First, to clear the streets of dogs, cats, this is actually a bad idea given that the cats might actually be the best defense against the rats. Second, expel vagrants, another bad idea in that it only spread the plague around, the vagrants would leave town and spread the plague. Third, they stopped ships in the Thames from ports where the plague was reported. Fourth, they prohibited attendance at funerals, but this was very hard to enforce. Fifth, they restricted attendance at inns and alehouses which was happening anyway. Sixth, they banned ballad singers and hawkers. Seventh, they closed schools, and eighth, they imposed quarantine on the sick.

Now this was city policy from 1581. Whenever plague broke out each parish was supposed to nominate "two discreet matrons" to be paid searchers to inquire in parishes and neighborhoods as to who was sick. Infected houses were marked with a red cross. Inhabitants were quarantined for 40 days. These measures were seen as a death sentence for the whole household. Think about it, being locked up with plague victims for 40 days. In fact, the quarantined often refused to stay put and die. So the city posted guards with halberds at infected houses.

By late summer 1665, people actually began to attack their guards, and throw themselves from upper stories into the streets. Some would run into the streets naked and delirious, foaming at the mouth. One physician reported seeing others crying and roaring at their windows. As this implies, community broke down. Masters turned out apprentices, physicians abandoned patients, and pastors abandoned flocks, but note that class still mattered.

> 22 of August, 1665: After dinner I by water to Greenwich, where much ado to be suffered to come into the town for fear I should come from London till I told them who I was.

Servants, abandoned by their masters, were enlisted to drive the notorious dead-carts calling on the inhabitants of London to "bring out your dead!" They would then carry the bodies out to mass graves or plague-pits just beyond the City walls. By the way, there is a legend, I can't verify this, that whenever you're on the Tube and it diverts one way and then comes back for no apparent reason, that's supposed to be a plague burial ground.

By late summer, the cart drivers and grave diggers began to be infected themselves; some died at the reins of their carts which, stacked with corpses, moved on aimlessly at the whim of the horses. Because of the sheer volume of corpses, bodies were stacked nearly up to the surface then covered over with a few inches of dirt and quick-lime by endless shifts of grave diggers who worked round-the clock, often drunk to get through their work.

As this implies, the greatest effect of the plague epidemics may have been psychological. Naturally, the first reaction of the plague was fear and uncertainty, hence Pepys's worry about his smell, above.

Then grief:

> 29 October, 1665: But in the street did overtake and almost run upon two women, crying and carrying a man's coffin between them. I suppose the husband of one of them, which me thinks is a sad thing.

Then there was obsession:

> 3 September, 1665: But Lord, how empty the streets are, and melancholy, so many poor people in the streets, full of sores, and so many sad stories overheard as I walk, everybody talking of this dead, and that man sick, and so many in this place, and so many in that. …

Some reactions might strike us as perverse, but are all too familiar from modern disasters. There were wild rumors of people infecting each other deliberately, that they would "breathe in the faces out of their windows of well people going by." So there's a kind of demonization of the victims, right, they're actually spreading it.

There was disorientation: "4 November, 1665: But now, how few people I see, and those walking like people that had taken leave of the world."

And perhaps finally resignation:

> 28 August, 1665: Thence to the office, and after writing letters, home to draw over anew my Will, which I had bound myself by oath to dispatch by tomorrow night, the town growing so unhealthy that a man cannot depend upon living two days to an end.

Years later, Daniel Defoe, who was a small boy during the 1665 epidemic, would capture all this in one of the greatest psychological novels in the English language, *Journal of the Plague Year*, I urge you to buy a copy and read it.

Londoners did not get a reprieve until spring. Still, Pepys could write in January, 1666, that the city was coming back:

> And a delightful thing it is to see the town so full of people again, as now it is, and shops begin to open, though in many places, seven or eight together and more all shut, but yet the town is full compared with what it used to be—I mean the

> City end, for Covent Garden and Westminster are yet empty of people, no Court nor gentry being there.

The court hadn't come back. Why did the plague go away? Nobody knows. Contemporaries thought that next year's Great Fire burned it out somehow, that, of course, is nonsense. The brown rat, *rattus norvegus*, did drive out the black, *rattus rattus*; but not until the 18th century. Maybe the rats themselves acquired immunity. In any case, 1665 was the last major plague epidemic in England, but London's *anni horibili* continued.

The summer of 1666 was hot and dry. Most people were grateful because they thought that that would kill off the plague. Once again, the Great Fire, which began on the 2 of September, was nothing unusual. London was continually burning. There had been fires in 60, in 675, which destroyed the first St. Paul's Cathedral. In 1087 which destroyed the third St. Paul's Cathedral.

A series of fires, 1132 to 1135, which destroyed lots of property from London Bridge north to—you guessed it—St. Paul's Cathedral. In 1212 a fire in Southwark destroyed St. Mary's Church and houses on London Bridge, and there was another major fire in 1632.

So why did London burn so readily? Daniel Defoe recalled the Old London of his childhood:

> The streets were not only narrow, and the houses all built of timber, lath and plaster, or, as they were very properly called paper work … But the manner of the building in those days, one story projecting out beyond another, was such, that in some narrow streets, the houses almost touched one another at the top, and it has been known, that men, in case of fire, have escaped on the tops of the houses, by leaping from one side of a street to another, this made it often, and almost always happen, that if a house was on fire, the opposite house was in more danger to be fired by it, according as the wind stood, than the houses next adjoining on either side. The buildings looked as if they had been formed to make one general bonfire whenever any wicked party of incendiaries should think fit.

Now don't forget, too, that lots of early modern London industry uses open flames, think of smithies and bakeshops, indeed all cooking takes place over open flame. Also there was lots of tar and combustibles down by the docks, the whole thing is ready to go up.

The Great Fire began on the morning of the 2 of September, just after midnight in the house and bakery of Thomas Farriner, the king's baker, in Pudding Lane, just north of the river. He probably failed to damp the fire properly. The family escaped by climbing through an upstairs window into the next house, all but one frightened maid who refused to make the leap and was burned, the fire's first casualty. Neighbors tried to fight the fire, but Londoners had few tools with which to do so, buckets, if a fountain was nearby, ladders to rescue those on upper floors, and staves with which to pull houses down to form firebreaks. Unfortunately, London's dryness and high winds overwhelmed their efforts.

Now, in contrast to the plague, local government did not distinguish itself. About 1:00 am the parish constables arrived and they suggested pulling down houses as a firebreak. The lord mayor, Sir Thomas Bludworth, was then awakened and brought to the scene and told the same thing.

But Bludworth was reluctant, the area was full of rich mercantile property, so he went back to bed, exclaiming with impeccable sexism, "Why, pish! A woman could piss it out!" These would become famous last words.

Speaking of women, that night the maids in the Pepys household were up late preparing food for the next day, Sunday's, dinner. At 3:00 am they woke their master and mistress, "to tell us of a great fire they saw in the City." But Pepys, like his mayor, dismissed it and went back to bed. When he awoke the next morning he decided to check the scene out. At 7:00 am he headed up to the Tower of London, what he saw appalled him.

> So I walked to the Tower and there got up one of the high places and there did see houses at the end of the bridge all on fire, and an infinite great fire on this and the other side of the bridge. So down, with my heart full of trouble.

By the way I think what he means by "the other side of the bridge" is looking a little bit west, it never crossed London Bridge.

People didn't flee at first, they tried to put out the flames, but by mid-morning they began to give up and tried to save their belongings. Some took their possessions to the crypt of St. Paul's; remember the idea of St. Paul's as being our local parish church, this great community facility. They thought that their goods would be safe there because, of course, the crypt was made of stone. Goldsmiths, who had vaults, also took in valuables. Some tried carting their goods to Westminster. On Saturday, a cart cost a few shillings to rent, on Monday, 40 pounds, so much for London's entrepreneurial spirit.

Pepys went to Whitehall to break the news to the king and Duke of York, and if you know Sam Pepys you know he must have reveled in this moment of supreme self-importance, he's the man who gets to tell the king. He found the king at Chapel. Now remember that Charles and the court had been criticized for fleeing the plague. They were determined they weren't going to make the same mistake twice. The king immediately ordered the pulling down of houses. Pepys tried to return and bring the order back by coach, but he found the streets so clogged with carts and refugees.

"Every creature coming away loaden with goods to save, and here and there sick people carried away in beds. Extraordinary good goods carried in carts and on backs." He eventually had to get out and walk; he couldn't make his way through the throng.

At this point he finds Bludworth, like a "fainting woman," whining, "Lord, what can I do? I am spent! People will not obey me. I have been pulling down houses. But the fire overtakes us faster than we can do it."

At least the king never turned to him and said, "Heck of a job, Bludy." Instead, when Charles arrived at the scene of he ordered the Coldstream Guards to start pulling down houses, he just ignored the mayor. By afternoon, about 2:00 pm, a firestorm arose, created by high winds and the chimney effect as heat rises in the narrow areas between London's buildings.

Remember, it's a conglomeration of narrow courts and alleys. That evening, the Pepys's and friends watched the flames, at first they rent a boat and they get out on the river; but they are actually getting hit by sparks and so they eventually retire to an alehouse on the South Bank and there they see, "one entire arch of fire from this to the other side of the bridge. And in a bow up the hill for an arch of above a mile long, it made me weep to see it."

On Monday, the 3 of September, the flames pushed north, west, and south. Now, in the south they were actually stopped by the river, but threatened to cross London Bridge, which, remember, is built over. In the City, the Royal Exchange and Cheapside all go up. The magistrates at this point actually order the city gates to be shut to persuade people to return and fight the fire. This stupid order was rescinded the following day. In the meantime people have had time to think and now rumors begin of foul play. Remember that contemporaries had lived through decades of plots and counter-plots. In this very decade, England was at war with the Dutch and there was always fear of Catholics. Since the wind carried sparks, houses, seemingly far away from the fire, combust because a spark will fly through the air and all of a sudden this house is going up. This led to rumors of spies throwing fireballs, French spies. French shops were attacked. A Westminster schoolboy, William Taswell, remembered seeing a Frenchman clubbed in the head with an iron bar, his brother saw another torn almost limb from limb; so perhaps not Londoner's finest hour here.

By this time, the lord mayor had fled. But Charles II put his brother the Duke of York in charge and he organized command posts headed by courtiers. He dragooned able-bodied men into teams to pull down houses, he rode up and down with the lifeguards to rescue foreigners; there is even semi-witness accounts, I'm not sure how trustworthy they are, of Charles and the Duke of York manning bucket brigades. But in any case, the court did better this time.

Tuesday, the 4 of September, saw the worst destruction. The fire leapt over firebreaks at Fleet Street and Cheapside, heading east, north, and west towards Whitehall Palace in the west and the Tower of London, with its gunpowder stores, in the east. The center of this conglomeration was St. Paul's, the old cathedral never had a chance. The crypt was loaded with goods and books from the nearby booksellers. The structure was surrounded by wooden scaffolding from current renovations, the lead roof started to melt, and it ran down the walls into the crypt igniting it.

According to John Evelyn:

> The stones of Paul's flew like Granados, the melting lead running down the streets in a stream, and the very pavements glowing with fiery redness, so as no horse, nor man, was able to tread on them.

The collapse of St. Paul's was the climax of the fire.

On Wednesday, the 5 of September, the winds died down. The firebreaks started to work and eventually the fire was put out, or died out is perhaps more accurate. Both Pepys and Evelyn witnessed the dazed refugees congregating in Moorfields on open ground just north of the City: "Many were without a rag or any necessary utensils, bed or board … reduced to the extremist misery and poverty."

The Fire, by the way, had begun in Pudding Lane and ended at Pye Corner. This led some wits to say that the Fire was a punishment from God for the sin of gluttony.

What was lost? The Fire destroyed 13,200 houses, 87 parish churches, St. Paul's Cathedral, and virtually all of the City of London within the walls. I do want to stress that the Fire never crossed London Bridge and so did not burn Southwark, nor did it ever get to Westminster and so a Whitehall and the Westminster complex survived.

Remarkably, it is thought that the fire killed less than 10, but Neil Hanson, the Fire's most recent historian, suggests that may be a vast under estimate. Poor people and vagrants were probably not reported. Now we know that the Fire was hot enough to melt imported steel at the docks. That implies temperatures between 1,200 and 3,000 degrees Fahrenheit. In such temperatures, bodies and bone would have melted. Teeth might survive, but then the poor wouldn't have many teeth, would they? The swiftness of the fire probably trapped "the old, the very young, the halt and the lame."

Hundreds more may have died that winter from poor nutrition and exposure. We estimate that 70,000 people were made homeless out of a population of 460,000, about 15 percent, mostly camping out in Moorfields.

Now, the government immediately sought scapegoats. Robert Hubert, a French immigrant confessed to setting the fire in Westminster. Never mind the fact that Westminster is nowhere near Pudding Lane and never burned. He was nevertheless hanged on the 28 of September, 1666. It was only later discovered that he hadn't even arrived in London until the 4. A Parliamentary Commission blamed Catholics generally. This was believable at the time considering the numerous failed plots against Queen Elizabeth, the failed Gunpowder Plot of 1605, the Irish Rebellion of 1641, whose deaths had been exaggerated but most Londoner's didn't know that. This explanation was eventually inscribed on The Monument, erected by Sir Christopher Wren, and finished in 1677. The monument, which you can still climb, is 202 feet tall and it stands 202 feet from the start of the fire, so I guess if you knocked it down it would point you in the direction of Pudding Lane. A relief at the base depicts the flames, Charles and James fighting the fire, and the reconstruction of London by architecture, liberty, and science.

In 1681, at the height of the exclusion crisis, a sort of orgy of anti-Catholicism, Whig aldermen helpfully added the concluding line, "but Popish frenzy, which wrought such horrors, is not yet quenched." This inspired the following couplet from the Catholic Alexander Pope: "Where London's column pointing at the skies, like a tall bully, lifts its head, and lies." The inscription was only finally chiseled out in 1831 on the eve of Catholic Emancipation.

Naturally of course, Puritan preachers thundered that London and the Restoration court were being punished for their sins. But here's the thing, London did not fold, nor did it drop to its knees after plague and fire. Londoner's picked themselves up and rebuilt, a story that would be told in the next lecture.

Now a part of that story goes that in the summer of 1673, Sir Christopher Wren went to the site of Old St. Paul's Cathedral to mark the spot for the center of the dome of its replacement, so you've got to imagine lots of rubble, maybe a make-shift table. Now according to legend, he asks a workman, "go fetch me a stone," and there's all this uncleared rubble. So the worker returns with a piece of masonry that contains the word "*resurgam*," I shall rise again. Wren instantly decrees this the motto of the new cathedral.

That I think is the spirit of London; like New York, or Chicago, or even Los Angeles today, all cities which have experienced major disasters, London was not about to turn back or to look back.

Timeline

B.C.E.

800–200 .... Celts migrate into Britain.

55 .... Julius Caesar invades Britain.

43 .... Aulus Plautius invades and establishes a permanent base in Britain.

C.E.

c. 50 .... Londinium founded.

60 .... Revolt of the Iceni; London sacked, resulting in 60,000 casualties.

c. 129 .... Londinium suffers a devastating fire.

409–410 .... Roman garrison abandons London.

c. 604 .... First St. Paul's Cathedral built.

839 .... Vikings sack London.

851–886 .... Vikings rule London.

1045–1065 .... Westminster complex built.

1066 .... William the Conqueror burns Southwark, and London capitulates.

1078 .... Tower of London begun.

1087 .... Much of London destroyed by fire.

c. 1130 .... London granted its charter.

1176–1209 .... Old London Bridge built.

1212 .... Major fire in Southwark kills about 3,000 people.

1245–1272 .... Rebuilding of Westminster Abbey.

1265 .... First parliament is held in Westminster Hall.

1326 .... London mob attacks royal officials.

1348–1349 .... Black Death kills at least 30,000 Londoners.

1361–1362 .... Plague returns to London; it returns again in 1368–1369, 1407, 1499, 1563, 1581, 1593–1594, 1603, and 1625.

1381 .... The Peasants' Revolt is put down when the Lord Mayor kills the rebel leader, Wat Tyler.

1407 .... Merchant Adventurers founded.

1411 .... Guildhall built.

1423 .... Death of Dick Whittington.

1450 .... Jack Cade's rebellion.

1517 .... Evil May Day riots.

1529 .... Henry VIII confiscates Whitehall and makes it his principal palace.

1536–1547 .... Dissolution of the monasteries, chantries, hospitals, almshouses, and so forth.

1553 .... Bridewell is donated to London.

1554 .... Wyatt's rebellion.

1555–1558 .... Protestant martyrs burned in Smithfield.

1566 .... The Royal Exchange founded; opened 1571.

1576 .... London's first purpose-built theater, The Theatre, opens in Shoreditch.

1587 .... Rose Theatre opens in Southwark.

c. 1590 .... Shakespeare arrives in London.

1598 .... John Stow's *Survey of London* published; Globe Theatre opens.

1600 .... East India Company founded.

1601 ....Essex rebellion.

1605 ....Gunpowder Plot to blow up James I and the House of Lords.

1627–1631..................................Covent Garden built.

1641–1642..................................Mass demonstrations in London against bishops, the Earl of Strafford, and the king.

1642–1643..................................London resists Royalist attack during the Civil Wars.

1649 ....Execution of Charles I.

1652 ....London's first coffeehouse opens.

1660–1669..................................Samuel Pepys keeps his *Diary*.

1665 ....Great Plague of London; possibly 70,000–100,000 die.

1666 ....Great Fire of London; 13,200 houses and 87 churches destroyed.

1667 ....Dutch sail up the Thames and destroy shipping.

1672 ....John Banister organizes England's first public concerts.

1675–1710..................................Rebuilding of St. Paul's Cathedral.

1678–1682..................................Exclusion crisis.

1688–1689..................................Glorious Revolution.

1694 ....Bank of England established.

1695 ....Lapse of the Licensing Act; beginnings of a free press.

1698 ....Whitehall Palace destroyed by fire.

1702 ....*The Daily Courant* (the world's first daily newspaper) premiers.

1710 ....Sacheverell riots.

1719–1720..................................Calico riots.

1720 .... South Sea Bubble stock market crash.

1720s–1740s .... Gin craze.

1741 .... Founding Hospital opens.

1750 .... Westminster Bridge opens.

1759 .... British Museum opens.

1773 .... London Stock Exchange established.

1780 .... Gordon riots.

1785 .... *Times of London* founded as the *Daily Universal Register*.

1807 .... First public demonstration of gaslight.

1825 .... First music hall opens.

1828 .... University College London founded.

1829 .... Metropolitan Police Department founded.

1831 .... New London Bridge opens.

1831–1832 .... Cholera epidemic; returns 1848–1849 and 1866.

1834 .... Westminster Palace burns down; replacement built 1837–1860.

1836 .... First railway train runs in London.

1837 .... Royal family moves into Buckingham Palace.

1851 .... Great Exhibition.

1855 .... Metropolitan Board of Works created.

1856 .... Big Ben installed.

1858 .... The Great Stink.

1863 ....Metropolitan Line (the first Tube line) opens.

1875 ....London's underground sewer system completed.

1888 ....Whitechapel murders.

1889 ....Establishment of the London County Council.

1891–1903................................Charles Booth's *Life and Labour of the People of London* published.

1912–1913................................Suffragette demonstrations in London.

1915 ....Zeppelin raids begin.

1923 ....Wembley Stadium opened.

1926 ....General Strike.

1933 ....London Passenger Transportation Board established.

1936 ....Battle of Cable Street.

1940–1941................................The Blitz.

1944–1945................................V-1 and V-2 missile attacks.

1951 ....The Festival of Britain.

1952 ....The Big Smoke; 12,000 die.

1956 ....John Osborne's *Look Back in Anger* premieres at the Royal Court Theatre.

1958 ....Notting Hill riots.

1964 ....The Beatles appear on *Ready, Steady, Go!*

1965 ....Funeral of Sir Winston Churchill; London County Council dissolved in favor of Greater London Council.

1974 ....IRA bombing campaign begins; resumed in 1981–83, 1991–1993, and 1996.

1981 ....Brixton riots; occur again in 1985 and 1995.

1986 ....Greater London Council abolished; "Big Bang" deregulation of financial markets.

1996 ....New Globe Theatre opens.

1997 ....Princess Diana's funeral.

2000 ....Ken Livingstone becomes the first elected mayor for the whole of London; millennium celebrations.

2005 ....The 7/7 Bombings kill 52; London carries on.

Glossary

alderman: Title originating in the 12th century; from 1377, the elected head of one of the City of London's wards. The Court of Aldermen (established in 1200) had the power to veto legislation passed by the Common Council and, with the lord mayor, to pass decrees for London regarding public health, traffic, regulation of alehouses, and so forth.

alehouses: The ad hoc counterparts to taverns, they served only beer and were associated by the authorities with lowlifes. Various attempts to suppress or regulate them usually failed. *See also* **taverns**.

apprentices: Young people, usually men aged 14–21, whose parents had bought them a place with a merchant or tradesman to learn his craft. In theory, after seven years' instruction, the apprentice became a journeyman worker and could then apply to become "free of the guild." In practice, they seem to have spent far too much time engaged in riot and other idle pursuits.

Bank of England: Established by parliamentary statute in 1694 and funded by subscription to loan money to the government, it soon became the Crown's biggest creditor and the regulator of its money supply. Always located in the City, the building and institution are popularly known as "the Old Lady of Threadneedle Street."

Big Bang: Deregulation of London's financial markets, which took place on October 27, 1986. Among the changes was the end of the distinction between stock traders and jobbers, the abolition of fixed commission charges, and the rise of on-screen trading. These measures were successful, leading to a reassertion of City dominance of world financial markets.

Big Smoke of 1952, the: A particularly deadly pea-soup fog caused by a combination of an inversion layer and the burning of large quantities of poor-quality coal in early December. Perhaps 12,000 people died.

Black Death, the: Plague that arrived in London via trade routes in 1348 and reached its deadly peak in 1349. Some 15,000 died in a city of 45,000.

Blitz, the: A campaign of Luftwaffe attacks around and on London between July 1940 and May 1941, with London particularly targeted from September 7. This campaign killed 43,000 civilians and made thousands more homeless, but Luftwaffe losses were such as to lead Hitler to abandon his plans to invade Britain.

Bow Street Runners: A protoprofessional police force established by Henry Fielding in 1749; eventually incorporated into the Metropolitan Police after 1829.

Brixton riots: Riots in 1981, 1985, and 1995 in a poor, largely Afro-Caribbean suburb of London that exposed the tensions between police and minority youth.

burnings at Smithfield: In an attempt to purge the nation of Protestants, Mary I ordered the burning at the stake for heresy of 286 men, women, and teenagers, most of them at Smithfield market. Their stories would be enshrined in John Foxe's *Acts and Monuments of These Later and Perilous Days* (better known as *The Book of Martyrs*).

Campaign for Nuclear Disarmament (CND): An organization formed in 1958 to protest the proliferation of nuclear weapons and Britain's support for the United States in the Cold War. Its membership included many luminaries in politics, the arts, and the sciences. It launched a series of massive protest marches in London during the 1960s.

Carnaby Street: Street just off Regent Street that became synonymous with high and mod fashion in the 1960s.

charter: Document granted by the Crown under the Great Seal of England that, in London's case, lays out its rights and privileges vis-à-vis the national government.

City, the: The square mile of London within the walls, plus parts of Southwark (Bridge Ward Without) and the area west of the wall up to Temple Bar (Farringdon Ward Without). Only this area is governed by the lord mayor, Court of Aldermen, Common Council, and Common Hall from the Guildhall. In modern parlance, tends to mean the financial district and its institutions.

coffeehouse: First established in the City in the 1650s, coffeehouses became popular rendezvous for Londoners because of the strong coffee, newspapers, and egalitarian conviviality. Particular coffeehouses tended to attract individuals from similar professions. An attempt to suppress them by royal proclamation in 1675 failed completely.

commercial revolution: Spurred by the Navigation Acts, the increasing dominance of overseas trade (in particular, sugar, spices, tobacco, and slaves) by mainly London merchants between 1660 and 1720.

Common Council, the: Council consisting of the lord mayor, 25 aldermen, and 210 councilors elected annually by the City of London's ratepayers (taxpayers) on a ward-by-ward basis. The Common Council regulated markets, street lighting, paving, and other day-to-day business that kept the city running, and it oversaw City finances. During the early modern period, it tended to be more Puritan and radical than the lord mayor and aldermen.

Common Hall: Body consisting of all the freemen of the City, about three-quarters of the male population. It was Common Hall that elected London's four members of Parliament.

constable: Unpaid, volunteer, and reputedly unreliable law-enforcement officer during the Middle Ages and early modern period.

Cornhill: The highest point in the city, site of a fortress in Roman times; site of the Royal Exchange and the heart of the financial district from early modern times onward.

dissolution of the monasteries, convents, and chantries: A series of legislative acts between 1536 and 1547 that dissolved and confiscated most of the church-owned land in London. Though the city was eventually allowed to take over a number of hospitals (Bridewell, Bedlam, Christ's, St. Bartholomew's, and St. Thomas's) to look after the poor and the sick, most of the land was eventually purchased or given to wealthy aristocrats like the Russells, who would build a new London.

doss-house: A low-class lodging house, often associated in the 18th century with the sale of gin.

Essex rebellion: Abortive rebellion against Elizabeth I of February 1601, led by Robert Devereaux, Earl of Essex, which failed when London did not support him.

exclusion crisis: The crisis over the succession that occurred in 1678–1681 over whether James, Duke of York (a Catholic) should be allowed to succeed his brother Charles II. The crisis, which was borne of the supposed discovery of the Popish Plot to kill the king, precipitated three elections and led to the rise of the first two political parties in England. Whigs opposed the Duke's succession, proposing that Parliament name a Protestant instead; Tories favored it. *See also* **Tories** and **Whigs**.

Festival of Britain of 1951: Held on the South Bank, a government-sponsored fair designed to recall the Great Exhibition of 1851 and cheer the nation up after World War II. A great success, it attracted 8.5 million visitors.

financial revolution: Term for the development of modern government deficit finance, a funded national debt, and the rise of public stock trading, all based in the City, in the 1690s. The financial revolution enabled the British Crown to field vast armies and navies in its wars with France.

freeman (a.k.a. free of the guild): Tradesmen who paid a fee called quarterage (paid four times a year) to their livery company were freemen or "free of the guild." This made them citizens and gave them the right to vote for municipal offices and members of Parliament.

General Strike of 1926: A series of sympathy strikes with the coal miners, the point of which was to paralyze London and, with it, the country. In the end, government preparations and the unwillingness of Londoners to put up with the paralysis scuttled the strike.

gin craze: Born of the fact that gin was easy to make and largely untaxed, the gin craze reached its peak in the 1730s and 1740s and was thought to have led to thousands of deaths. Satirized in Hogarth's *Gin Lane* and *Beer Street*, the craze faded with the regulatory Gin Act of 1751 and a subsequent rise in the price of grain.

Glorious Revolution of 1688–1689: A series of events, including the invasion of William of Orange, the abandonment of London by James II, and the naming of William and his wife Mary to the Crown by Parliament as William III and Mary II, which established constitutional monarchy in England and precipitated the Nine Years' War with France.

Gordon riots: A series of anti-Catholic riots inspired by the incendiary speechmaking of Lord George Gordon in early June of 1780. Newgate, the Fleet Prison, and the Bank of England were attacked by mobs numbering as high as 60,000. About two dozen rioters were executed, marking an end to tolerance of large public demonstrations in London.

Great Exhibition of 1851: The first world's fair. It originated with Prince Albert as a way to show off the goods of the world, but it was dominated by British manufacturers. It was held in a glass and iron building in Hyde Park: Sir Joseph Paxton's Crystal Palace.

Great Fire, the: On September 2–5, 1666, this fire burned 13,200 houses, 87 parish churches, St. Paul's Cathedral, and virtually all of the City within the walls. The official death toll was less than a dozen, but this is in dispute.

Great Plague, the: Epidemic of (probably) bubonic plague that raged in London from the spring of 1665 into 1666, peaking that summer. Mortality estimates range from 70,000 to 100,000.

Great Stink, the: In the hot, dry summer of 1858, the sewage system backed up near Westminster, river traffic stopped, and the windows of the Houses of Parliament had to be draped with curtains soaked in chloride of lime to mask the smell. Tons of chloride of lime and carbolic acid were dumped into the Thames, but to little effect. The result was the Thames Purification Act and the beginning of a proper underground sewer system.

Grub Street: Early modern street near Moorfields where hack writers and journalists worked in the early 18th century. The term applied to them and their work on newspapers, essays, almanacs, political broadsides, advice books, travel books, true crime narratives, and so forth.

Gunpowder Plot: Catholic plot organized in 1605 by Robert Catesby to blow up King James I and both Houses of Parliament at the state opening on November 5 by detonating barrels of gunpowder stored in the basement of the House of Lords. The plot was uncovered, and one of the conspirators, Guy Fawkes, was caught red-handed with the explosives the night before. The conspirators were executed, and anti-Catholic legislation was toughened.

inn: Originally simply a large house, more particularly a large full-service hostelry usually located at the London end of a major road and coaching line, providing accommodation, stabling, food, drink, and the occasional play in its open courtyard.

Licensing Act: A statute passed in 1662 that limited the number of master printers in Britain to 20, with a few additional journeyman printers. All publications were required to carry the name of the author and printer and to be approved by a Licensor of the Press, who was empowered to search out unauthorized presses and publications. Expired 1679; renewed 1685–1695.

livery company: An organization of London tradesmen granted privileges by a royal charter as well as by the lord mayor and aldermen to set prices, wages, and standards of quality for all its merchants and tradesmen. Only its members could trade within the walls and vote in municipal elections for all sorts of local officials, including London's members of Parliament. Livery companies also distributed charity to sick or unemployed members, widows, and orphans and, before the Reformation, often endowed hospitals, schools, and almshouses.

London Bridge: There has been a bridge linking Southwark to London since Roman times. Most famous was the bridge built from 1172 to 1209, which lasted into the 19th century. It was the only bridge linking London's two banks until 1750.

London County Council: Established in 1889, the overarching government authority for maintaining public works, health, housing, and so on, in London until its replacement by the Greater London Council in 1965.

London Wall: First built by the Romans, the wall demarcated and protected the City into the 17th century. Punctuated by eight gates that often incorporated prisons and atop which the heads of executed malefactors were often placed. Most of the wall was subsequently torn down to make way for development.

Long Parliament: The Parliament summoned in the autumn of 1640, which sat in one form or another from the spring of 1641 to December 1648, at which point its more moderate members were purged to form the Rump Parliament, which in turn governed the Commonwealth until 1653. First the Rump and then the whole of the Long Parliament was recalled during the period of instability prior to the Restoration, 1659–1660. *See also* **Rump Parliament**.

lord mayor: The old walled City of London was granted the right to elect annually a mayor (soon called the lord mayor) under King John. By the early modern period, he was usually simply the senior alderman. Only in 2000 were the inhabitants of Greater London granted the right to elect a mayor for the whole of the city.

Merchant Adventurers: A lobbying group for overseas wool merchants founded in 1407. For much of the 16th century, one had to be a Merchant Adventurer to have the right to participate in the wool trade.

Metropolitan Board of Works: Established in 1855, the first overarching authority for Greater London. It built London's sewer system, created new roads, and bought Hampstead Heath to provide additional green space for London. It was superseded by the London County Council in 1889.

Metropolitan Police Act: Proposed by Sir Robert Peel, this act established London's first professional police force in 1829.

mods: A 1960s youth group who wore tailored Italian clothes and well-coiffed hair and rode motor scooters. They tended to embrace modern jazz and existentialist philosophy. *See also* **rockers**.

music hall: Entertainment venue combining theater and drink, patronized by the working class in the early 19th century. They put on comedy acts, animal acts, and singers, with the audience joining in on the chorus.

Navigation Acts: Parliamentary legislation that passed in 1651, 1660, and 1663 that required goods shipped to and from the English colonies in America to be transported in English vessels through English ports. This legislation ensured England's commercial supremacy. After 1707, it was applied to Britain as a whole.

ordinary: The early modern word for a restaurant.

pleasure garden: An early modern version of an amusement park—for adults (e.g., Vauxhall, or later Ranelagh). Patrons could saunter along meandering walks behind high hedges, stroll beautifully manicured gardens, retreat to secluded booths where they could order dinner and drinks, listen to the latest music, and delight to the fires of numerous small lamps as the twilight descended.

poor laws: Series of parliamentary statutes (1536, 1563, 1598, 1601, and 1662) designed to provide relief for the "deserving" poor (i.e., those who could not work because of gender, age, or illness) out of taxes called the poor rate, collected and distributed on a parish-by-parish basis. Some of these laws also had punitive provisions for "sturdy beggars," (i.e., those who would not work). In London, both groups were often sent to Bridewell Prison. The law of 1662 allowed parishes to send itinerant poor back to their parishes of origin.

Puritans: Protestants who sought the continued reform of the Church of England after its establishment in 1559–1563. Puritans tended to be Calvinists, favoring plain church ritual consistent with scriptural injunction. Many, though not all, favored a Presbyterian form of church government. After a brief moment in the sun following the Civil Wars, they were driven out of the Church of England by parliamentary legislation and so are properly known after the Restoration as Dissenters.

Rebuilding Act of 1667: This post–Great Fire law mandated that, in London, houses built in by-lanes could not exceed two stories, houses built along the river could not exceed three, and houses built along high streets "for citizens of extraordinary quality" could not exceed four. Also mandated construction of wider streets; that the docks were to be kept clear of houses; and, above all, that London was to be rebuilt in brick and stone.

Riot Act of 1715: Defined a riot as any assemblage of 12 people "unlawfully, riotously, and tumultuously assembled together." It became a felony to cause damage to places of worship, houses, barns, or stables. Most famous was the requirement that it actually be read before rioters.

rockers: A 1960s youth group associated with riding motorcycles, wearing leather jackets, and a penchant for American rock and roll (Elvis, Eddie Cochran, Bo Diddley). Compared to the mods, they were angrier, more macho, and more violent. *See also* **mods**.

Rump Parliament: Popular nickname for the radical remnant of the Long Parliament that continued to sit after Pride's Purge in December 1648. The Rump was the effective legislature of the Commonwealth. It was dissolved by Oliver Cromwell in 1653 but was briefly revived in 1659–1660 during the chaos leading to the Restoration. *See also* **Long Parliament**.

Sacheverell riots: After the High Anglican preacher Henry Sacheverell was found guilty of a charge of seditious libel, Tory mobs attacked Dissenting meeting houses in March 1710.

Southwark: Area south of London Bridge, established by the Romans but mostly unincorporated with the City until 1550. Because it was outside City authority, it became notorious as the home of brothels; bear rings; and, from the late 16th century, theaters. In 1951, it was the site of the Festival of Britain. Today it is home to the National and New Globe Theatres and the Royal Festival Hall for music.

Spectator*, *The: Along with *The Tatler*, London's first literary magazine, in which the anonymous-yet-omnipresent "Mr. Spectator" would offer his witty, often caustic, opinions on London life, drawn from its very streets.

suffragettes: Active in the 19th and early 20th centuries, suffragettes wanted a parliamentary statute granting women the vote. Militant suffragettes like the Pankhursts engaged in civil and violent disobedience before World War I.

sweated labor: Unskilled labor, divided up into easy-to-learn tasks, performed in attics and basements by newly arrived immigrants for starvation wages. Its emergence in the 19th century was cause and consequence of the demise of guild regulations.

taverns: Large and well-established facilities serving wine, spirits, beer, and food and providing rooms for meeting and even overnight accommodation. *See also* **alehouses**.

Teddy Boys: Working-class white teenagers of the 1950s who liked exaggerated Edwardian dress (velvet collared jackets, bootlace ties, tapered trousers, suede shoes), Brylcreamed hair, and hanging out at cafés ("caffs").

Tories: English political party that arose in response to the exclusion crisis of the 1680s. The Tories began as a court party defending the hereditary succession in the person of James, Duke of York. They favored the rights of the monarch, the Church of England, and the interests of landowners. During the 1690s, as they became associated with Jacobitism and lost power, the Tories became more of a country party. Their name derives from a cant term for Catholic-Irish brigands. *See also* **exclusion crisis**.

trading companies: Generally (with the exception of the East India Company) not investment opportunities but lobbying groups that achieved monopolies on overseas trade to particular areas (Spain, the Baltic, and so forth). Most of these monopolies were granted in the second half of the 16th century; most were broken by 1700.

trained bands: London's militia, often deployed in royal military campaigns; arguably, the best-trained fighting force in Britain until the advent of the New Model Army in the 1640s.

Tube, the: London's underground railway system, begun in the 19th century and electrified at the beginning of the 20th century.

Westminster: The borough of Greater London just west of the City. Edward the Confessor began to lay it out in 1045, establishing an abbey and a palace there. The Normans made it England's capital. Westminster Hall was added by William II; the abbey was rebuilt by Henry III. The palace was given for Parliament's use by Henry VIII; it burned down in 1834 and was replaced by the present Palace of Westminster designed by Charles Berry and Augustus Pugin. The area was for many years governed by the Abbey Chapter. It was finally incorporated into Greater London in the 19th century.

Whigs: English political party that arose in response to the exclusion crisis of the 1680s. The Whigs began as a country party demanding the exclusion of the Catholic James, Duke of York from the throne, emphasizing the rights of Parliament and of Dissenters, and championing a Protestant (pro-Dutch) foreign policy. In the 1690s they became a party of government and grew less radical. *See also* **exclusion crisis**.

Wyatt's rebellion: Insurrection led in 1554 by Sir Thomas Wyatt against Mary's intended marriage to Phillip, King of Naples. Mary rallied the palace guards and remnants of Northumberland's army and beat back the rebels, many of whom were executed.

Zeppelin: Invented by Count Ferdinand von Zeppelin, an airship borne aloft by helium. The Germans used these to rain bombs on London from May 1915 to August 1918, with greater psychological effect than economic or military consequences.

Biographical Notes

Note: With one exception, monarchs designated with the Roman numeral "I" bore no such designation in life: Charles I was "King Charles," Elizabeth I was "Queen Elizabeth," and so forth. They only acquired their distinguishing Roman numerals posthumously, when a second of that name succeeded. The exception was King James I, who was actually so designated in his proclamation of accession to distinguish his English title from his Scottish, as James VI.

Alfred the Great (849–899): King of the West Saxons from 871 to 899 who united England and spent most of his reign trying to unite the country against the invading Danes. He is often credited with establishing the first English navy, reforming the militia, and initiating or perfecting many of the institutions of Anglo-Saxon government. Captured London in 886 and established a street plan and an early taxation infrastructure.

Anne (1664–1714): Queen of England, Scotland, and Ireland from 1702 to 1714, successfully pursued the War of the Spanish Succession against France. Her attempt to maintain her freedom of action in the face of party partisanship was less successful, but her reign saw the Act of Union between England and Scotland, creating the state of Great Britain; maintenance of religious toleration for Dissenters; unprecedented British military success; and the expansion of the British territorial and commercial empire as a result of the Treaty of Utrecht (1713).

Bazealgatte, Sir Joseph (1819–1891): Civil engineer who was chief engineer to the Metropolitan Board of Works (1855–1889). Carried out the design and construction of London's sewer system (1858–1875) and the Thames Embankment (1862–1874). Knighted 1874.

Booth, Charles (1840–1916): English ship owner and social reformer; author of *Life and Labour of the People of London* (1891–1903), a systematic and comprehensive study of its subject. Played a major role in securing passage of the Old Age Pensions Act (1908).

Boudicca (d. 61): Queen of the Iceni who, after she was flogged and her daughters were raped by the Romans, sacked London, killing perhaps 70,000 people. Eventually defeated and took poison. Some 80,000 of her people were slain by the Roman commander Suetonius Paulus.

Charles I (1600–1649): King of England, Scotland, and Ireland from 1625 to 1649. His support for the Duke of Buckingham's failed foreign policy early in his reign, combined with his High Church religious policies and suspected Catholic sympathies, poisoned his relationship with Parliament. His attempt to rule without it, the Personal Rule of 1629–1640, saw a much-needed reform of the royal administration, but his financial exactions, never approved by Parliament, were very unpopular. His attempt to impose an Anglican-style liturgy on Presbyterian Scotland in 1637 provoked the Bishops' Wars, which provoked, in turn, the Long Parliament, which sought to limit his power. After neither king nor Parliament could agree on how to deal with the Irish Rebellion of 1641, civil war broke out. After some opening successes, the king lost the conflict by 1646. When, after much negotiation, it became clear that he would never agree to a limitation of his powers, he was tried by order of the Rump Parliament and executed in January 1649.

Charles II (1630–1685): King of England, Scotland, and Ireland from 1660 to 1685, though committed Royalists dated his reign to the death of his father in 1649. Prince Charles fought in the Civil Wars on the Royalist side, escaping to Europe in 1646, but he returned in 1650 to accept the Scots' acclamation as king. Defeated by Cromwell at the Battle of Worcester in 1651, he was forced to hide in a tree—"the royal oak"—and make his way incognito back to European exile. Restored in 1660, Charles II initially attempted to pursue a combination of absolutism, religious toleration, and friendship with France, culminating in the Treaty of Dover of 1670. But after the disaster of the Third Anglo-Dutch War, he employed the Earl of Danby to repair his relationship with the ruling elite by working to manage Parliament, embracing an Anglican religious policy, and pursuing, albeit fitfully, a Protestant (pro-Dutch) foreign policy. The climax of his reign was the Popish Plot and the exclusion crisis, in which he coolly refused to accept that there was such a plot and, after some hesitation, continued to back his brother, James, Duke of York, as his heir until a Tory reaction set in.

Chaucer, Geoffrey (c. 1340–1400): English poet, government official, and native Londoner. He served abroad in the Hundred Years' War (1359–1360) and on several continental diplomatic missions thereafter. He was Comptroller of the Customs in London (1374), a member of Parliament (1386), Clerk of the Works (1389–1391), and the author of *Troylus and Cryseyde* and *The Canterbury Tales*, among other works.

Churchill, Sir Winston Leonard Spencer (1874–1965): British statesman and author; served abroad in India, the Sudan, and the Boer War (the last as a correspondent) from 1897 to 1899. Became a member of Parliament in 1900; president of the Board of Trade in 1908; and First Lord of the Admiralty from 1911 to 1915, from which post he fell as a result of the disaster at Gallipoli. He held various cabinet positions in the 1920s, was reappointed First Lord in 1939, and became prime minister in May 1940. Famously rallied London, the nation, and then the alliance that defeated Hitler. Voted out of office July 1945; returned as prime minister from 1951 to 1955. The author of numerous works of history, including histories of both world wars and a four-volume biography of his ancestor John Churchill, Duke of Marlborough, he was awarded the Nobel Prize in Literature and was knighted in 1953. Refused the title of Duke of London.

Cromwell, Oliver (1599–1658): Lord Protector of England from 1653 to 1658, Cromwell began life as an obscure gentleman from Huntingdonshire. Educated at the strongly Puritan Sidney Sussex College, Cambridge, he proved himself a brilliant general of horse during the Civil Wars. By their end, he was the commander of the New Model Army and, arguably, the most important man in England. In 1649 he recaptured Ireland, gloating over the massacres at Drogheda and Wexford. In 1650–1651 he defeated the Covenanting and Royalist Scots, securing the control of the Commonwealth over the whole of the British Isles. However, he soon became disillusioned with the Rump Parliament and used the army to send them home in 1653. Named lord protector by the Instrument of Government later that same year, he gave England good government and an aggressive and successful foreign policy but also a more intrusive state and higher taxes than it had ever known previously. Though he was succeeded by his son, Richard, after his sudden death in 1658, his regime collapsed soon after.

Dickens, Charles (1812–1870): English author. Born in Portsmouth, he arrived in London in 1822 and spent his youth in sweated labor and in getting to know the city. After spending time as a reporter, he wrote over a dozen novels, plus short stories and essays, nearly all of which advocate social reform.

Edward I (1239–1307): Warlike medieval English king who reigned from 1272 to 1307, he fought in the Seventh Crusade in 1270 and was responsible for the conquest of Wales in 1282–1284, as well as repeated wars to secure the submission of Scotland from 1290 onward. Domestically, he reformed government and called what became known as the Model Parliament in 1295. He expelled the Jews from England in 1290. He did not get along with the City of London and, as a consequence, strengthened the fortifications of the Tower.

Edward VI (1537–1553): King of England and Ireland from 1547 to 1553, he was too young to direct policy on a day-to-day basis. The first part of his reign was dominated by his uncle, Edward Seymour, Duke of Somerset, was named Lord Protector within days of Edward's accession. Somerset pursued Protestantism at home and an aggressive foreign policy against Scotland but fell in 1549 over his failure to deal effectively with the Western Rising and Kett's rebellion. He was replaced as leading minister by John Dudley, Duke of Northumberland, who pursued Protestantism more aggressively. Since this would make his position untenable if the Catholic Mary succeeded, he persuaded Edward to divert the succession to the Protestant Lady Jane Grey as Edward's health failed in the spring of 1553. The king died that July.

Edward the Confessor (c. 1002–1066): King of England from 1042 to 1066. He was deeply religious, taking a vow of celibacy, though he was forced to marry in 1045. Refounded a monastery at Westminster soon after his accession and built a great abbey and palace there, thus laying the foundation for the transfer of the capital to London.

Elizabeth I (1533–1603): Queen of England and Ireland from 1558 to 1603. As a princess, Elizabeth had a checkered career, sometimes in royal favor, sometimes—especially under her Catholic sister Mary I—well out of it and in some danger of her life. She preserved herself by avoiding all plots to put her on the throne prematurely. As queen, she inherited a great many problems from Mary. She solved them by pursuing extreme frugality and a moderately Protestant compromise on religion (the Settlement of 1559–1563) and by placating the great Catholic powers of Europe (Spain, France, the Holy Roman Empire) for as long as possible. This last was difficult, as Elizabeth found it in her interest to offer support to Scottish Presbyterian rebels against Mary, Queen of Scots, and (covertly) Dutch Calvinist rebels and English privateers against Phillip II of Spain. Spain only retaliated after Elizabeth sent an army to the Netherlands in 1585 and executed her cousin Mary in 1587. The defeat of the Spanish Armada in 1588 was only the beginning of a long war, the climax of which was the English suppression of the O'Neill rebellion in Ireland in 1603. By then, Elizabeth's well-cultivated aura as Gloriana, the Virgin Queen wedded to her adoring people, was wearing thin due to high taxes, poor harvests, and a sense that the reign had run its course.

Fielding, Henry (1707–1754): English novelist and playwright. Born in Somersetshire, he became a barrister in 1740 and was named justice of the peace for Westminster in 1748. Author of, among other works, *Joseph Andrews*, *Tom Jones*, and the *History of Jonathan Wild the Great*, he was also a reformist who established the Bow Street Runners.

George I (1660–1727): King of Great Britain and Ireland and Elector of Hanover from 1714 to 1727. His family was placed in the succession to the British throne by the Act of Settlement of 1701. The Hanoverian claim having received the wholehearted support of the Whigs prior to his accession, George I employed the Whigs in office exclusively. In particular, he placed his affairs so fully into the hands of Sir Robert Walpole that the latter is considered the first real prime minister in British history.

Henry III (1207–1272): King of England from 1216 to 1272, though the realm was governed by a regency until 1232. He clashed frequently with his barons, led by Simon de Montfort, and with London in the 1250s and 1260s especially. After his son, Edward, defeated the barons at Evesham in 1265, he retreated from active participation in government. He rebuilt Westminster Abbey in a high gothic style.

Henry VII (1457–1509): King of England from 1485 to 1509. As Henry Tudor, Earl of Richmond, he inherited a claim to the English throne from his mother, Margaret Beaufort. Acting on that claim in 1485, he defeated Richard III at the Battle of Bosworth Field and seized the throne. He kept it by wooing London; reducing the power of the greatest nobles; promoting trade; building alliances with France, Scotland, and Spain through threats of war or diplomatic marriage; and reforming the administration and finances of the Crown to a point where he no longer had to trouble Parliament for funds. This, in turn, meant that they would not trouble him.

Henry VIII (1491–1547): King of England from 1509 to 1547 and Ireland from 1541 to 1547, he deployed his considerable intelligence and energy during the first 20 years of his reign on pleasure and wars with France, leaving the administration of the country to Thomas, Cardinal Wolsey. Wolsey fell in 1529, after failing to secure for Henry a papal divorce from his first wife, Catherine of Aragon, necessitated in Henry's eyes by her failure to give him a male heir. Wolsey's replacement, Thomas Cromwell, made possible the divorce by making Henry supreme head of the Church of England through a series of acts passed in 1533–1536. These acts initiated the English Reformation and a virtual revolution in the Crown's relationship to its subjects. Henry was a popular monarch, despite the fact that he exploited, exhausted, or liquidated a series of wives, ministers, and courtiers and the contents of the royal treasury. His wars wrecked the economy, and his dissolution of the monasteries initiated a major shift of land ownership in London away from the church and toward the nobility. Although a political and religious conservative, his constitutional and religious changes did much to propel England down the path of parliamentary sovereignty and Protestantism.

Hogarth, William (1697–1764): English painter and engraver and a native Londoner. Though a painter of great accomplishment, his fame rests on his prints and print series (*The Rake's Progress*, *Marriage à la Mode*, *Industry and Idleness*), many of them satirical of London life. His artistic support for the London Foundling Hospital was important in its survival.

James I (1566–1625): King of England and Ireland from 1603 to 1625 and, as James VI, of Scotland from 1567 to 1625. James succeeded his mother, Mary, Queen of Scots, as ruler of Scotland after she was deposed by the Presbyterian nobility. Raised a somewhat reluctant Presbyterian, James grew up to be an effective ruler of Scotland, particularly good at balancing its various factions. He was also something of a scholar, writing in support of divine-right kingship. He succeeded Elizabeth I on the strength of his Tudor great-grandmother, Margaret. As king of England, he forged peace with Spain and pursued a moderate religious policy, avoiding persecution of either Catholic or Puritan extremes when possible. He had more difficulty balancing English political factions and never quite figured out how to manage Parliament so as to supply the extravagance of his court. Nor did he make any attempt to woo London. Increasingly lazy as he grew older, he turned his affairs over to his principal favorite, George Villiers, Duke of Buckingham. This explains the ill-advised resumption of hostilities with Spain begun in his last year on the throne.

James II (1633–1701): King of England and Ireland and (as James VII) of Scotland from 1685 to 1688. As a young man following the Civil Wars, James, Duke of York, escaped to the Continent. There, in the service of the French king, and after the Restoration as Lord High Admiral (1660–1673), he distinguished himself by his bravery. In 1678, after allegations of a "Popish Plot" to kill Charles II and place James on the throne, the Whigs organized, unsuccessfully, to try to ban him from it. As king, he proved a far-sighted administrator, but his major policy initiative—to grant both Catholics and Dissenters a toleration—was widely unpopular. In 1688 he was deposed by William of Orange and fled once more to France. The following year he attempted to launch a second Restoration from Ireland, but following his defeat at the Battle of the Boyne in July 1690, he left his former kingdoms for good. He lived out his days on the hospitality of Louis XIV.

John (c. 1167–1216): Weak medieval king of England from 1199 to 1216 as well as Duke of Normandy, Anjou, Maine, and Tourraine until he lost them by 1205. His refusal to recognize the papal nominee, Stephen Langton, as archbishop of Canterbury in 1206 led to an interdict against England in 1208 and his deposition by the Pope in 1212 before he submitted, receiving England back as a feudal fief in 1213. He granted many of London's privileges, including the right of the City to govern itself and elect a mayor, in order to secure loans and City support. This did him little good as, following his return from the disastrous French military campaign of 1214–1215, the city opened its gates to the rebels who forced the Magna Carta on him.

Johnson, Samuel (1709–1784): English lexicographer, writer, and raconteur. Born in Lichfield, he moved permanently to London in 1737 and began to work on *The Gentleman's Magazine*. Over the next half century or so he produced an astonishing amount of work, including a literary magazine (*The Rambler*), poetry, plays, an edition of Shakespeare, and the first comprehensive dictionary of the English language (1749–1755). In 1763 he met James Boswell, who became his biographer. His Literary Club included Garrick, Burke, Reynolds, Goldsmith, and others.

Jones, Inigo (1573–1652): Architect and scenic designer to James I and Charles I and a native Londoner, he is credited with designing the neo-Palladian Banqueting House at Whitehall, the portico to Old St. Paul's, and London's first square, Covent Garden.

Livingstone, Ken (b. 1945): Labour politician who was head of the Greater London Council in 1981–1986 and became London's first elected mayor in 2000. Known to the press as "Red Ken" for his left-wing policies, he was defeated for reelection in 2008.

Mary I (1516–1558): Queen of England and Ireland from 1553 to 1558. Educated to be a consort, not a queen; delegitimized by her father, Henry VIII, in 1533; and taken out of the succession by her brother, Edward VI, in 1553; Mary survived the attempted coup of Lady Jane Grey to succeed in July 1553. She precipitated another crisis, Wyatt's rebellion, in 1554 by choosing to marry Phillip, King of Naples, the future Phillip II of Spain. The rebellion failed, but the marriage proved unhappy: It never produced the heir that Mary so desperately wanted, but it did land her in a disastrous war with France that saw the loss of Calais. The major policy initiative of her reign, the restoration of Catholicism as the state church, failed, not so much because of the burnings at Smithfield, which earned her the sobriquet "Bloody Mary," but because she had neither time on the throne nor an heir to continue her policies. In their absence, hers is generally considered the only failed Tudor reign.

Mary II (1662–1694): Queen of England, Scotland, and Ireland from 1689 to 1694. The daughter of James, Duke of York (James II), Mary was raised a Protestant at the Restoration court. She was matched in a diplomatic marriage with William of Orange, Stadholder of the Netherlands, in 1677. In the Glorious Revolution of 1688–1689, she was offered the throne with William as king, in whom administrative power was vested. Serving as regent when he was out of the country on campaign, Mary was frequently urged by the Tories to exercise her power, but she remained loyally subordinate to her husband. Her importance to the regime was in giving it a face that was English, Anglican, charitable, fun-loving, and attractive. She was also important as a patron of the arts and was much lamented at her sudden death from smallpox in December 1694.

Mayhew, Henry (1812–1887): English journalist, humorist, and playwright who cofounded *Punch* in 1841. Best remembered for his inquiry into *London Labour and the London Poor* (1851–1864).

Pankhurst, Emmeline (1858–1928): Militant English suffragette. With her eldest daughter, Christabel, founded the Womens' Social and Political Union in 1903. From 1905 she advocated radical, even violent methods to obtain votes for women, including window smashing, arson, and hunger strikes.

Pepys, Samuel (1633–1703): English government official and diarist, a native Londoner. After his education at Cambridge, he was appointed clerk of the acts of the Navy Board in 1660, then was appointed secretary of the Admiralty and was elected to Parliament in 1673. He was made a fellow of the Royal Society in 1665 and became its president from 1684 to 1686. Closely associated with the king's brother—James, Duke of York, who as James II was overthrown in the Glorious Revolution—Pepys fell with his master, resigning from the Admiralty in 1689. He spent the rest of his life as a leisured London gentleman, pursuing scientific and artistic hobbies. The shorthand diary he kept in the years 1660–1669 recreates his own life and 17th-century London in amazing, fascinating detail.

Plautius, Aulus: Roman general designated by Claudiuis to invade Britain and establish a Roman presence there in 43 C.E.

Shakespeare, William (1564–1616): English playwright, born at Stratford-upon-Avon, Warwickshire; moved to London by 1592. He became an actor-playwright in the Lord Chamberlain's Men and a shareholder in the Globe Theatre, built in 1598. He produced 37 plays (including histories, tragedies, and comedies), plus poems and sonnets, before retiring to Stratford around 1611.

Stow, John (c. 1525–1605): English historian and antiquary, a native Londoner whose greatest work is *A Survey of London* (1605).

William I (the Conqueror; 1027–1087): Duke of Normandy from 1035 to 1087; King of England from 1066 to 1087. As Duke of Normandy, he defeated King Harold II at the Battle of Hastings on October 14, 1066. When London refused to capitulate, he marched on and burned Southwark, leading to London's reversal of course. Crowned at Westminster Abbey on Christmas Day 1066, he built the Tower of London to keep an eye on his new capital. This was one of many castles he established to safeguard his rule. He also established the feudal system in England and commissioned a thorough survey of his realm, entitled Domesday Book (1085).

William III (1650–1702): King of England, Ireland, and (as William II), Scotland from 1689 to 1702; Prince of Orange from 1650 to 1702; and Stadholder of the Netherlands from 1672 to 1702. William was the only child of William II, Prince of Orange, and Mary, the daughter of Charles I. Chronically unhealthy but of exceptional intelligence, William was kept from power in the Netherlands by a republican faction during his youth. He was catapulted to the leadership of the Dutch Republic by Louis XIV's attempt to wipe it off the map in 1672. For the remainder of his life, he worked to build a Grand Alliance to stop the Sun King, an important stage in that project being his marriage to Princess Mary of England in 1677. His great opportunity to take advantage of this match came in 1688 when he was invited to invade England. After extensive preparations, the invasion was a success, and on February 13, 1689, William was offered the English crown, jointly with Mary II but with administrative power to be vested in him. The Glorious Revolution precipitated the Nine Years' War, in which he secured first Ireland by 1692, then a favorable peace with Louis via the Treaty of Ryswick in 1697. As William's reign ended, he was preparing a second war to stop Louis XIV from placing his grandson, Philippe, Duke of Anjou, on the Spanish throne, and James II's son, Prince James, on the British throne.

Wren, Sir Christopher (1632–1723): English architect, Professor of Astronomy at Oxford from 1666 to 1673, Surveyor of the King's Works from 1668 to 1718, charter member of the Royal Society, and its president from 1680 to 1682. After the Great Fire of London, his designs resulted in the rebuilding of St. Paul's Cathedral in 1675–1716, 52 churches, and the Customs House. Among other notable buildings in London, he was responsible for work at Whitehall Palace, St. James's, Greenwich, Chelsea, Temple Bar, and the Monument. Knighted 1673.

Bibliography

Acknowledgement: Professor Bucholz would like to thank Jeannette Pierce, head of reference and history bibliographer at Cudahy Library, Loyola University Chicago, for supplying him with many books necessary to the preparation of the course and this bibliography.

Ackroyd, P. *Dickens's London*. London: Headline, 1987. Lavishly illustrated with contemporary photographs, this book quotes from Dickens's writings to recreate his city through his eyes.

Barker, F., and P. Jackson. *The History of London in Maps*. New York: Cross River, 1994. This is the most comprehensive and beautiful compilation of maps of London, including Tube maps, novelty maps, and so forth.

———. *London: 2,000 Years of a City and Its People*. London: Macmillan, 1974. Richly illustrated history of London, including many iconic images.

Brigden, S. *London and the Reformation*. Oxford: Oxford University Press, 1989. Authoritative and groundbreaking, based on archival sources, this standard work on the subject stresses religious conflict and turmoil in the city.

Brooke, C., and G. Keir. *London 800–1216: The Shaping of a City*. Berkeley: University of California Press, 1975. Two eminent medievalists examine the crucial period when medieval London came together.

Castle, I., and C. Hook. *London 1914–17: The Zeppelin Menace*. Oxford: Osprey, 2008. An illustrated narrative of the Zeppelin raids.

Davis, J. *Reforming London: The London Government Problem 1855–1900*. Oxford: Oxford University Press, 1988. This, the most comprehensive scholarly work on how London began to organize itself in the 19th century, is also lucid and readable.

Gurr, A. *Playgoing in Shakespeare's London*. Harmondsworth, UK: Penguin, 1987. This is the now-standard work on the composition of Shakespeare's audience and, in particular, on the question of just how plebeian it really was.

Hansen, N. *The Great Fire of London: In that Apocalyptic Year, 1666*. Hoboken, NJ: John Wiley & Sons, 2002. The most recent treatment of the fire, taking into account the most recent scholarship and based on eyewitness accounts.

Harris, T. *London Crowds in the Reign of Charles II*. Cambridge: Cambridge University Press, 1987. Detailed study of mob action during the Restoration period makes clear that there was never a single London mob but rather different groups who took to mob action.

Harrison, T. *Living Through the Blitz*. New York: Schocken, 1976. Based on eyewitness accounts of Londoners' experience of the Blitz from the archives of Mass Observation, this account is full of telling day-to-day detail and harrowing reminiscence.

Hewison, R. *Too Much: Art and Society in the Sixties*. London: Methuen, 1986. A wide-ranging and comprehensive survey of the popular arts in Britain, concentrating on Swinging London, that argues that we are still influenced heavily by the styles and assumptions of the 1960s.

Hiley, M. *Victorian Working Women: Portraits from Life*. London: Fraser, 1979. Examines the situations of textile workers, nontextile workers, dressmakers, governesses, and the idle across Britain.

Holmes, M. *Elizabethan London*. New York: Prager, 1969. A readable if discursive account of Shakespeare's London.

Humphries, S., and J. Taylor. *The Making of Modern London, 1945–1985*. London: Sidgewick and Jackson, 1986. Based on a popular television program in Britain, this book focuses on the human story of London's postwar development.

Inwood, S. *A History of London*. London: Macmillan, 1998. The magisterial, essential, and most comprehensive history of London.

Manley, L. *London in the Age of Shakespeare: An Anthology*. London: Croom Helm, 1986. A fascinating anthology of contemporary writings about Shakespeare's London by natives and foreign visitors.

Marshal, D. *Dr. Johnson's London*. New York: John Wiley & Sons, 1968. A comprehensive account of 18th-century London.

Moote, A. L., and D. C. Moote. *The Great Plague: The Story of London's Most Deadly Year*. Baltimore: Johns Hopkins University Press, 2006. Written by a historian and a microbiologist, this book combines documentary evidence with a modern understanding of the pathology of the plague.

Myers, A. R. *London in the Age of Chaucer*. Norman: University of Oklahoma Press, 1972. Eminently readable and logically laid out, this is the best guide to Chaucer's London.

Paterson, M. *Voices from Dickens's London*. Cincinnati, OH: David and Charles, 2006. A fascinating collection of contemporary quotations about aspects of London life addressed in the novels.

Pearl, V. *London and the Outbreak of the Puritan Revolution*. Oxford: Oxford University Press, 1961. The authoritative standard work on London's contribution to the start of the English Civil Wars.

Pepys, S. *The Illustrated Pepys*. Edited by R. Latham. Berkeley: University of California Press, 2000. Lavishly illustrated, brief selection from the *Diary*, with good maps.

Perring, D. *Roman London*. London: Routledge, 1991. Based on the most recent archeological findings, this book traces the rise and fall of Roman Londinium.

Reddaway, T. F. *The Rebuilding of London after the Great Fire*. London: Jonathan Cape, 1940. The standard account of the rebuilding, with special attention to plans to redesign the City and the problems of sorting out land ownership.

Robertson, D. W. *Chaucer's London*. London: John Wiley & Sons, 1968. Quixotic organization but much fascinating local detail about late medieval London.

Rudé, G. *Hanoverian London, 1714–1808*. Berkeley: University of California Press, 1971. The most scholarly treatment of 18th-century London is also a good read with a strong sense of life on the streets.

Saint, A., and G. Darley. *The Chronicles of London*. New York: St. Martin's Press, 1994. A rich chronological anthology of eyewitness accounts, newspaper stories, diary entries, and so forth.

Seaman, L. C. B. *Life in Victorian London*. London: Batsford, 1973. The most comprehensive treatment of London life toward the end of the 19th century.

Strong, R. *The Cult of Elizabeth*. London: Pimlico, 1999. A series of fascinating case studies using the techniques of modern art history and iconography to understand how the Elizabethans created the image of Gloriana.

Tomalin, C. *Samuel Pepys: The Unequalled Self*. New York: Vintage, 2003. The most recent and authoritative biography of the great diarist goes well beyond the *Diary* both thematically and chronologically to present the man in full.

Weightman, G. *London's Thames: The River that Shaped a City and Its History*. New York: St. Martin's Press, 2005. An absorbing account of the Thames that takes into account its commercial, sanitary, and symbolic significance to London.

Weightman, G., and S. Humphries. *The Making of Modern London, 1914–1939*. London: Ebury, 1984. Based on a popular television series, this book gives a readable account of how the city changed in the 20th century.

Weinreb, B., and C. Hibbert. *The London Encyclopaedia*. Bethesda, MD: Adler & Adler, 1987. The authority on all things London, organized by place and concept rather than proper names.

Wilson, A. N., ed. *The Norton Book of London*. New York: Norton, 1993. Among many competitors, this is the best and widest-ranging recent anthology of poetry and prose on London.

Notes